Joseph Edwin Roy

Pilgrim's Letters

Bits of Current History Picked Up in the West and the South

Joseph Edwin Roy

Pilgrim's Letters
Bits of Current History Picked Up in the West and the South

ISBN/EAN: 9783337293277

Printed in Europe, USA, Canada, Australia, Japan

Cover: Foto ©Lupo / pixelio.de

More available books at **www.hansebooks.com**

PILGRIM'S LETTERS.

Bits of Current History

PICKED UP IN THE WEST AND THE SOUTH, DURING THE LAST THIRTY YEARS,
FOR THE INDEPENDENT, THE CONGREGATIONALIST, AND THE ADVANCE,

BY

JOSEPH E. ROY.

BOSTON AND CHICAGO:
Congregational Sunday-School and Publishing Society.

Electrotyped and Printed
By Stanley & Usher, 171 Devonshire Street, Boston, Mass.

To Mrs. Pilgrim,

WHO, DURING ALL THE YEARS OF THIS PILGRIMAGE,

HAS TARRIED BY THE STUFF,

BEARING THE DOUBLE BURDEN OF THE HOME,

REARING THE FAMILY,

AND PRESERVING IN GROWING VOLUMES THESE ORIGINAL LETTERS,

THIS BOOK, THE SUBSTANCE OF THEM,

IS GRATEFULLY INSCRIBED

By Pilgrim.

PREFACE.

How did I come to take the name Pilgrim? Of Huguenot and New Jersey lineage, a son of the west, all the Pilgrim blood in me comes from a Yankee step-mother; but they which are of faith the same are the children of Abraham. Then my mode of life for these twenty-seven years, as superintendent of missions in the west and in the south, calling me to all parts of the country, has been that of a pilgrim. Moving about during this epoch-making period I have sought to catch some of its peculiar features by a sort of instantaneous photography; and for all of this time the press of *The Independent*, or of *The Congregationalist*, or of *The Advance* has been printing them. Out of these letters, seven hundred of them, I have sifted material which seemed to have a permanent interest. As they cover the period of the Kansas Struggle, the War of the Rebellion, the process of civil and moral reconstruction, and of the phenomenal development of our new territories, they afford glimpses of the real life of those times in which history was rapidly made — a history big with destiny. These are not war letters, but sketches, rather, showing what the men and the women were doing at home during the war to give material and moral support to the government and the army, and what they have since been doing for our country in supplementing the war and in maturing the national life.

It is a royal hospitality which Pilgrim has enjoyed every-where these many years. This title has often made ready for him a welcome where he had supposed himself a stranger. For all of this he once more expresses thanks, as he invites these and other friends to tread again with him some of the paths of this Pilgrim's progress.

CONTENTS.

PERIOD I.
BEFORE THE WAR, 1857-60.

                                                                                              PAGE.

"Bleeding Kansas." — A State with a History. - The Missouri Plan in North Carolina and in Kentucky 11

PERIOD II.
DURING THE WAR, 1861-63.

The South Pushing at the North. — Emancipation Memorial. — Soldiers from Western Colleges. — Trip to the Army. — United States Sanitary Disbursements. — Surgery in the Army. — Emancipation Meeting. — Boston Tract Society in the Army. — A May Anniversary in New York. — The Morgan Raid. — First Sanitary Fair 23

PERIOD III.
DURING THE WAR (Continued), 1864-65.

The Virginia Union Flag. — Death of Owen Lovejoy. — Triennial Convention on the State of the Country. — Deaths of Colonels Mulligan and John A. Bross. — Tour Among the Bushwhackers. — Quantrell's Raid. — Lincoln's Second Election. — Plot to Release Rebel Prisoners at Chicago. — Illinois Responds to the Call for Five Hundred Thousand More. — Blatchford's Sanitary Report. — Revolutionary Incident. — Turner and Pratt go to Missouri. — Rebel Prisoners in Camp Douglas. — Richmond Fallen. — Lee's Surrender. — Lincoln Assassinated. — The National Pageant. — Chicago's National Fair. — "Little Tad." — Boston National Council. — American Missionary Association Accepts the Trust Proffered by the Boston Council   52

PERIOD IV.

AT THE END OF THE WAR.—TOUR THROUGH THE SOUTH, 1865.

Mammoth Cave. — Freedmen's Bureau and Bank. — Knoxville. — Chattanooga. — Battle-fields. — Mississippi Legislature. — Natchez. — New Orleans. — Sea Island Negroes. — Alabama Legislature. — Black Heroes. — Charleston Shelled and Burned. — Emancipation Celebration in Charleston. — Virginia Legislature. — Generals Thomas and Fisk   81

PERIOD V.

AFTER THE WAR.—TO THE FIRE, 1866-71.

Soldiers from Congregational Churches in the West. — "Blue Laws" of South Carolina. — Iowa Quarter-Centennial. — Chicago Christian Commission. — Roll of Boston Council: Analysis of it. — Illinois Responds to President Johnson. — Four Western War Books. — Abraham Lincoln, "Surveyor." — Grinnell. — Quarter-Millennial of Plymouth Rock   109

PERIOD VI.

FROM THE FIRE TO THE CENTENNIAL, 1871-76.

The Chicago Fire. — National Council. — Tour in Connecticut. — The Ohio an Ancient Highway. — An Exploration of Colorado. — Among the Dakotas. — The Boston Fire. — Philo Carpenter. — Lake Superior. — Lone Star State. — The Woods of Northern Michigan   129

PERIOD VII.

AN INTERVAL OF SILENCE.

The Centennial. — The Gilded Dead-fall. — Transfer South . .   151

PERIOD VIII.

IN THE SOUTH, 1878-79.

Atlanta. — Emancipation Day. — Talladega, Ala. — Chattanooga. — Mardi Gras and Washington's Birthday in New Orleans. — The Acadians in Louisiana. — San Antonio. — Corpus Christi. — Alabama Anniversary Week. — Hampton, Va. — Fisk University   156

PERIOD IX.

IN THE SOUTH, 1880-82.

Berea. — National Cemeteries at the South. — Prohibition in North Carolina. — East Tennessee. — Anniston. — Memphis. — The Congregational Methodists. — A July Vacation. — Atlanta Cotton Exposition. — Crossing Boston Mountain. — Confederate Memorial Day in New Orleans. — Presbyterian Missions in the South. — North and South : Some Things in Common. — Colored Work of Southern Churches 181

PERIOD X.

IN THE SOUTH, 1883-84.

Miss Willard in the South. — Secretary Dunning. — The New Birmingham. — Canon Farrar. — Concord Council. — Mountain Work. — Wesleyans and German Reformed in North Carolina. — The Georgia Association in Charleston, S. C. 217

PERIOD XI.

IN THE SOUTH, 1885.

Itinerary from Austin to Corpus Christi. — Black Men and Big Pastures in Texas. — Negroes in the New Orleans Exposition. — Grant's Canal Caving in 239

PERIOD XII.

BACK IN THE WEST, 1885-87.

Transition. — Woman's Work for Woman at the South. — Methodist Episcopal Work Among the Freedmen. — Dakota Indian Conference. — In Colorado. — New West Commission. — Slater Fund. — Centennial of Territory of the North-west and of Louisiana Purchase. — Georgia's Prison and Chain Gang for Missionaries and Teachers. — An Old Experiment in Indian Land Severalty. — The Martyrdom of Elijah P. Lovejoy . . 252

PILGRIM'S LETTERS.

PERIOD I.

BEFORE THE WAR, 1857-60.

"Bleeding Kansas." — A State with a History. — The Missouri Plan in North Carolina and Kentucky.

LETTER I.

"BLEEDING KANSAS."

LAWRENCE, Kansas, September 28, 1857.

HERE I am on the soil of "Bleeding Kansas." I came on to arrange the affairs of my deceased brother, Aaron D. Roy, who had settled in this country that he might have a hand in the free state cause. He was soon enlisted among the Kansas defenders, and was in several encounters under General Lane. He was in the company that was captured at Hickory Point and thrust into prison at Lecompton by the United States troops, who are now made to serve the "border ruffians." After some weeks in this vile place, he dug out and escaped to the woods, afterwards finding harborage in the home of S. Y. Lum, that earnest patriot, who was the first minister from the east to reach the territory. The exposure of that imprisonment had so worn upon my brother's health that when attacked by fever he soon succumbed. They tell me that his funeral, directed by the Oread Guards, was the largest the town of Lawrence has ever seen.

Repairing to his grave, was it any wonder that I should kneel upon its fresh earth and renewedly devote myself to the cause of the slave? I became an abolitionist when a little child, through a mob. William T. Allen, son of a slave-holding minister in Huntsville, Alabama, one of the Lane Seminary "rebels," out from Oberlin on a lecturing tour, had come to our town of Mount Gilead, Ohio, to be entertained at my father's house. There a mob broke up his lecturing, and as he was returning with my mother and her little boy to our house, egg-shells filled with tar were thrown upon them. Before his lectures I had never heard of the slave, and had never seen a black person, but there and then I date the birth of my abolitionism. As it has been proposed to abrogate that old landmark of freedom, the Missouri Compromise, and let slavery into these new territories, I had to preach in my Plymouth pulpit: "Cursed be he that removeth his neighbor's landmark." When Chief Justice Taney, in the Dred Scott decision, claimed as the sentiment of the fathers of the republic that "black men had no rights which white men were bound to respect," I had to preach: "Cursed be he that perverteth the judgment of the stranger." And when this town of Lawrence was sacked and Charles Sumner was assassinated, I had to preach on "Kansas: Her Struggle and Her Defence." The text was Daniel 11: 11, 40: "And the king of the south shall be moved with choler, and shall come forth and fight with him, even with the king of the north: . . . And at the time of the end shall the king of the south push at him: and the king of the north shall come against him like a whirlwind, with chariots, and with horse men, and with many ships ; and he shall enter into the countries, and shall overflow and pass over." The sermon predicted : " If the south still persists in rushing this nation on to civil war, 'at the time of the end' of forbearance, the north will come 'like a whirlwind, with chariots, and with horsemen, and with many ships,' and will sweep from Mason and Dixon's line to Florida, from New York all around the coast to the Gulf."

After preaching in Mr. Lum's church on national affairs, Governor Robinson said that I must go out with him on a political canvass among the settlements. The free state men who had heretofore repudiated the bogus territorial government had now decided to vote. The election would come in a month. The treasurer of the state of Massachusetts, T. J. Marsh, Esq., who was also the treasurer of the Emigrant Aid Society, was present and was going along. It was important to lay before the people the true issue. So I joined their company ; and for three weeks, with printed placards ahead, we went lecturing day by day, the statesmen talking politics and the churchman preaching abolitionism. We had no disturbance along the way except when going to our appointment at Fort Scott, when we had to turn back upon learning that the border ruffians had possession of that stronghold. Striking off in another way, we got lost and were driving on far into the night. At last, following the barking of dogs, we came upon a settler's cabin. All the family were in bed, and nearly all were sick. After a repast of slapjacks and pork, we were allowed to lie down on our own buffalo robes with our feet to the fire. In the morning, giving the woman a five-dollar gold piece, we started on to our next appointment. The friends there finding where we had been lodged, told us that the man was one of the biggest border ruffians in all the region, and that if he had not been sick, and had known what game he had within reach, he certainly would have routed out the neighbors and bagged it all. Getting back to Lawrence, the people must needs give us a reception. It was an open-air meeting, with Jim Lane for presiding officer. Coming to introduce the young Chicago pastor, he said: "He's the fighting preacher; them's the sort we love."

I have had ample opportunity to see the people and to learn their spirit. They are united in the policy of voting at the October election. Keeping aloof from the sham government, they have made it appear the farcical thing it is. Its taxes could not be collected; its laws could not be enforced. When their ballot boxes were stolen and carried over into Missouri, they declared that they would not vote again until those boxes were brought back and a fair election secured. Nobly have they stood these two years for self-government. They have suffered in their personal interests rather than resort to the bogus authorities for their rights. They have lived here without justices of the peace, without constables and sheriffs, without courts, without registers. That a heterogeneous population scattered over a vast region have not only been a law unto themselves, but have successfully resisted a merciless tyranny, is a new proof of the inherent capacity of the people to govern themselves. And now when the President and the governor have promised to restore the ballot box and to assure a fair election, when the test oath of obedience to the fugitive slave law is abolished, and when the tax-paying qualification for voting is removed, the people resolve to try these fair offers and to assume the government which had been wrested from them, or make a new one in its stead. But this was the last thing that the administration had desired. Supposing that the free state men would not vote at all, it had thus thrown the doors wide open so that it might be said that they were factious and hypocritical in their clamor for freedom.

The population of Kansas is estimated here at one hundred thousand, and the immigration of this season at forty thousand, the most of which is free state, and will be cut off from voting by the six months' stipulation. Everywhere they are confident of success, if not in the October election, yet in a final victory for freedom. It has not been in vain that the cause of Kansas was espoused in the east. It has been that general movement that has saved this territory for freedom. The Emigrant Aid Society, which invested thousands of dollars in mills, the first want of a new country, and in school-houses ; and also the National Kansas Committee, which sent seven hundred and fifty boxes of clothing, arms, and provisions to the value of several hundred thousand dollars ; the thundering of the press and the pulpit and the platform ; the general burst of sympathy that could not be cut off by the blockade of the national highways, — all these have conspired to save Kansas from the doom of slavery. It has been pleasant to hear the people express such views and tell how much good this aid has done. It was but our duty, for their cause was ours.

But you ask me about the sufferings of the Kansas people. Were the reports exaggerations, abolition lies ? I have taken great pains in this matter, and am constrained to say that scarcely the half has been told. In the distant settlements along the streams there were enough such incidents unpublished to fill a volume. Every cabin we entered would tell us some new tale of house robbing and burning, of stealing horses and cattle, of destruction of crops, of personal insult and injury, of constant fear and alarm. Many had been driven out of the country after their all had been taken from them. In the wake of the invading guerrillas followed the pro-slavery settlers, appropriating their neighbors' chickens, cattle, hogs, and grain. As I have stood upon the ashes of hundreds of homes; as I have stood by the graves of the martyrs, Phillips, Roberts, Dow, Hoyt, Barber, and Shomber, the last of whom died saying, "I give myself a cheerful sacrifice on the altar of Kansas freedom"; as I have heard the tales of outrage from men and women, my realization of these facts has made my indignation burn, and I have wondered how the freemen here could have the moral courage to stand as they did only on the defensive, and not to annihilate their savage invaders as they might have done. It is a strange feeling I have had in passing over these prairies to have the driver or my traveling companion saying, "On this spot Roberts was murdered, and here is the pile of stones at his grave; at this spot another was butchered; here that woman at the home of Mr. Hyatt was seized, gagged, kicked, and left for dead; here this house was burned, there that; here the presses of the *Herald*, the *Free State*, and the *Times* were destroyed." We stopped two nights with the family of Ottawa Jones, an Indian who, having received a college education, married a white woman who had come as a missionary to his tribe twenty years ago. He has a farm of two hundred and fifty acres under the best of cultivation. He had a house two stories high, twenty by fifty feet, well finished and furnished. He sympathized with the free state cause but took no part. A company of eighty cowardly brutes came to his house one night and aroused him by breaking in the windows. Mr. Jones fled through a shower of bullets out of the back door into the cornfield, and his wife was robbed of eight hundred dollars in gold which she was bringing out of the house, which was burned to the ground. A sick man in the house was dragged down-stairs, had his throat cut, and his body thrown into the stream near by, though he still survives the horrid gashes. The large stone chimney still stands upon the ruins, a monument of barbarism more savage, as the family said, than they had ever known in savage life. And the leader of this gang was Captain H., of Missouri, who boasted of the hospitality he had shared in that house! It was refreshing to enjoy the family devotions of Mr. Jones. He had just returned from Washington, where a treaty was made by which his tribe, numbering two hundred and thirty, is received into citizenship, each one taking two hundred and forty acres of land. They will vote the free state ticket.

I was present at the opening and adjourning of the Constitutional Convention at Lecompton. The printer was chosen because he had distinguished himself in the Kansas war, and so it was publicly avowed. But this is only one section of that gigantic crime to be incorporated into that constitution. Taking the ayes and nays upon adjournment to Leavenworth or Lecompton, Randolph arose at the call of his name to explain his vote, and said: "Yesterday I was strongly in favor of adjourning to Leavenworth, for the whiskey was getting tolerably weak; but since we began to talk about leaving, the whiskey is getting quite decent; now I am in favor of staying here." That, you may take for the *spirit* of the convention.

LETTER II.

A STATE WITH A HISTORY.

SAINT JOSEPH, Mo., October 1, 1857.
KANSAS will be a state with a history. Probably the history of no state in the Union, since the founding of Massachusetts upon Plymouth Rock, has had so much of stirring incident. Almost every other state has had in its early history a chapter upon its warfare with the savages of the forest. In Kansas the conflict has been with white savages, the Indians having given them no trouble. This new state has been the scene of our first civil war, a war in which the Federal army, stationed here to protect the frontier, has been used to sustain invasion and usurpation, to crush out liberty. The history of Kansas will bristle with reminiscences of heroism and of martyrdom. It has its Bunker Hill and its Lexington; its Warrens and its Putnams. The chapter upon the early legislation of Kansas will hardly be believed by the future reader of history. It will seem to him like a burlesque upon all jurisprudence, upon all right and justice The early history of Kansas will be marked by the rapid transitions in its government. Within four years, two territorial and two state governments; two conventions, convening and forming constitutions, and a third provided for; seven governors and acting governors succeeding upon the throne of this ruffian dynasty, all crucified upon this gubernatorial Golgotha as fast as they come short of the bidding of the slavocracy! But freedom and peace and prosperity will come. The American Home Missionary Society and the American Missionary Association have shown a just appreciation of the importance of Christian ministers in this

struggle for civil and religious freedom, by early sending, each of them, four or five home missionaries. The influence of these men is acknowledged as very great in behalf of liberty as well as of religion ; and now as society settles down, they will have a hold upon the people which will be of great service in their specific work. A band of four young men is soon to come from Andover under the American Home Missionary Society. These are Storrs, Cordly, Parker, and Marsh.

LETTER III.

THE MISSOURI PLAN IN NORTH CAROLINA AND KENTUCKY.

SYRACUSE, N. Y., October 12, 1860.
HERE at the fourteenth annual meeting of the American Missionary Society in Rev. M. E. Strieby's Plymouth Church, we have a lot of refugees, our missionaries, driven out of North Carolina and Kentucky by mob violence on account of their liberty-loving sentiments. Here is Rev. Daniel Worth, of Quaker origin, a native of the old North State, where he had served as a justice of the peace. *The New York Herald* says he "is a large, portly man, with a large head and intellectual and expressive countenance and a large, commanding eye. He looks enough like Burton, the comedian, to be his twin-brother. He is fluent in speech, and the general style and manner of his speaking are calculated to win attention." He was arrested in Guilford County and thrown into the Greensboro' jail. He was released upon three thousand dollars of bail. This sum the friends at the north have raised, and now he is a free man. The punishment, if he had been convicted, would have been pillory, whipping, and

imprisonment. The sole charge on which he was imprisoned, after the preliminary examination, was the circulating of "Helper's Impending Crisis," a book written by a southern man, and dwelling, not upon the moral aspects of slavery, but solely upon its economic bearings. Now we have here a pamphlet entitled "An Address to the People of North Carolina on the Evils of Slavery," printed in that state and in that very county in the year 1830, by the "Manumission Society of North Carolina," which a newspaper in that state declares to be ten times worse than Helper's book. It maintains these propositions: "First, Our slave system is radically evil. Second, It is founded in injustice and cruelty. Third, It is a fruitful source of pride, idleness, and tyranny. Fourth, It increases depravity in the human heart, and nourishes a train of dark and brutal passions and lusts, disgraceful to the human nature and destructive of the general welfare. Fifth, It is no less contrary to the Christian religion than to the dictates of justice and humanity." Mr. Worth and his associates had eight Wesleyan churches under their charge. Rev. Alfred Vestal was driven back north by violence. Another was seized by the throat in the pulpit and shamefully treated. They were all under commission of this body.

The whole Kentucky force has been driven out. Reverends George Candee and William Kendrick were seized in Laurel County by a committee; their hair and beards were sheared off, and then their heads and faces were tarred. Rev. J. C. Richardson was teaching a school in Whitley County; being suspected of anti-slavery sentiments, upon search a copy of Wesley's tract on slavery was found in his possession. He was seized and bound with ropes at the house of Mr. Rockhold, where was the post-office, to which he had gone for his mail. There he was kept under an armed guard of three men. He was released by two Elliott brothers and their father, powerful men, who took away their man, covering his escape by their rifles. The whole of the Berea community were driven out upon the demand of a committee of sixty of the first citizens of Madison County, who in martial array rode around from house to house. Among those thus compelled to leave were the families of Reverends John G. Fee, J. A. Rogers, and James S. Davis. This, after the burning of their mill, and mobs and whippings not a few. It was the shiver of the John Brown raid that had aroused the people to these atrocities. I spent the evening with John Brown not long ago at the house of John Jones, a colored man in Chicago, when he was on his way with a batch of fugitives from Missouri to Canada. He said he was showing the people at the south what could be done. He did the same at Harper's Ferry. On the evening of his execution we had a prayer-meeting in Plymouth Church, to pray for the emancipation of the slave.

This has been a grand meeting of the Association. The refugees have added greatly to the enthusiasm. Dr. John Morgan preached the sermon. In the home field there were last year 112 missionary pastors, who served 145 churches. Of these churches there were in the states east of the Ohio, 15; in Ohio, Michigan, and Indiana, 35; in Illinois, 23; in Wisconsin and Minnesota, 14; in Iowa, 10; in Kansas, 4; in Missouri, 1; in Kentucky, 8; and in North Carolina, 2. Among these may be mentioned: in Michigan, those of Charlotte, Augusta, Allegan, Eaton Rapids, Grand Haven; in Illinois, DeKalb, Dundee, Paxton, Sandwich, New England of Aurora, Morrison, and Waukegan; in Wisconsin, Broadhead, Reedsburg, Burlington, and Sparta; in Iowa, Cedar Falls, Waterloo, Mason City; in Minnesota, the Plymouth Church of Minneapolis. It was to labor among these churches that I resigned my pastorate last July.

PERIOD II.

DURING THE WAR, 1861-63.

The South Pushing at the North. — Emancipation Memorial. — Soldiers from Western Colleges. — Trip to the Army. — United States Sanitary Disbursements. — Surgery in the Army. — Emancipation Meeting. — Boston Tract Society in the Army. — A New York May Anniversary. — The Morgan Raid. — First Sanitary Fair.

LETTER IV.

THE KING OF THE SOUTH PUSHING AT THE KING OF THE NORTH.

NORWICH, Conn., October 25, 1861.

IN 1856 was printed that sermon with a prophecy on the king of the south coming forth to fight against the king of the north. So soon has it come to pass. At Sumter did that king, moved with choler, push at our king to rouse him to come like a whirlwind, with chariots and with horsemen and with many ships, to enter into the countries and pass over. The American Missionary Association, holding its anniversary in this ancient city, by its identification with the cause of freedom now finds itself brought to the forefront of the battle. By General Butler's stroke of genius the colored people coming through our lines at Fortress Monroe are not to be sent back to their masters, but are to be treated as "contraband of war." There are now eighteen hundred of them, in great destitution. Rev. L. C. Lockwood has been sent forward as a missionary, General Wool heartily approving.

He is to preach at the fortress, the seminary, and at the Tyler House. A week-day school was opened on the seventeenth of September, under Mrs. Mary E. Peake, a colored person of English education; and Sunday-schools were opened at the three places named, the last being the residence of ex-President Tyler. Not only Bibles, Testaments, and school-books, but clothing has been sent forward to meet the necessities of the "contrabands." This body, moved by the grandeur of the opportunity, declared its purpose "to follow the armies of the United States with faithful missionaries and teachers." How grand the opening when God, by the issues of war, shall set before us a "wide and effectual door" in all the south for teaching and propagating the gospel, and when four millions of ex-slaves shall be thrown upon our hands for nourishment into Christian citizenship!

The Association, in this changed order of things, while expressing thanks to God for the work accomplished in the north-west by its missionaries and by its organic testimony against slavery, has determined now the more to concentrate its effort along the fifteen hundred miles of border-ground and over in the slave states as rapidly as possible. This, as is contemplated, will leave the missionaries and the district secretary of the north-west to fall over into their natural relation to the American Home Missionary Society.

LETTER V.

THE EMANCIPATION MEMORIAL.

CHICAGO, September 20, 1862.

THE idea of such a memorial was born in the brain of Dr. William W. Patton. I had the honor of circulating the call for the meeting that adopted the memorial. We agreed that the call should be limited to those who were ready to ask for emancipation, thus shutting off discussion on that question. In passing about the streets for signatures, I was deeply impressed with the fact that so many of our business men of first position were Christian men. The call was also signed by the Congregational, Baptist, and Methodist ministers. After the meeting had been held and the memorial adopted, the following circular was issued, calling upon the people in other places to hold similar meetings : —

CHICAGO, September 8, 1862.

Dear Sir, — At the call of more than one hundred of the prominent citizens of this city, a meeting of all denominations was held in Bryan Hall, Thursday evening, September 4, Hon. L. B. Otis in the chair, to take measures to memorialize the President to issue a proclamation of national emancipation. At this meeting the Hon. Grant Goodrich, Hon. John M. Wilson. Rev. T. M. Eddy, D.D., Rev.W.W. Everts, D.D., Hon. Mark Skinner, Rev. Nathaniel Colver, D.D., Rev. W. W. Patton. D.D., and Hon. S. B. Gookins were appointed a committee to report a memorial and resolutions to be adopted at a subsequent gathering.

On Sabbath evening, September 7, in the same immense hall, which was crowded to overflowing, and from which hundreds went away unable to gain entrance, the following memorial and resolutions, recommended by the committee, were adopted unanimously by a solemn rising vote.

A delegation, consisting of Rev. W. W. Patton, D.D., Hon. Mark Skinner, Rev. John Dempster, D.D., and Charles Walker, Esq., was appointed to carry the memorial in person to Washington and present it to the President.

Read it! Read it carefully! Call your Christian fellow-citizens together, without distinction of sect, and adopt it, or something like it, and send it to the President. The united voice of the Christians of this whole land should go up to the executive mansion, calling for justice to the oppressed. We must as a nation learn righteousness, or our poor, bleeding, imperiled country is undone. Religious men everywhere at such a time as this should act and speak fearlessly and promptly. They should also pray unceasingly that God would incline our President to do that great act of justice and mercy which this memorial implores.

Dear sir, as you love your God, we beg that you will not delay to act in this matter.

    JOSEPH E. ROY,
    S. B. GOOKINS,
    NATHANIEL COLVER,
    LUCIUS H. BUGBEE, *Committee of Correspondence.*

To His Excellency, Abraham Lincoln, President of the United States, — Your memorialists of all Christian denominations in the city of Chicago, assembled in solemn meeting to consider the moral aspects of the war now waging, would utter their deepest convictions as to the present relation of our country and its rulers to the government and providence of Almighty God; and would respectfully ask a hearing for the principles and facts deemed fundamental to a right judgment of this appalling crisis. And to this we are encouraged by the frequency with which, on various public occasions, you have officially recognized the dependence of the country and its chief magistrate upon the divine favor.

We claim, then, that the war is a divine retribution upon our land for its manifold sins, and especially for the crime of oppression, against which the denunciations of God's Word are so numerous and pointed.

The American nation, in this its judgment hour, must acknowledge that the cry of the slave, unheeded by man, has been heard by God and answered in this terrible visitation. The time has at length come of which Jefferson solemnly warned his countrymen, as he declared that the slaves of America were enduring "a bondage, one hour of which is fraught with more misery than ages of that which occasioned the war of the Revolution," and added: "When the measure of their tears shall be full, when their tears shall have involved heaven itself in darkness, doubtless a God of justice will awaken to their distress by diffusing a light and liberality among their oppressors; or at length by his exterminating thunder, manifest his attention to things of this world, and that they are not left to the guidance of blind fatality."

The slave oligarchy has organized the most unnatural, perfidious, and formidable rebellion known to history. It has professedly established an independent government on the avowed basis of slavery, admitting that the federal union was constituted to conserve and promote liberty. All but four of the slave states have seceded from the Union, and those four (with the exception of Delaware, in which slavery but nominally exists) have been kept in subjection only by overwhelming military force. Can we doubt that this is a divine retribution for national sin, in which our crime has justly shaped our punishment?

Proceeding upon this belief, which recent events have made it almost atheism to deny, your memorialists avow their solemn conviction, deepening every hour, that there can be no deliverance from divine judgments till slavery ceases in the land. We can not expect God to save a nation that clings to its sin. This is too fearful an hour to insult God or to deceive ourselves. National existence is in peril; our sons and brothers are falling by tens of thousands on the battle-field; the war becomes daily more determined and destructive. While we speak, the enemy thunders at the gates of the capital. Our acknowledged superiority of resources has thus far availed little or nothing in the conflict. As Christian patriots we dare not conceal the truth, that these judgments mean what the divine judgments meant in Egypt. They are God's stern command, " Let my people go."

This work of national repentance has been inaugurated by the abolition of slavery in the District of Columbia, and its prohibition in the territories, as also by encouragement to emancipation in the border slave states, offered by Congress at the suggestion of the President.

But these measures do not meet the crisis, as regards either the danger of the country or the national guilt. We urge you, therefore, as the head of this Christian nation, from considerations of moral principle and as the only means of preserving the Union, to proclaim without delay national emancipation.

However void of authority in this respect you might have been in time of peace, you are well aware, as a statesman, that the exigencies of war are the only limits of its powers, especially in a war to preserve the very life of the nation. And these exigencies are not to be restricted to what may avail at the last gasp prior to national death, but are to be interpreted to include all measures that may most readily and thoroughly subdue the enemy. The rebels have brought slavery under your control by their desperate attack upon the life of the republic. They have created a moral, political, and military necessity which warrants the deed, and now God and a waiting world demand that the opportunity be used. And surely the fact that they have placed in our power a system which, while it exposes them, is itself the grossest wickedness adds infinitely to the obligation to strike the blow.

In this view of a change of power involving an equal change in duty, we will not conceal the fact that gloom has filled our hearts at every indication that the war was regarded as simply an issue between the federal authorities and the rebel states, and that therefore slavery was to be touched only to the extent that the pressure of rebel success might absolutely necessitate. Have we not reason to expect rebel success on that policy? Are we to omit from our calculations the necessary conditions of divine favor? Has the fact no moral force that the war has suddenly placed within the power of the President the system that has provoked God's wrath? Is there not danger that while we are waiting till the last terrible exigency shall force us to liberate the slave God may decide the contest against us, and the measure that we would not adopt on principle prove too late for our salvation? We claim that justice, here as every-where, is the highest expediency.

At the time of the national peril of the Jews under Ahasuerus, Mordecai spake in their name to Queen Esther, who hesitated to take the step necessary to their preservation, in these solemn words: "Think not with thyself that thou shalt escape in the king's house, more than all the Jews. For if thou altogether holdest thy peace at this time, then shall there enlargement and deliverance arise to the Jews from another place; but thou and thy father's house shall be destroyed: and who knoweth whether thou art come to the kingdom for such a time as this?" And your memorialists believe that in divine providence you have been called to the Presidency to speak the word of justice and authority which shall free the bondman and save the nation. Our prayer to God is that by such an act the name of Abraham Lincoln may go down to posterity, with that of George Washington, as the second saviour of our country.

RESOLUTIONS.

Resolved, That universal emancipation seems pointed out by providence as the most effectual, if not the only, means of saving our country.

That in the appalling loss of blood and treasure and repeated reverses to our arms, pressing the nation to the verge of destruction, should be heard the voice that sounded above the wail of desolated Egypt: "Let my people go."

That universal emancipation as a mere act of political justice would be without a parallel in the annals of the world.

That it would be the abandonment of a wrong long perpetuated against the oppressed race, to the contravention of impartial liberty, the reproach of free institutions, and the dishonor of our country.

That it would be a consummation of the expectations of the founders of the republic, who, deploring while tolerating slavery, anticipated its early disappearance from the continent.

That it would accord with the world's convictions of justice and the higher teachings of Christianity.

That we should not expect national deliverance till we rise at least to the moral judgment of Jefferson, who, in view of slavery, exclaimed: "I tremble for my country when I reflect that God is just; that his justice can not sleep forever; that, considering numbers, nature, and natural means only, a revolution of the wheel of fortune, an exchange of situation, is among possible events; that it may become probable by supernatural interference. The Almighty has no attribute which can take side with us in such a contest."

That all assumed right to slavery under the Constitution is forfeited by open and persistent rebellion; and therefore emancipation, to preserve the republic, would only vindicate and honor the Constitution.

That, as slavery is a principal reliance of the rebellion, conserving its property, tilling its plantations, feeding and clothing its armies, freeing the slaves would take away its support, recall its armies from the field, demoralize its conspiracy, and organize in its midst a power for its overthrow.

That putting down this rebellion is as obvious a Christian duty as prayer, preaching, charity to the poor, or missions to the heathen.

That the postponement of emancipation jeopards countless treasure, the best blood and the existence of the nation.

That no evils apprehended from emancipation are comparable to those that would arise from the overthrow of the republic, and they would fall upon those madly provoking the catastrophe.

That as the perpetuation and extension of slavery were a primary aim of this rebellion, its overthrow would seem a fitting and signal retribution upon its authors, like hanging Haman upon the gallows he erected for Mordecai.

That it were better for this generation to perish than that the American Union should be dissolved; and it is a delusion that those disloyal and belligerent under the Constitution and traditions of their fathers would become peaceable citizens, observant of treaties and oaths in rival states.

E. W. BLATCHFORD, *Secretary*.
L. B. OTIS, *Chairman*.

Doctors Dempster and Patton were the bearers of the memorial. President Lincoln heard them graciously, bringing out such arguments on the other side as occurred to him. These were reported in the papers, and *The Chicago Times* suggested that the President had put a bee in the doctors' ears. But Dr. Patton came home expecting a favorable issue, and so set his people to praying in a daily morning prayer-meeting for that result; and while they were praying the announcement came of the preliminary proclamation.[1]

LETTER VI.

REVIVALS IN WAR TIME. — CONSUL ZEBINA EASTMAN.

CHICAGO, November 11, 1862.

THE war times do not seem altogether unfavorable to revivals. The excitement of the public mind breaks up that lethargy which is antagonistic to Christian influences. The people are now communing with great moral principles, and this arouses sensibility. It is comparatively easy now to illustrate the moral government of God. The churches of God are not left without the manifestations of the Spirit. This is true at Cairo, Ill., where Rev. John T. Avery, the evangelist, is assisting the pastor, and many citizens and soldiers have found hope in Christ. The pastor is the only Protestant minister in the county except the United States chaplains. At this point and along up the Illinois Central Railroad there are located three thousand troops.

---

[1] Some months after this Joseph Medill, of *The Chicago Tribune*, who had recently been in Washington, told me that Secretary Stanton had said to him: "Tell those Chicago doctors that their interview did the business; that before their coming the President had been undecided."

Mr. Zebina Eastman, who for twelve years was editor and proprietor of the first anti-slavery paper in the state, *The Western Citizen*, which was incorporated into *The Chicago Tribune*, and who is now our consul at Bristol, England, is doing a good work over there in giving the English people correct ideas of our national affairs. "Our Civil War and Slavery" is the title of an address delivered by him in Arley Chapel, Bristol, and now passed to the third edition in London. His former acquaintance with the abolitionists of England must give weight to his influence there. President Lincoln has honored our country by honoring this old emancipationist. The Wisconsin General Convention of Congregational and Presbyterian ministers and churches, recently in session at Beloit, devoted an evening to the state of the country. Addresses were made by President Chapin, Rev. Joseph E. Roy, and Senator Doolittle, in the strain of sustaining the President in his preliminary proclamation, which was endorsed by a solemn rising vote of the assembly.

LETTER VII.

SOLDIERS FROM OUR WESTERN COLLEGES. — ILLINOIS CHAPLAINS.

CHICAGO, December 15, 1862.

THE war has brought into strong light the influence of our western colleges in nourishing patriotism. When the firing upon Fort Sumter echoed the call to arms, no class sprang into line with greater alacrity than did the sons of our colleges. At Oberlin, two companies, formed mostly of students, responded at once to the call of the President, and were incorporated in the second regiment of Ohio. The present senior class, that entered with eighty, is now reduced to eight. General Cox, a son-in-law of President Finney, is an alumnus of Oberlin, and many of the alumni are officers in the army. In all, Oberlin has sent nine theologues, ninety-two collegians, one hundred and fifty "preps," and five hundred former students, a total of seven hundred and fifty-one, a regiment of young ironsides. Besides these a company of "squirrel hunters" went for two or three weeks to the defence of Cincinnati. The Baptist theological school at Kalamazoo, Mich., has been nearly emptied of students. Illinois College has enlisted thirty-two graduates and fifty-one under-graduates, while former students have doubled this number, making one hundred and sixty-six in all. Knox College has furnished seventy graduates and under-graduates; Wheaton sends sixty-seven; Beloit, sixty-two in all. *The Beloit College Register* in its army list shows that of these student soldiers, sixteen are officers. Shurtleff counts her forty-five soldiers in the army. Generals Pope, Cook, Palmer, and many other officers of less note were once students there. Marietta has her sixty-one graduates and under-graduates in the service, besides quite a number who did not complete the course. Prof. E. B. Andrews, of this college, has gone up from the position of major to that of colonel. Wabash has sent off seventy-six of her sons. She is represented by General S. S. Fry, General Charles Cruft, General Lew Wallace, General J. J. Reynolds, and a plenty of minor officers. Adrian College counts out its forty-eight; Hillsdale, one hundred; and little Olivet, seventy-eight. Of the hundred and forty-three scholars in Liber College, Jay County, Ind., who were of a proper age, eighty-three have gone into the army. Evanston Biblical Institute sends ten, and the

Chicago Seminary, forty-two soldiers, one chaplain, and one surgeon. An average of seventy to each of these institutions would probably be too small, and yet they are all comparatively young and some of them have hardly come to the dignity of a list of alumni. The other colleges of the west would probably range in this respect with these. When you add the army lists of eastern colleges you will make out several regiments. Then to all this must be added the influence of these institutions in disseminating the spirit of patriotism. Surely, then, this is no time to allow these institutions to languish for want of support.

In this connection I may mention that Illinois has furnished ten Congregational chaplains. These are: Reverends Jeremiah Porter, J. H. Dill, S. Day, Joel Grant, A. L. Rankin, W. G. Pierce, S. S. Morrill, H. E. Barnes, W. C. Scofield, and Daniel Chapman. These pastors have each a son in the army: Reverends S. G. Wright, S. H. Emery, J. D. Baker, M. Bushnell, D. Andrews, D. Mattison, E. Morris, O. Miner, E. Jenney, and probably many more. It is worthy of mention that Mr. Porter began his ministry in 1831 as a chaplain at Fort Brady on the Sault Ste. Marie River, whence in 1833 he was transferred to Fort Dearborn (Chicago), where he organized the first church of the city. His commission from the Home Missionary Society instructed him to look after Fort Howard also (Green Bay) and Fort Crawford (Prairie du Chien), which he has literally done by subsequent pastorates at those places. He is accompanied by his wife, who is equal to most of the chaplains.

LETTER VIII.

A TRIP TO THE ARMY.

CAIRO, Ill., January 5, 1863.

I AM in charge of a car-load of stores, two hundred and twenty-seven packages, from the Chicago branch of the United States Sanitary Commission, and *en route* to minister to the soldiers wounded in the late battles down the Mississippi. I find here one thousand "contrabands," well cared for by the government, while a chaplain has been detailed to look after their spiritual welfare. Friend Headley, from Indiana, with his wife and niece, has opened a school, now in its second week, for the children. The teachers told me that on the first day of the school twenty of the pupils learned the alphabet, and I had the pleasure of hearing them read in words of three letters. It is a fine bit of retribution that the United States government furnishes transportation for these people to all the north-western states, except Illinois, which had set up such a howl over this "negro inundation." The recent message of our governor, Richard Yates, aside from its eminent ability and statesmanship, is worthy of mention in this place for its reverent recognition of God's hand in our delays and defeats, in order to bring about emancipation, and for his generous word as to New England. He says: —

It seems that providence has protracted this war and subjected our people to repeated humiliations and reverses for the purpose of making the destruction of slavery inevitable.

He also says: —

I regret that appeals are being made to the masses by a few public presses in the country for separation from New England. Not a drop of New England blood courses in my veins; still, I should deem myself an object of commiseration and shame if I could forget her glorious history; if I could forget that the blood of her citizens freely commingled with that of my own ancestors upon those memorable fields which ushered in the millennial dawn of civil and religious liberty. I propose not to be the eulogist of New England; but she is indissolubly bound to us by all the bright memories of the past, by all the glories of the present, by all the hopes of the future. I shall always glory in the fact that I belong to a republic in the galaxy of whose stars New England is among the brightest and best. Palsied be the hand that would sever the east from the west!

LETTER IX.

ON BOARD STEAMER SIR WILLIAM WALLACE.

JANUARY 8, 1863.

THIS steamer has been chartered by the United States Sanitary Commission. We have our Chicago stores on board, and in all we now have one thousand and twenty-seven packages, about one hundred tons of necessaries and delicacies for hospital use. At Columbus we took on the balance of the stores. The agency there is to be united with that at Memphis. As a sample of what the Commission is doing, I was informed by the agent at the other place that during the last six months he had given out 2,346 bed-ticks, 308 blankets, 22,363 comforts, 8,558 pairs of drawers, 4,960 pillows, 8,402 pillow-cases, 7,387 sheets, 13,913 shirts, 3,003 pairs socks, 9,119 towels, 97 boxes of bandages, 3,946 pounds of butter, 2,260 pounds of codfish, 570 pounds of corn-starch, 1,067 dozen eggs, 16,279 pounds of dried fruit, 6,774 cans of fruit, 2,921 bushels of vegetables, 491 bottles of wines and cordials, and so on through a list of seventy-four articles. This is a minor agency with but one man, while that at Pittsburg Landing has had five busily engaged. The Commission has followed up every battle with its ministrations. The aggregate of such articles furnished would be astounding, and the good accomplished simply incalculable. As to the producers of this immense treasure, it can only be said that the patriotic ladies of the north have vied with their brothers in doing for their country, while noble men have not spared themselves nor their business in managing the central and the branch commissions. Of the Chicago branch I can say that Hon. Mark Skinner, its president, E. W. Blatchford, its secretary, Rev. Dr. W. W. Patton, and the other members have given themselves to this work with a zeal only equaled by their patriotism. And now with one hundred thousand soldiers in our hospitals, while the government is doing all that is needed for those in active service, the country ought not to slacken its efforts in this great and glorious work of comforting our sick and wounded soldiers. Columbus, scarcely recovered from its recent big scare, is an immensely strong position from a military point of view, but a miserable town. Island No. 10, since the recent surprise which spiked so many guns, looked desolate and had but a few soldiers. The several rebel fortifications along the eastern bank will soon be washed away, but there are enough more of the mementoes of Commander ·Foote's patriotic deeds. The sweep from some of these fortifications up and down the river, as well as across the narrow channel, is truly awful. The great wonder was the sight of the narrow and crooked slough through which General Pope passed his men across the bend.

It is night. It is densely foggy. We hasten on to reach our moorings here under the guns of Fort Wright, fearing to tie up elsewhere, lest the sweeping guerrillas should gobble us up. A strange feeling this, coming from the presence of our artillery and our soldiers. We have but one pilot along, his partner having left the boat at Cairo, notwithstanding the usual wages of $250 per month, fearing, as we expected to go below Memphis, that he might be picked off by the sharp-shooters, though the pilot-house was guarded with boiler iron.

LETTER X.

MEMPHIS, Tenn., January 11, 1863.

THE weather is that of mid-October days. The city, located upon a high bank, built of brick, with a population of thirty thousand, is one of fine appearance. In its rapid growth and in the bluster of its business men, it reminds one much of Chicago. At present it is said that the only truly loyal people here are the soldiers and the negroes. As the place of residence, in palatial style, of nabobs, whose plantations are below on the river, it has been one of the most spiteful of rebel towns. Here is the great factory where the cloth for rebel uniforms was made. Here I find Rev. Jeremiah Porter, chaplain of the first regiment of Illinois artillery, but now detailed for duty in the garrison. He and his wife are very angels of mercy to the soldiers. Rev. Z. K. Hawley, also of Illinois, is acting as chaplain to the Overton Hospital, a grand hotel building formerly used by the rebels for the same purpose. With nine hundred patients it is under the best of management. Here there is a contraband village of two thousand people. Here is Miss Rose M. Kinney, who, under the American Missionary Association, had been with our garrison at Corinth, and connected with the hospital and school for the colored refugees at that place; and who, as the post had to be abandoned to the rebels, fled to this city with our soldiers and the refugees, pursued and fired upon by the enemy. But no sooner had she arrived than she was again at work in hospital and school service, a heroine indeed. In two months fifty children had learned to read. On New Year's day they had a celebration, at which an exhibition of the school, worship, and addresses by chaplains Porter and Hawley and a colored minister were the exercises. It was a gala day. Their pastor, a quadroon, having returned to Mississippi to get his wife and children, had found that they had been sent farther south for safety. He had been kidnapped and sold for $1,100 and was still in the care of the buyer, bound, when, our forces coming up, the tables were turned, the minister set free and the man-stealers made prisoners, being now as such in this city, while the man of God is dispensing the Word of Life to the people, a freeman.

The heroism of this war is not all on the side of the men. Besides the missionary lady named, here are Miss Babcock, of Chicago, in care of sanitary goods; Miss Mary Burnell, of Milwaukee, my niece, under the Christian Commission; and "Aunt Lizzie" Aiken, a former parishioner of mine, serving as a nurse out of the greatness of her heart. Here are also Mrs. Hoge, of Chicago, and Mrs. Colt, of Milwaukee, women of great experience, on a tour of exploration among the hospitals and camps, dispensing wisdom in counsel and in personal attention. We find that General Sherman has been repulsed at Vicksburg, and with his army on the transports is on his way up to capture Arkansas Post, and we are ordered forward to that point. General Grant has arrived here and his army will be joined to Sherman's. Then, in conjunction with Banks and Farragut, another move will be made upon Vicksburg. With a gun-boat escort we are off to Arkansas Post.

LETTER XI.

DISBURSEMENTS BY THE SANITARY COMMISSION. —
SURGERY IN THE ARMY.

CHICAGO, January 22, 1863.
As I have just returned from a trip down the Mississippi to the mouth of the White River, in charge of the stores of the Chicago Branch of the United States Sanitary Commission, I desire to say a few words to the friends of this enterprise in the north-west in regard to the disbursement of goods by this patriotic and philanthropic agency. An impression has gained some currency that these sacred benefactions are not used as exclusively for the use of soldiers as they ought to be. As an arm of the government, appointed by the President and by him entrusted with the important function of the inspection of hospitals and camps as to their sanitary condition, and yet performing their service independent of the national treasury, this Commission deserves profound respect. The several branches at Cleveland, Cincinnati, Louisville, Chicago, are but the correlative parts of the central organization at Washington, of which Rev. Dr. Bellows is President, and Fred. Law Olmstead Secretary. The appointees, as inspectors, general superintendents, and local disbursing agents, are all amenable to the one organic body. Thus in the south-west, Dr. H. A. Warriner, a man of eminent qualifications, is sanitary inspector of camps and hospitals, and general superintendent of sanitary agencies in General Grant's army. These are at Cairo, Columbus, Memphis, Corinth, and Jackson. He also controls the movements of the steamboat Sir William Wallace, chartered for the uses of the Commission in that

region, a boat which, paying one half of its surplus earnings to the chartering party, does much towards meeting its own expense, while enabling the agents to carry their stores to such places and at such times as the exigencies of battle or the uncertain movements of war may demand. This boat is in charge of Dr. R. G. McLean, who is also United States inspector of hospitals, for which double responsibility his professional and military experience (in Mexico) eminently qualify him. On her last trip down, she carried one thousand and twenty-seven packages, or one hundred tons of stores, gathered up from the several branches.

The local agencies are usually in buildings confiscated by the government and so costing nothing for rent, while the agents are held to a strict account for the goods in their charge, giving and receiving vouchers for the same. They or the general superintendent, if at hand, make appropriations to camp or general hospitals as needed. Then these goods are delivered into the possession of the head nurse of the hospital, who carries the keys of the rooms containing sanitary clothing and delicacies. She administers upon written requisition of the surgeon for each particular patient. Thus, at Memphis, the Overton Hospital, in a new hotel, and the Jefferson Hospital, and several others there, all confiscated property, are supplied by the agency of the Commission, which occupies and fills a store in one of the above-mentioned buildings, equal to any in Lake Street, Chicago.

One reason why soldiers return home from the hospitals and sometimes say that they never received any thing from the Commission, is that the articles furnished through the system described above seem to them to come from the government. A soldier upon his cot eating canned peaches made a remark to that effect, when it was shown by the marks that his peaches and his shirt and the bedding he had were all from the Chicago Commission.

Another element of strength in this arm of the public service is that, while its sphere is not that of fighting, it yet hangs upon the rear and even seeks the front for its ministrations. Dr. E. Andrews, of our city, who was one of the three who were detailed to do all the amputating at Vicksburg, told me at Memphis, where he was then in charge, that before the battle began he had sanitary stores from the Chicago branch on hand, and that they did great good. And while from our distance from the scene of action we could not, as we had hoped, reach that field of carnage, we were glad to learn that the agent at Helena, Mr. Pattenburg, had hastened down with stores and was able to administer to the six hundred and fifty wounded on their way up the river, and, as he said, he was never so happy before in his life. At the mouth of the White River our boats found one hundred of the slightly wounded from Vicksburg on board the Adriatic, used as a hospital, and left there, that when recovered they might be within easy reach of the army. But in that by-place they were in great destitution of any thing like comforts. We supplied them with apples, tea, crackers, concentrated milk, beef, and delicacies, and necessaries of under-clothing and bedding. Never were poor fellows more grateful for such favors. At the same place our boat also discharged a supply for General McClernand's army up the Arkansas River. At Memphis, on my return, I found five companies of the one hundred and thirteenth Illinois, and I supplied them with the balance of the goods sent them by the Board of Trade, and also other articles as they needed. Some of them were sick, and all of them, having been upon boats for six weeks, were living upon hard bread and salt meat. Their apples, tea, crackers, etc., were all the sweeter for being a remembrance from friends at home.

Let us not be weary in well doing. The one hundred thousand soldiers lying in the hospitals, sick and wounded, who have fought our battles for us, have a claim upon our material sympathy. Our obligation is not simply that of humanity, but that of debt.

A valuable addition has been made to the literature of the war by Dr. Edmund Andrews, professor of surgery in the Chicago Medical College, and late surgeon of the first regiment of Illinois artillery, in a "Complete Record of the Surgery of the Battles fought near Vicksburg, December 27–30, 1862." Seeing that by the confusion of battle, the scattering of the wounded, and the imperfect registration, the vast statistics of the war were slipping away, and that this costly experience of blood and life were giving but little aid to the settlement of many difficult questions in surgery, the doctor determined to secure a record of the wounded of that battle up to the latest period possible. Here is an entire surgical history of the wounds up to the twentieth day, at which time the question of life or death is usually settled, giving the case, name, operation, anæsthetics, and remarks. Of the 750 wounds, 50 were of the head, 10 of the neck, 164 of the trunk, 69 of the arm, 77 of the hand, 14 of the elbow, 43 of the forearm, 41 of the hip, 107 of the thigh, 25 of the knee, 79 of the leg, 50 of the foot. Of the wounds of the head, 10 died; of the trunk, 20; of the arm, 4; of the hip, 3; of the leg, 7; of the foot, 1. A predominance of wounds on the right side comes from skirmish-firing from behind trees, which is usually on the right-hand side. Of the 88 cases of amputation, 13 died. Dr. Andrews was detailed as one of three surgeons to perform these operations, and it is not likely that any poor soldier lost his limb or his life unnecessarily under his skillful hand. The result of his observation on ventilation is: "Let the surgeon see that he gets fresh air for his men in preference to food, warmth, or shelter. Men will live on snow, on wet ground, or under open sheds, and do well on bacon and hard tack; but in closed hospitals they will die, though they have all the luxuries of the world around them."

LETTER XII.

EMANCIPATION MEETING.

CHICAGO, January 31, 1863.

IT is the year of jubilee! Our colored brethren, on New Year's day, celebrated the glorious event. Future generations of all climes will hallow this era of emancipation. Glory to God, good-will to men! Addresses were made by Hon. John Wentworth, Rev. J. E. Roy, and E. C. Larned, Esq. The last speaker told this story of himself: Recently he had been over in England. At his lodgings, coming down the first morning to his breakfast, he saw a colored man sitting at the table. He shrank back at first at the thought of sitting by the side of the black man. Then he mentally thus addressed himself: "Larned, you are an old abolitionist; are n't you ashamed of yourself?" He went and took his seat by the side of the sable man, and found him to be an English barrister; a man well-traveled, a courteous gentleman, whose company he ever afterwards sought and enjoyed. "That experience," said he, "cured me of all color prejudice."

The Chicago Sanitary Commission having requested the churches of the north-west to take up a collection on the third Sabbath of January for its uses, the result, as reported thus far, is an aggregate of $7,760, of which $3,444 was from the churches of this city. Such a simultaneous remembrance of our wounded soldiers in our places of worship was a material expression of our religious sympathy. As a sign of the times, it is worthy of mention that on the same day two of the local associations of this state were in session upon slave soil : the Illinois, at Hannibal, with pastor Sturtevant ; the southern Illinois, at St. Louis, with Dr. T. M. Post. Telegrams of Christian fellowship and of patriotism were exchanged. At St. Louis the camps were visited, and it was cheering to see how much the loyal Christian people of that city were doing for the temporal and spiritual welfare of the soldiers brought among them.

Those who propose to re-construct our disrupted Union by leaving out New England, would do well to consider such facts as those presented by Dr. Kitchel in his " New England Zone," and by Dr. Joseph Clark in his " New England in the West." The Puritan commonwealth of ideas, institutions, enterprise, stretches across the continent. Emigration and evangelization have sown the seed broadcast, disseminating the spirit and the privileges of the Pilgrims from the Atlantic to the Pacific. The colleges and the theological seminaries of the west are distinctively New England in their origin, officers, and early endowments. Marietta, as shown by its report of a quarter-centennial celebration, has sent out two hundred and twenty-two graduates, of whom ninety-two have entered the ministry. In the same time, at the beginning, Harvard graduated one hundred and forty-seven, and Yale one hundred and forty-five. No man can estimate the influence of these institutions to mold society, to sustain the state; and he would be a madman and a traitor who should propose to eliminate Puritanism from the west.

LETTER XIII.

CHICAGO BRANCH, BOSTON TRACT SOCIETY.

CHICAGO, April 30, 1863.

THE Western Agency of the American Tract Society, Boston, under Rev. G. S. F. Savage, whose headquarters are in this city, and whose field runs from the Ohio westward, has already come to a large degree of prosperity. Its catholic spirit and its devotion to the moral needs of the soldiers are calling out the benefactions of our western people. The annual report of the Agency, besides books sold, shows the receipt of $5,335. The larger part of this amount went to the supply of gospel rations to the army of the south-west. During the year the secretary has made five trips to "Dixie" for the purpose of visiting the soldiers in camp, on the battle-field, and in the hospital, and of distributing the tracts, books, and papers so elegantly prepared by this Society for this use. In this way he has given out twelve hundred hymn-books and one hundred dollars' worth of Bibles and Testaments. In the year, besides doing an overwhelming amount of office work, he has visited all the north-western states, traveling in all, 15,245 miles. The Tract Society, which opened its mouth for the dumb, is now brought into such usefulness in this the time of our nation's distress.

Dr. Patton, a member of the Chicago branch of the United States Sanitary Commission, having just returned from a trip to Vicksburg on business for that arm of the service, made a report to his church last Sunday evening, using as his text the passage of Jesse's sending David to the army with the loaves, ten cheeses, and parched corn, to see how his brothers fared. He had little hope of the speedy capture of that stronghold. Dr. Charles Jewett, that old temperance war-horse, in a recently published report of his labors in Illinois, says that in traveling over the state promiscuously, he has found only one temperance man disloyal or reading a disloyal paper. He thinks that liquor and disloyalty go together.

LETTER XIV.

A MAY ANNIVERSARY.

NEW YORK, May 20, 1863.

A WESTERN man notices that the New York anniversaries have not the numbers and the fervor they once had on the boards of the old Tabernacle, which must somewhere yet be resonant with truth and eloquence. The anti-slavery society always produces a sensation and receives the commendation of the *Herald* for spice. The Boston Tract Society made a grand report of work among the colored people. Mr. Beecher had an anniversary of his own before the Home Missionary Society, with another western man to stand as preface to the volume which he unrolled in his own strain of eloquence. Mr. Beecher was not ashamed to say, "When I was out west as a missionary." It was worth a trip to New York to witness the baptism of a slave child, to gain the sight of a vast congregation responding by their tears as godfathers and godmothers to the little stranger.

They say that it gives breadth to an eastern man to go out upon the western prairies. It certainly gives a western man elevation to come down among the hills. Every visit to them has given me a thrill. As they flitted by us on the railway, such individuality had they, that they seemed as old acquaintances. The Hudson is a neverending glory. But the climax of my delight was a trip over the Erie Railroad by daylight. Seated in the rear of the rear car, with a view sidewise and backward, from morning till night my eyes were strained and my heart subdued. Such majesty, such kaleidoscopic beauty, such thrilling surprises! What a path-finder is the locomotive! On this track it coquets with four different rivers: the Passaic, the Delaware, the Susquehannah, the Chenango, shooting from one to the other as if by instinct; now creeping along the sides of precipices, now snorting through cavernous tunnels, now bidding defiance to altitude. But who ever discovered, who ever cut out these water-courses, and why this piling of land into such unserviceable shapes? For the same reason that the common Author used up in a Lord Bacon enough material to make many ordinary men, and that to inspire reverence for His works. While thus musing upon the hills so carelessly tumbled together, and wondering what could be raised upon them, a friend pointed out a little farm, with its plain homestead nestling between the base of a tall mountain and the Delaware, as the boyhood home of William Bross, one of the editors of our *Tribune*. Here nine boys had been "raised" and educated and then sent West — an editor, a doctor, a lawyer, a railroad operator, and such like. Then I saw the utility of that soil in producing men to people, subdue, and govern the empires springing out of the regions beyond.

But those horrid fences! The grand old stumps of the field saturated with pitch, extracted by a mammoth dentistry, and then set upon edge and in line for miles, as fences defying all intruders! So may it be with the forest growth of rebellion in this land: chopped down, turned up by the roots, and then made to hedge in our government and our freedom, a warning against all future treason. And so may it be with that other conspiracy, the liquor traffic.

LETTER XV.

THE MORGAN RAID.

CHICAGO, July 31, 1863.

ON a trip through central Indiana, during the late Morgan raid, I saw something of the patriotism of the Hoosier State. In forty-eight hours after the governor's call sixty thousand men had volunteered. At Terre Haute eleven hundred men came in from two counties, and five hundred others were under way when orders came that they were not needed. At Kokomo, the call was received at ten o'clock A.M., and at one o'clock P.M. a company of eighty men, made up on the spot, of lawyers, doctors, ministers, editors, county officers and clerks, was on the cars bound for the seat of war, and four hundred more were at once raised from that county of Howard. And so it was all over the central and southern parts of the state. Although the country had been drained before so that the women were taking care of the crops, as soon as the hoof of the invader struck the free soil, its loyalists seemed to rise up out of the ground. On former Fourth of July occasions we have had the rhetoric of leaving the plow in the furrow, but here was a literal leaving of the reaper in the swath, for the harvest had just begun. Such demonstrations reveal the fact that the country is safe, after all, in the hands of the people. At Noblesville a squad of forty Americo-African recruits had come to take the cars for rendezvous at Indianapolis, and during the hours of waiting were scorching in the sun. A citizen, Joseph Gray, Esq., told them to go to the court-house green and hold up their heads. A crowd assembled, and Gray made a speech, and called upon the people to treat these soldiers as they had treated their white comrades before, with a dinner. Soon the tables were built and a bountiful repast provided, and then the sable warriors moved off with light hearts. Now Gray's harvest is ripe and no hands can be found. Driving to the capitol, he finds the leader of the squad he had befriended, and, telling his story, he is furnished with a half-dozen men whom the examining officer had rejected for inconsiderable disabilities. The jolly fellows put up the harvest in good style and received their two dollars a day — a generous reciprocity all around.

LETTER XVI.

THE FIRST SANITARY FAIR.

CHICAGO, October 30, 1863.

ON the second and third of September a convention of ladies was held in this city to arrange for a great north-western fair and festival for the benefit of the Sanitary Commission. Congressman Owen Lovejoy, Senator Chandler, and others made addresses. And now the women's fair is reported to be a great success. It has surpassed all expectation. We have had the glow of the feast of tabernacles protracted through two weeks and with culminating effect. The opening was an ovation. In eight year's residence here I have witnessed many civic, military, and patriotic demonstrations, but never any thing that thrilled the mass of the people as this did. Banks, schools, stores, and shops were closed, and the people turned out in a procession three miles long, that took fifty-eight minutes to pass a given point, while the city every-where was a-flutter with flags, and resounding with vocal music and jubilations. Instead of the captive kings who were wont to grace the old Roman triumphs, a half-dozen captured rebel flags were borne upon a band chariot, while the convalescents from the Soldiers' Home and Hospital were carried in the wagons of the express companies. Most notable in the procession was the delegation of farmers from Lake County, who drove one hundred teams that were loaded with the choicest stores of their farms, dairies, poultry-yards, and cellars, to the value of three thousand dollars, which was immediately dispatched to the army in camp and hospital. At the dinner given to the farmers, in responding to the presentation address, Dr. Patton, in behalf of the Sanitary Commission, but expressed the experience of many of the people when he said that the sight of the farmers' procession entirely overcame him. On a later day, sixty-four loaded farm-wagons from four townships in Cook County marched through our streets, amidst the enthusiasm of our people, to the sanitary rooms. But these farmers, by their contiguity to the city, became only the representatives of their brethren of the soil, who for more than a year have been making their contributions through other channels to this blessed cause, and the honor done was as to their class. The conception, preparation for, and the management of this stupendous affair seems a marvel. None but the ladies could have conciliated and consolidated so many interests, and could have done that only in the interests of the soldiers. The skill which managed this scheme would have engineered a battle or a campaign.

I do not go into the details of the fair. Suffice it to say that Bryan Hall was a wonder for the beauty and elegance of its adornments; that it was filled with articles of value, of luxury, and of curiosity, from thousand dollar shawls, six hundred dollar pianos, and threshing machines, down to fancy-work and trinkets; that it was visited by an average of five thousand and ninety persons daily; that the dinners served by the ladies were patronized by an average of fifteen hundred persons; that the curiosity shop was a Barnum's Museum; that Metropolitan Hall was kept warm every night by concerts, readings, and lectures, of which two were given by Anna Dickinson, at a dollar a seat, to enthusiastic, crowded audiences, and several on the last evenings by governors of the north-western states and Hon. Owen Lovejoy; that on the last day a dinner was given to the sick and wounded soldiers in the city; and that the total receipts were sixty-five thousand and fifty dollars! Besides the vast amount of comforts that will be dispensed to the sick and wounded braves from the magnificent donation, it will carry to them a flood of sympathy from their friends at home. As a demonstration of the patriotism of the people at home, and of the enthusiasm in prosecuting the war, the fair was worth all it cost. It was a fitting accompaniment of the recent political triumphs that were worth as much to the government as sanguinary victories.

PERIOD III.

DURING THE WAR (*Continued*). 1864-65.

The Virginia Union Flag. — Death of Owen Lovejoy. — Triennial Convention on the State of the Country. — Death of Colonels Mulligan and John A. Bross. — Tour Among the " Bushwhackers." — Quantrell's Raid. — Lincoln's Second Election. — Plot to Release Rebel Prisoners at Chicago. — Illinois Responds to the Call for Five Hundred Thousand More. — Blatchford's Sanitary Report. — Revolutionary Incidents. — Turner and Pratt go to Missouri. — Rebel Prisoners in Camp Douglas. — Richmond Fallen. — Lee's Surrender. — Lincoln Assassinated. — The National Pageant. — Chicago's National Fair. — " Little Tad." — Boston National Council. — American Missionary Association Accepts the Trust Proffered by the Boston Council.

LETTER XVII.

UNION FLAG FROM VIRGINIA. — DEATH OF OWEN LOVEJOY.

CHICAGO, April 5, 1864.

DROPPING in to-day at Bryan Hall, where were dining the eighth Illinois cavalry, under Lieutenant-Colonel D. R. Clendenin, whom I had prepared for college (how we like to stand related in some way to these brave fellows!), and who had led that splendid raid down between the Rappahannock and the James, I found Mr. T. B. Bryan, the proprietor of the hall, one of our noblest patriots, standing upon one of the tables and holding up a beautiful flag. "Here," said he, with suffused eyes, "here is the first Union flag presented by Virginia, given to this regiment for its good conduct while in Alexandria, by the Union ladies of that city. God bless them! I know that place. I was born and brought up there. I know some of the ladies." When some one proposed three cheers for eastern Virginia, Mr. Bryan replied: "No; not till she is redeemed." Then it went, three cheers for the future of Virginia, and three more for the Union ladies of Alexandria.

The death of Owen Lovejoy occurred on the twenty-fifth of March, at Brooklyn, N. Y., when he was a little over fifty years of age. Born at Albion, Maine, the son of a Congregational minister, graduated at Bowdoin, then a student in theology, he came to Illinois in 1836, and in 1839 was ordained pastor of the Congregational church at Princeton, in which service he remained for seventeen years. In 1854, as an indication of the Liberty party movement, he was elected to the legislature of the state. In 1856 he was elected to Congress, and then was re-elected three times, so that he had served a longer period, with four exceptions, than any man ever elected to that position from Illinois. This fact, as he had always championed the unpopular anti-slavery party, shows the hold he had upon the people. His death has been a personal bereavement to the old anti-slavery men who have known the devotion of his life to the cause of the slave. Twenty-four years ago, in 1840, when he was moderator of the Rock River Association, which had met in Lyndon in my father's house, my young blood was fired by his recital of the murder of his brother, Elijah P. Lovejoy, at Alton, and of his solemn oath of enmity to slavery, taken over his lifeless body. I well remember one item in the charge he gave to a young man, George B. Gemmel, who was ordained at that time: "I charge you not to preach that there were two Adams; one white and one black." He was a brave man. Indicted once by a grand jury for giving food and raiment to a poor woman who came, footsore and starving, to his door, on her weary way from a land of chains to a land of freedom, he faced court, jury, witnesses, and, against their statutes and their special pleading, beat them with the righteousness of his act. At another time he faced an armed and threatening mob, who had seized a man and bound him, whose only crime was a dark skin, cut his fetters and let the oppressed go free, while the mob, awe-struck, slunk away in silence. This bravery the nation was made to know when, on the fifth of April, 1860, in Congress, after having repeatedly endured the insults and felt the oppression exercised upon those who battled for freedom and the rights of free speech, he met the confronting bullies of the south, who strove to silence him, and declared: "You shall hear me. I will speak. I stand here to say what I have to say upon the great crime of the nation. I will not yield the floor."

The congressional committee bearing his remains were met in this city by a large delegation from Princeton. The funeral was held in the church where he had preached for seventeen years. It was fitting that the sermon should be delivered by Dr. Edward Beecher, who, as President of Illinois College, having attended at Alton the organization of the anti-slavery society, and having witnessed the safe landing of the press, had returned to Jacksonville only the day before the murder of Elijah P. Lovejoy, supposing that all would remain quiet. The sermon, an hour and a half long, delineated accurately and gratefully the character of the deceased and the crisis in which he was called to act. The preacher stated that Mr. Lovejoy, having sought ordination in the Episcopal church at the hands of Bishop Chase, was required by him to pledge in writing that he would not agitate the subject of slavery. His answer was: "My right arm shall drop off before I will sign that pledge. If I should sign it I should expect it to drop off." The bishop then agreed that he might lecture on slavery if he would not preach against it. "Promise not to preach against prevailing sin? Never!" And so he turned to the freedom of the Congregational way. Dr. Beecher also stated that at the funeral services in Brooklyn, a common soldier, a stranger, came and knelt by his coffin and kissed him; also that an old colored woman kissed him and held up her child to kiss him. President Lincoln said that there was no man he could so ill afford to lose.

The American Home Missionary Society seems to be marching into this battle of the great day of God Almighty, reëntering the field from which it had been driven by its anti-slavery testimony. Besides Dr. T. M. Post's church in St. Louis and Rev. J. M. Sturtevant's in Hannibal, a mission has just been started in Kansas City by Superintendent L. Bodwell and Pastor R. Cordley, both of Kansas, while two or three freedmen's churches have sprung up in that region. At Memphis, Tenn., Rev. T. E. Bliss has organized a church. I learn that there is one Congregational church in Mississippi, one in Georgia, and one in South Carolina. The friends of the American Missionary Association at the west are delighted with the appointment of Rev. M. E. Strieby, of Syracuse, as one of the secretaries of that institution. With a western training, an eastern pastoral experience, with eloquence and executive capacity, and with a lifelong devotion to the cause of the slave, he will make a very effective officer.

LETTER XVIII.

THE TRIENNIAL CONVENTION ON THE STATE OF THE COUNTRY.

CHICAGO, May 30, 1864.

THE deliverance of the triennial convention of the Chicago Seminary upon the state of the country met the living issues. It was in two parts : one by President Sturtevant, approving the policy of arming negroes, demanding for them a parity of treatment and protection with the white soldiers, asking that the same measures in the Fort Pillow case be resorted to as though the same number of white soldiers had been massacred in like circumstances, and endorsing the movement in Congress to amend the Constitution so as to exterminate slavery. The other part of the report, by Dr. T. M. Post, set forth the duty of the Congregational churches of the United States to inquire what they owe to this vast and solemn crisis, recommended correspondence among friends and associations in regard to calling another National Convention, and declared the duty of self-extension as coördinate with the right of existence in any ecclesiastical order, and the duty of indoctrinating our seminaries, ministers, and churches in the Puritan ideas.

The Association of Illinois, held at Quincy, approved the idea of a National Council and appointed C. G. Hammond and Drs. Sturtevant and Bascom a committee to confer with other bodies upon the matter. Rev. M. E. Strieby, the new secretary, was warmly greeted. He presented eloquently the idea of a new element in civilization, to be introduced by the Africans. The great theme of the meeting was the war, the soldiers, the freedmen, and the relation of all this to the kingdom of God. A telegram of congratulation and of assurance of prayer and sympathy was sent to President Lincoln. A visit was made to a camp of six hundred freedmen, and to the four hospitals, where prayer and addresses were offered. Dr. Milton Badger, whose heart has not grown old in his twenty-nine years of service in the American Home Missionary Society, assured us that the society was ready to press into the opening fields of the west and south. Well may Abraham Lincoln say: "Praise God for the churches!"

LETTER XIX.

THE DEATH OF COLONEL MULLIGAN AND OF COLONEL JOHN A. BROSS.

CHICAGO, August 3, 1864.

THE funeral of Colonel Mulligan in this city yesterday was a grand pageant. At Lexington, Mo., when summoned by General Price, to surrender, he replied: "If you want us, come and take us." At the recent encounter at Winchester, after he had fallen, pierced by two balls, a squad of men picked him up and were about to carry him off when the flag being endangered, he ordered them: "Lay me down and save the flag." They did so. He fell into the hands of the enemy and died among them. He was a rising young lawyer of high repute and a zealous Catholic.

Yesterday we learned of the fall of Colonel John A. Bross of the twentieth United States colored regiment, the first raised in this state. He went down in that terrible assault after the explosion at Petersburg. He first raised a company for the eighty-eighth Illinois, and fought with them at Perryville, Stone River, and Chickamauga, and then came home to raise a colored regiment. A brother of the Hon. William Bross of *The Chicago Tribune*, and an honored member of the bar in this city, a Christian gentleman, he went into the service from pure patriotism, and early identified himself with a movement for arming the black men. He was a faithful officer, caring for the spiritual as well as the physical wants of his men. The horrors of Fort Pillow did not deter him from the service so precarious in its risks. It is ascertained after the assault, foremost among the bodies found and furthest inside the rebel works, was found the body of Colonel Bross. A surviving captain says that not a man of the regiment faltered, and that every one that came out shed tears over the fall of their commander and friend. A private letter from one of those black warriors to a friend in this city, after detailing the incidents of the night of preparation and the explosion, says:—

> The rebels poured a heavy volley upon us, wounding Corporal Maxwell severely, and he was compelled to let the colors fall. Corporal Stevens then seized the colors and bore them up to the top of the works. He was quickly cut down. Corporal Bailey seized the colors and was killed instantly. Thomas Barret, a colored private, seized the colors and bore them up to the top of the fort again. He quickly fell dead. Captain Brockway then seized the flag and was mortally wounded, and was obliged to let the colors fall. Colonel Bross then seized the flag, rushed upon the top of the fort, planted it upon the parapet, drew his sword, took his hat in his hand and cried: "Rally, my brave boys, rally!" The boys did instantly rally up to him. He quickly fell.

LETTER XX.

A TOUR AMONG THE "BUSHWHACKERS."

St. Joseph, Mo., September 10, 1864.
The field superintendent had orders to explore the land of Missouri with reference to opening church work in this state. On the first night out we had a collision which killed six passengers and wounded fifteen. I came out unhurt. At Hannibal I found Pastor Sturtevant intrepidly leading on his church. Along the Hannibal and St. Jo, at the crossing of the rivers, were yet standing the block forts which had guarded the bridges in the earlier days of the war. And still, at Hannibal, St. Joseph, and many other places on the route the boys in blue are guarding the peace of the country. General Price is moving his rebel army up this way. As I passed along, two trains had been stopped and robbed on the North Missouri by guerrillas. At Brookfield, the halfway place, General C. B. Fisk, in command of the district, had been pouncing down with his train of soldiers to set things right and to collect of the secesh the value of the property stolen. The day before I stopped at New Cambria the "bushwhackers" had robbed nine citizens in daylight. The house at which I was entertained at Callao has since been searched by the banditti, who, finding a returned Union soldier at the bedside of his sick child, took him out to the edge of the town and shot him.

Nearly all of the old churches in this region, by the conflict of unionism and secessionism, have fallen into disorganization. Their congregations have been broken up and their houses closed. Farther south, within the Confederate lines, the people have kept up their church life.

The great work here will now be to re-organize upon the basis of loyalty and spirituality. Many of the people, weary of the conflict in the church as well as that in the state, seem now disposed to welcome a church that has been free from this entanglement, and which, by its liberal polity, offers a rational ground for union. Population will be flowing into Missouri, which is really a western state. New towns will be springing up on these fair prairies. I shall recommend that a superintendent be secured, and that the work be pushed with vigor.

LETTER XXI.

QUANTRELL'S RAID.

LAWRENCE, Kansas, September 21, 1864.

THE last time I visited this place, seven years ago, I found a regiment of federal soldiers encamped here to watch this Yankee, liberty-loving town. Then all over the territory the United States troops were used in complicity with the plot of the border ruffians to throttle the freedom of Kansas. Now I find Lawrence and all the eastern border of Kansas under the protection of Uncle Sam's boys, the difference being caused by a change of administration. Besides the fortifications on Mount Oread, a battery of one hundred and twenty men, a company of infantry, and some cavalry, the militia of this town and neighboring country is under organization and drill. Recently, fifteen hundred of them had a review and a sham-fight, in which the Lawrence Sable Company bore off the palm, receiving a cavalry charge under an old army officer in splendid style. Five block-houses in different parts of the town are garrisoned every night by these men. One of the forts is under the care of the colored company. And this is the preparation for a return of Quantrell. If he should come every year with his recruits, fiends from the infernal regions, he could not dislodge the genius of liberty from this historic spot.

That raid was on Black Friday, August 21, 1863; and so it is just a year and a month since the deed was done. It burned two hundred buildings, among which were seventy-five business houses, and destroyed property to the amount of $1,500,000. And now Massachusetts Street is nearly re-built, and in better style than before. In all, two hundred new houses have been put up on the ruins of the old ones. Business is now lively. But how can those satanic emissaries atone for the slaughter of one hundred and fifty citizens? There was method in their insanity. Some of them had heard Pastor Cordley preach a national sermon the Sabbath before in Kansas City, and so they were looking for that "one-eyed abolition preacher who had preached in Kansas City." But he escaped, with the loss of home, library, sermons and all, and the next Sunday he was ready to preach from the text: "The morning cometh." And now he stands his night-watch on guard. His friends have made up the $1,500 of his loss. And so did Superintendent Bodwell escape for other years of usefulness.

A visit to the grave of my brother, Aaron D. Roy, who had given his life to Kansas in her early single-handed struggle with that power which has since struck at the life of the nation, revealed to me a glimpse of the horror of the raid, in the long trench where, in rough boxes, lay the mangled and charred remains of fifty or sixty of the victims. As every man who could find a horse and a revolver had gone in pursuit of the flying demons, it was not possible to get separate graves dug for all. But one hundred of the raiders, it is said, have already been made to bite the dust.

LETTER XXII.

LINCOLN'S SECOND ELECTION. — PLOT TO RELEASE REBEL PRISONERS. — ILLINOIS RESPONDS TO THE CALL FOR FIVE HUNDRED THOUSAND MORE. — BLATCHFORD'S REPORT. — REVOLUTIONARY INCIDENT.

CHICAGO, November 10, 1864.

THANK God, Lincoln has been reëlected! We had here in the summer a convention that voted "the war a failure." It was a painful and significant fact that in the scores of speeches made in the convention and from the hotel balconies, scarcely a word was uttered of sympathy with the government as engaged in a deadly conflict with gigantic treason, or of condemnation of secession, or of generous recognition of the soldiers and their service. The harp of a thousand strings was thrummed by almost every speaker upon the despotism of Abraham Lincoln. The only way to save our property, liberty, and life is to overthrow the reigning dynasty. In all the reported speeches it would be hard to find an honest word of reprobation of Jeff Davis. Vallandigham has been the admired of all admirers. A friend, sitting by my side, a refugee from Mississippi, who with three brothers fled before bloodhounds from the conscription, has been into the great convention. He says that by the spirit of the convention he was made to feel as though he were back in Columbus, Miss. The tone and the talk were just such as he had been accustomed to there. But now the answer to all this is the people's return of Abraham Lincoln.

The discovery on the day before the election of the plot to release the nine thousand prisoners here in Camp Douglas, to pollute our ballot-boxes and to burn the city; the arrest of rebel officers and of home traitors and of one hundred butternut accomplices imported for the occasion; and the seizure of cartloads of arms and ammunition secreted near the camp, was a merciful and a providential deliverance. The navy revolvers, already loaded and capped for the use of the rebel prisoners, were used in part by the four hundred volunteer mounted patrolmen who have guarded our city the last two days. I have never seen a general election more quiet; but there was intense feeling and every body worked. I had myself the honor of driving a neighbor's carriage for half a day to bring to the polls invalid citizens and the halt and the blind from the soldiers' home. Chicago gave a majority of 1,776 — a significant number for the Union and for the war until the rebellion is dead.

A new story of the President may come in here. During our state fair at Decatur, a friend was calling upon the family of Rev. Mr. Crissey, who is now a chaplain in an Illinois regiment. The mother stated that many years ago her little boy, when playing out in the street, had fallen down and was crying. A tall young man came along, driving a yoke of oxen. Picking the little fellow up and setting him inside the gate, he remarked: —

"You will never make a soldier if you cry like that."

His ambition touched, the little soldier cleared up his face. The mother, after relating this, turned to a young captain just returned on a furlough, and said: —

"This is the son, and the tall young man is the commander-in-chief of the army and navy of the United States!"

Illinois responds with men as well as with votes. On the new call for five hundred thousand more, we have thirty-five thousand ahead of all former calls, and the remaining twelve thousand of our quota we can call out any day. We have reënlisted sixteen thousand three-year veterans. General Oglesby, the Union candidate for governor, who, like our President, was of lowly Kentucky origin, told us recently in this city how he became an anti-slavery man. One old negro, Uncle Tim, who belonged to his father's estate, was sold to a man whose son laid one hundred lashes upon the back of the noblest black man he had ever seen. Though but a boy he determined, if he ever could get the money, to buy the old man free. Coming to manhood, a cruise in California brought him the money. He returned, set the old man free, and swore vengeance upon the institution of slavery.

Mr. E. W. Blatchford, treasurer of the Chicago Sanitary Commission, in a published report, shows that in three years and two months 68,803 packages have been sent to the army, at a cash valuation of $964,059.71. This was at an expense of $32,154.01. This is only three and one half per cent. of the value of the supplies distributed. How grand this tributary uprising! An incident of Revolutionary times, just brought to my knowledge, illustrative of the patriotism and suffering of that day, finds its counterpart in this present struggle. My great-grandsire, a young man in New Jersey, engaged to be married, with his wedding-suit ready, was plowing in the field, barefoot, and with only the rustic dress of a shirt and pants, when the British came to the house and stole all he had. Leaving his team in the field he went seven miles that night in his plowman's rig and enlisted for the war. On the next day he recognized the buttons of his wedding-dress on the hats of the enemy. Captured, he lay six months in the "block-house" in New York, where many were *starved* to death. That must have been the place where our modern cavaliers learned this refinement of torture. After a service of seven years, for which he never got one cent of pay, as he was leaving Washington's Guard — so the domestic legend runs — the patriot general cried because his soldiers were no better clad. With a blanket, but with no hat or shoes, the soldier marked his track home for fourteen miles with the blood of his feet upon the frozen ground. "His blanket he had cut into a coat and was married in that." My great-grandfather on the other side was one of five brothers in the Revolutionary army, their father being a justice of the peace under the king.

LETTER XXIII.

TURNER AND PRATT GO TO MISSOURI. — REBEL PRISONERS IN CAMP DOUGLAS.

CHICAGO, February 21, 1865.

ON New Year's day Rev. E. B. Turner left to become missionary superintendent of Missouri, taking with him Rev. C. H. Pratt as his "son Timothy." The man who got Mr. Turner away from his people is called by them "Rob Roy." When these men left my house at midnight of New Year's in the teeth of a terrific storm to go and breast a fiercer commotion of the moral elements, my heart sank within me for the moment as being accessory to their running a fool's errand or making a sacrifice of themselves. But they are now getting well under way in their work. Leaving Hannibal, they were obliged to wear their old clothes and to carry material weapons. Timothy is located at Brookfield, the halfway place on the Hannibal and St. Jo, where he preached his first sermon in the barroom of the hotel. The Congregational ministers of Kansas evidently belonged to the Church Militant. When Price was pushing across Missouri for the invasion of Kansas, Storrs and Robinson, and Rice and Harlow, and McVicker and Guild responded to the call for troops. Adair was already in the field. Cordley was on duty day and night with his company, which was left as a part of the garrison for the block-houses in Lawrence, Kansas. On the day of that battle, Sunday, there were present in one of their congregations one hundred and fifty women and only six men, and these all physically unfit for duty and legally exempt.

Of the eleven thousand prisoners here in Camp Douglas, three thousand refuse to be exchanged, Major Hosford, the commissary, having made it so pleasant for them. They occupy the barracks which were built for our own soldiers. They have splendid hospitals. He bakes his own bread for them. He took pride in showing me through his stores of inspected flour and beans. Our home is near. We hear the reveille every night, and every day we see heavily loaded wagons, hauling fresh meat to the prisoners. How does this contrast with Andersonville and Libby and the other soldier prisons of the south! The government has put in a grand sewer from the camp to the lake shore. Alas, for the filth of those southern prison pens!

LETTER XXIV.

RICHMOND FALLEN. — LEE SURRENDERS. — LINCOLN ASSASSINATED. — THE NATIONAL PAGEANT.

CHICAGO, April 4, 1865.

RICHMOND has fallen. Yesterday Chicago ran riot with joy. It blossomed all over with red, white, and blue. Never before such excitement here; business stopped; streets crowded; merchants marching; fire departments out; guns firing all day. Nor was the Author of all this joy forgotten. Besides the noonday prayer-meeting, which throbbed with the great emotion, at four in the afternoon there were meetings for thanksgiving in the three divisions of the city: at the First Baptist, Grace Methodist, and the First Congregational churches. Then on Monday there was a mammoth street parade.

April 5, 1865.

General Lee has surrendered. Praise God! The exuberance of joy is tempered with reverence in the presence of the mighty providence. And what shall now be done with the leaders of the rebellion? General Grant's magnanimity with Lee and his men, approved at home, must surely be appreciated at the south. The most notable thing in this second Monday's celebration was, that in a procession, which was an hour in passing a given point, and between the Board of Trade and the Commercial College, marched three hundred colored citizens, with manly bearing. And well might they find their place, for had not their brethren marched shoulder to shoulder with the white soldier? When a base fellow pulled a black man off from his dray in the march, he was at once seized and sent to the lock-up.

April 19, 1865.

"My father, my father, the chariots of Israel and the horsemen thereof." In the hearts of the people, Abraham Lincoln has made for himself the place of a father. Illinois gave Mr. Lincoln to the nation, but she claims no preëminence in grief; yet her wail of sorrow is deep. This city has become a Bochim. On Saturday, business stood still; strong men cried upon the streets; an overcrowded prayer-meeting was held at four o'clock in one of the largest churches; and in the evening our two largest halls were filled with mourners. On the Sabbath all the churches were filled to repletion, all were draped, all resounded to the tones of lamentation. . Of course all the pulpits sought to give the Word of God for the crisis. In the absence of Dr. Patton at City Point on sanitary duty, I was called upon to preach in his church. The text was: "The Lord alone shall be exalted in that day," and this was followed in the evening by a discourse on the Christianizing of the south. In our South Congregational Church, Pastor W. B. Wright, who had entered Richmond with the President, and who had pulled the first bell-rope there to call the soldiers to worship in one of the forsaken sanctuaries, enriched his funeral service by an account of what he had seen, as a delegate of the Christian Commission, of God's work of grace in the army. At an inquiry-meeting one morning at Point of Rocks there were more inquirers than five of them could converse with. He feared not the return of the soldiers. To-day all business places are closed, and nearly all the churches have been open for worship during the time of the funeral services at Washington.

Peter Glass, a German from Wisconsin, is now in this city, halted by the national tragedy on his journey to

Washington, bearing as a present to the late President and his wife a superb center-table and work-stand of mosaic art. The stand cost him three months of work and the table nine. The two are composed of twenty-two thousand pieces of wood with exquisite polish. Without the use of paint or varnish there are twenty-one colors. Upon the top of the table there are vases of flowers, twenty-five kinds in all, fifteen kinds of birds, five kinds of pears, besides apples, peaches, plums, cherries, and strawberries. There are also portraits of Messrs. Lincoln, Johnson, Grant, and Butler. All are wrought in black walnut from rails on the farm of the father of the late President, and in white holly, colored to suit the varied articles represented. The whole was designed as an offering of patriotism by an adopted citizen.

May 2, 1865.

The solemn national pageant has reached our city. Yesterday the remains of the beloved Abraham Lincoln were followed to the rotunda of state by a procession, six abreast, that occupied four hours in passing a given point, while scores of thousands lined the track of the mournful cortege. Through the entire night and now on to the day the mourners have passed in solemn step to behold the face of their departed father, at the rate of seventeen thousand per hour. It is much for a strong man to bow in grief; now a nation bows in sorrow and in reverence too, for all do see that God alone is great.

LETTER XXV.

THE WOMAN'S NATIONAL FAIR AT CHICAGO. — "LITTLE TAD."

CHICAGO, May 30, 1865.

TO-DAY the last of the patriotic fairs, the second of the north-west, is in process of inauguration in this city. How strange the contrast of this gala day with that on which the cortege of our dear Lincoln passed through our streets! It was the first plan to open the fair on the twenty-second of February and to close it on the fourth of March, both notable days in the national annals. But so had the idea grown, even to the aspiration of half a million of income, that the time of opening had to be postponed. The crowning glory was to be the presence of Mr. Lincoln, which he had assured, if it were possible, to Mrs. Hoge and Mrs. Livermore, who had been on to Washington to see him. The day had been set for commencing the building, which was to cover the whole of Dearborn Park. The mayor had issued a proclamation requesting a suspension of business to honor the ceremonies. Military companies were to give brilliancy to the procession. A long line of teams was to come to the site, loaded with the lumber that had been given for the structure. Public school children, a thousand or more of them, were to sing in the park. Several companies of rebel prisoners, who had taken the oath of allegiance, were to enhance the occasion. But that day brought news of the assassination. There was no procession; there was no ceremony; so sharp was the precipitation from exultation to horror. But the opening on this the thirtieth day of May has been a grand pageant, though softened by an undertone of sadness. As in the grief, as in the joy, as in the funeral procession, so now in this of the fair celebration, are our colored citizens again participants.

June 20, 1865.

The great Sanitary Fair has moved along grandly. It has lasted three weeks, and is now to close. It has netted nearly $85,000. Of this, $50,000 was given to the Christian Commission, and the remainder was equally divided between the Sanitary Commission and the Soldiers' Home. This total was not the half a million at first planned for, nor had this ending of the war then been anticipated. In the place of the President we had his youngest and much-loved son, "little Tad." He wandered from booth to booth, and was finally found by a lady sitting apart in bitter weeping. To her inquiries he replied: "I can not go anywhere without seeing a picture of my father." "You did love your father very much?" said the lady, her own eyes humid with sympathy. "Oh, yes!" exclaimed the little child, "nobody ever had such a good father! He was always kind, and there was one thing that he never forgot, never!" said the child, with loving emphasis. "And what was that?" inquired his interested auditor. "Every day, no matter how busy he was, he never forgot to say a prayer with me. If he had time for only four or five words, he would lay his hand on my head and say them."

The glory of the exhibition is Carpenter's national painting of the Reading of the Proclamation. Native genius must have been touched with patriotism to have produced this crowning representation of our country's achievement. In the Hall of Trophies a coincidence appears, though not perhaps designed. Upon the front of the platform stands the immense catafalque on which rested in state the remains of Abraham Lincoln, and just below and in front is an ox-yoke manufactured by John Brown, with the carbine placed upon it with which he and seventeen others had attacked the sovereignty of Virginia; and down by the side of the yoke is a walnut rail, split by the late President, as testified to by his old friend, Mr. Hanks. John Brown tried to break the yoke of four million of bondmen, but he had not the power. Abraham Lincoln came to have the power and he used it so, as is evinced in symbol by the pile of fetters, chains, iron yokes, and whips which lie by the side of these larger emblems. The old John Brown song, having served the purpose of rallying our soldiers, of comforting the enslaved, and of terrifying the rebellious south, now comes to our aid at the north in toning up public sentiment to the dignity of justice, as expressed in the line,

"We'll hang Jeff Davis to a sour apple-tree;"

and when it shall have been relieved from this judicial application, its "Glory, Hallelujah" may go on into the millennium.

LETTER XXVI.

THE BOSTON NATIONAL COUNCIL.

BOSTON, Mass., June 24, 1865.

THE idea of this National Council took its rise in the west. Judge Warren Currier proposed it. Dr. Post presented it at the triennial convention of the Chicago Theological Seminary, held in May, 1864. That body approved the plan and referred it to the Congregational General Association of Illinois, to meet the same month. This body endorsed it and appointed a committee to bring the matter before other associations and to act with any committees that they might appoint for fixing the time and place of meeting and for making arrangements for the same. The several such committees, meeting at the Broadway Tabernacle, New York, in November last, issued letters missive by which this body of delegates from the Congregational churches of the United States was convened. It has representatives from twenty-five states and territories. It numbers five hundred and nineteen; of whom fourteen are honorary members, and eleven from foreign countries. It has for moderator Governor W. A. Buckingham; for assistant moderators, Colonel C. G. Hammond and Rev. Dr. Joseph P. Thompson; and for chief scribe, Rev. H. M. Dexter, D.D. The idea of the convention grew out of the state of the country, out of the patriotic inquiry, What will be the duty of this denomination toward the south and toward the west, as the war shall come to an end? What can we do in the matter of moral re-construction and of spiritual healing?

And so the invitation of the national committee, addressed to all the churches of this order in the land, named as the first subject to be considered: "The Work of Home Evangelization devolving on our Churches — a work including all the efforts which they are making, or ought to make, for the complete Christianization of our country, particularly by planting churches and other institutions of Christian civilization at the west and at the south; by coöperating in labors for the instruction and elevation of the millions whose yoke of bondage God has broken; by helping to build houses of worship in destitute places; and by providing the wisest and most efficient methods for the supply and support of an able, learned, and godly ministry."

To this end for ten days the Council has addressed itself. The grand opening sermon, by Pres. J. M. Sturtevant, of Jacksonville, Ill., from the text, "Ask for the old paths," was an inquiry after the seeds of our national life in the early history of New England, the causes which have hindered the sowing of them more generally in our country west and south of the Hudson, and the line of practical wisdom and Christian duty in this crisis. Here is the nub of the sermon: "Negro slavery shall no longer resist the organization of the Church on the basis of equality of the Christian brotherhood over half our country." The Council, in the line of its patriotic impulse, made haste to telegraph President Johnson their Christian salutations, assuring him of their profound sympathy in his great and trying labors, promising him loyal support and prayers, and expressing to him their solemn conviction that the hundreds of thousands of worshipers in their churches would most heartily coöperate with him in extending the institutions of civil and religious liberty throughout the land.

On one day was observed a special service of devotion for the acknowledgment of the marvelous and merciful dealings of Almighty God in connection with the war, and for supplicating a gracious dispensation of the Spirit of God upon our land, that our restored national unity may be consecrated to righteousness and in the peace and joy of the Holy Ghost. The Council, declaring the late rebellion a crime transcending the enormity of treason recorded in the history of other countries, — a crime against freedom, civilization, and human nature itself, — held it as due from our government, in its final adjudication upon this highest of crimes, that, while blending mercy with justice, it shall so deal with treason that the sense of its guiltiness be not impaired, and the majesty of the law and the divine sanction of legitimate government be sustained in the mind of the nation. It also declared the present to be a crisis in the nation's life, demanding the immediate appliance of the most efficient means of education and evangelization in our power.

And so with this view accorded the action of the Council, which determined to raise $750,000 this year for that object, and of this amount to assign $300,000 to the American Home Missionary Society, $250,000 to the American Missionary Association, and $200,000 to the American Congregational Union. As to the American Home Missionary Society and the American Missionary Association, the Council also said: " Nor do we find any difficulty in recognizing the respective spheres of these two societies. For while no separation is or can be made by a geographical line, and still less by any invidious distinction of color, we yet discover in the past labors of the American Missionary Association among the colored people of America, the West Indies, and Africa, and in the ready facility with which it has adapted itself to the peculiar condition of this people at the south, an instrumentality providentially provided for their evangelization." And still further: "In Virginia, North and South Carolina, and along the banks of the Mississippi, the colored people began early in the war to come within our lines and were immediately provided with teachers and schools by this association. In the progress of the war this work has continually grown in magnitude and importance until, by the overthrow of the rebellion, the whole colored population of the south is to be brought within the reach of teachers and missionaries. Never was a missionary field more inviting." The Council also found that the American Home Missionary Society had already ten new churches in Missouri, one in Memphis, and openings in Washington, Baltimore, and other places in the south.

The fellowship was enriched by a delegation from Canada, by one from Nova Scotia, by one from France, by one from Wales, and by one from England. The members of the last-named delegation were Rev. Drs. Robert Vaughan, Alexander Raleigh, and James W. Massie. Pastor Theo. Monod said: "We of the three hundred churches of France were with you to a man, a woman, a child. Our families observed the days of prayer and humiliation appointed by your Executive. The fall of Richmond pervaded all hearts with joy. We draped our sanctuaries at the tidings of the death of Lincoln and mourned at the loss of a dear friend." "We," said the Welsh, "were with you from the first and all the time. Many a Welsh mother in our homes across the sea mourns her son slain on your battle-fields in this holy cause." The English seemed not only to have come to bring the salutations of the mother country, but to rejoice with us in the making good, after nearly one hundred years, of our declaration of independence and of freedom; they having been stanch friends of our country in its late trial. Dr. Vaughan said: "It is your joy to know that your institututions, which deceived and false prophets had affirmed would snap at the touch of adversity, had borne the strain and the snap had not come. Your struggle for liberty has taken place in the sight of all nations. Your victories have given a new song to humanity and sent a message of despair to tyrants. Your triumphs were ours. Your armies have gained victories that have placed you in the first rank of nations, and what now more fitting than that you should show yourselves capable of realizing the victories of peace." Dr. Massie had made a visit to our country during the war as the messenger of many thousands of friendly Englishmen who desired that our troubles should end in the abolition of slavery. But after these friends had been heard, on motion of Henry Ward Beecher, a committee was appointed to prepare a suitable reply to these delegates, inasmuch as the attitude of various religious bodies in Europe toward the United States, during the past five years, requires a careful discrimination and statement. Dr. Leonard Bacon brought in that committee's report, which did make discriminations, giving undiluted praise to the Welsh Congregationalists and French Evangelicals for their sympathy and their prayers. Duly acknowledging the sincerity of friendship of not a few Englishmen, and especially of the operatives, he yet had to give vent to the grieved affection occasioned by the turning toward us of the cold shoulder on the part of the English people and even of many of our Puritan ancestors. The report said : —

> Our brethren who bring to us in this assembly the congratulations of the English Congregational Union must not be permitted to return under any impression that we have not felt deeply and sorrowfully, through these four years of national agony, the actual position of the English Congregationalists. Faithfulness to them and to Christ forbids us to forget that honored brethren who went from us to them, for the purpose of explaining our position and asking their sympathy and their prayers, were refused a hearing. Yet we accept the presence of the beloved and honored delegates who have stood in our assembly as a proof that they do now understand us, and that the ancient fraternity and unity between them and us shall be perpetual.

Dr. Quint, who had been a chaplain, in moving the adoption of the report, took occasion to make a pungent arraignment of the British government and sentiment in reference to our cause. He said that when he found his men dead, killed by English rifles in the hands of rebels who were clad in English garments, he had a right to express his indignation. Dr. Raleigh rallied with a story of a Scotch exegete, who, coming to a hard passage, was wont to say: "Let us look the difficulty straight in the face and pass right on." Then Henry Ward Beecher, who, in the interest of our country having subdued a Manchester mob, had a right to speak, in one of his transcendent addresses, laid his hands upon both parties; and then Governor Buckingham, in his persuasive way, pronounced the bans of peace.

While the glow of the great occasion is on, it may be too early to speak of resultant influences; but all the great measures proposed have been enthusiastically carried through. The grand object of the convocation as an evangelical expedient has been met. Men, measures, and money are to be provided to aid in the Christianizing of our country. The system by which these churches are to carry the gospel throughout the land has been burnished. The faith which is to be propagated has been declared in its historic and in its living relations. Great organizations of evangelism have been reëmpowered. Adoring thanks to God who, through his Spirit, hath brought out such conclusions!

LETTER XXVII.

THE AMERICAN MISSIONARY ASSOCIATION ACCEPTS THE TRUST PROFFERED BY THE BOSTON COUNCIL.

BROOKLYN, New York, October 26, 1865.
THIS Association in its annual meeting, just held in Plymouth Church, this city, gratefully accepted the proffer of the Boston Council to make it the national organ for

work at the south, and to raise for this object the current year two hundred and fifty thousand dollars. This the Executive Committee recommended in its annual report and the society approved. The same report, in order to assure the confidence of the enlarged constituency, set forth a statement as to the history, character, aims, and plans of the Association. Although the Association had taken its rise in order to bear testimony against complications with slavery, its report also states: "It rejoices to find itself and the American Board, the American Home Missionary Society, and the kindred organizations working in harmonious coöperation in the great endeavor to advance the Redeemer's kingdom among men."

The purpose declared at Norwich in 1861, "to follow the armies of the United States with faithful missionaries and teachers," has been pursued; as fast as the army has advanced the line of these missionary teachers has been set forward until now, with the close of the war, it has its gospel garrisons planted across the south. At the meeting it reported missions in Washington, Maryland, Virginia, North Carolina, South Carolina, Georgia, Florida, Mississippi, Louisiana, Arkansas, Kentucky, Tennessee, and Missouri. And in these states there were employed the last year two hundred and eighty-eight teachers and fifty-five ministers. Seventeen days after our troops had entered Richmond schools were opened there under the auspices of the Association. The work of administering physical relief to these wretched people has been kept up all along. The treasurer reports the sum of $61,674 as the value of goods received and delivered among the freedmen. The receipts, which before the war were ranging from $40,000 to $50,000 a year, have this past year, besides the sum named for the value of goods, gone up to $139,660. The annual discourse preached by Dr. Kirk, of Boston, was upon the supreme topic of the times, "Only One Human Race." Our common manhood and the duties growing out of it were set forth in Dr. Kirk's profoundly impressive manner. Dr. Kirk was made president in the place of the lamented Rev. David Thurston, of Maine, who had died in the eighty-seventh year of his age. The Association was also called to notice the death of Arthur Tappan, one of its earliest officers, whose name has been throughout the land a synonym for a friend to the slave. Lewis Tappan, who had been the treasurer from the first, serving for the most part gratuitously, by advancing age was constrained to decline a reëlection. How well do I remember the genuineness of his friendship for the colored people as shown by the fact that he furnished me every Lord's day for six months, while I was in the Union Seminary, the use of his family horse and carriage to drive out through mud and storm and sunshine to preach for one of their Presbyterian churches in the suburbs of this city. The meeting came to its climax on the last evening, when addresses were made by Secretary Whipple, Rev. Henry Ward Beecher, and Rev. R. S. Storrs, D.D., all of whom had been on hand from the beginning, serving on committees.

PERIOD IV.

AT THE END OF THE WAR. TOUR THROUGH THE SOUTH, 1865.

Mammoth Cave. — Freedmen's Bureau and Bank. — Knoxville. — Chattanooga. — Battle-fields. — Mississippi Legislature. — Natchez. — New Orleans. — Sea Island Negroes. — Alabama Legislature. — Charleston Shelled and Burned. — Black Heroes. — Emancipation Celebration in Charleston. — Virginia Legislature. — Generals Thomas and Fisk.

LETTER XXVIII.

MAMMOTH CAVE. — FREEDMEN'S BUREAU AND BANK. — GENERAL FISK.

CHATTANOOGA, Tenn., October 29, 1865.
Now for a pilgrimage through Dixie. I was glad when, in allusion to a text from which he had heard me preach, word came from Dr. Badger: "Will Joseph arise and go toward the south?" Here I am in company with Rev. Drs. I. P. Warren and G. S. F. Savage, secretaries of the Boston Tract Society, who are to study the south with relation to supplying it with literature. Pilgrim is here with reference to the planting of churches as proposed by the Boston Council. From Louisville to Chattanooga, the single line of communication with our army in the southeast, barricaded at every stream and station, the line of Bragg's march across two states and of his retreat before the Federals, — how much of anxious thought and prayer have throbbed along this same highway! The first part

of the trip was on the day of the great eclipse, which with thin clouds for smoked glass gave us a grand exhibition; not so grand, however, as that which revealed to us the passing off of the eclipse from our country and its freedom. At Elizabethtown, in Hardin County, we passed the place where was the boyhood home of Abraham Lincoln. Stone River, Munfordsville, Bowling Green, Nashville, Murfreesboro', Tullahoma, are places of classic interest, while almost every station on the road has its story of skirmish or battle.

Leaving the road at Cave City, we took stage ten miles to Mammoth Cave, through whose wonders in one day we traveled eighteen miles. The Star Chamber, with its twinkling stars and flaming comet; Gornu's Dome, with its awful chasm; Echo River, on which we had a boat-ride for three quarters of a mile, and whose echoes are charming; the maelstrom; the bottomless pit; Cleveland's cabinet, well stored with specimens and ornamented on wall and ceiling with the most delicate and rich of fresco work in gypsum, are some of the wonders. The feeling of reverence rises. In our case it manifested itself in a season of prayer at the most distant point of exploration. In the ceiling of one of those halls, dazzling in its ornaments of crystal, is cut "the cross," its parts being about eight and twelve feet long, and near it our nation's flag is kept unfurled; and so while Christianity has its emblem cut in these rocks under the earth, the symbol of our country's sovereignty claims this whole land from surface to center. Our guide, a black man, said that occasionally visitors knocked down the stars and stripes, but he always fell back and put them up again; and in like manner as traitors have struck down the national emblem, black men have helped to put it back again and to maintain its authority.

At Nashville we were delighted with the working of the Freedmen's Bureau, under General C. B. Fisk, assistant commissioner. Preëminently this is a bureau of justice; coming in between the freedmen and their late masters on the one hand and the government on the other, it is a most useful department. General Fisk is the protector. He is protecting the laborers. He is getting up schools for their children. He has a court in which a chaplain is judge for the rendering of justice to the black man. He has a legislature, as he calls it, an advisory council consisting of twelve of the most intelligent colored men in the city. I dropped in upon this body. With a black man on the bench, business was dispatched in a way of example to the other legislature upon Capitol Hill. The ten members who were present while I was in pay taxes on $250,000. Can't take care of themselves! Some curious things occur at General Fisk's headquarters. Here is one: A lady comes in wearing silk and feathers. "You have my land, sir, and I want to see about it." Her husband had been killed in the rebel service and his land had come under the head of "abandoned." "How far out do you live?" "About thirty mile." The general requests her to write out her case. She says: "I can't write very well." Then get some one to do it for you "I have no friends in the city, and lawyers will charge too much." A colored clerk was sitting near there at a table, a graduate of Oberlin. "Well," says the general, "you just sit down and dictate it to that gentleman, and he will write it out for you." With an expression of mortification and scorn she sat down, and when she took off her glove to make her mark, her finger glistened with a diamond ring. That is negro equality for you! Another: Up in Macon County a negro who had stolen a pig had been tried before a justice. By the old state law the negro had been sentenced to thirty-nine lashes for the theft and five for lying, and his mother was sentenced to five lashes for eating of the pig. The constable had laid on the lashes lustily. Both officers are brought before the court. They confess that they did not know that slavery had been abolished. The general tells them that he can fine them $100 and send them to jail. They admit that they ought to pay the fine for not knowing any better, but they don't want to go to jail. The general lets them off with the fine. Another: A woman appears and swears her three children upon her old master, who has turned her off without any provision for their support. He is summoned before the chaplain. Her affidavit was read to him. The father proposes to settle, and is let off with the payment of $540, the penalty affixed by the state for bastardy. A son of the rebel General Bragg is a porter about General Fisk's headquarters. A son of the rebel Governor Isham G. Harris was a member of the black legislature, bearing his father's name; and, as the Irishman said: "If half a nagur is so smart, what must a whole one be?" In a church of colored people I expressed surprise at seeing white women sitting among the black ones, but was told that these fine-looking women were of the proscribed race. A beneficent institution is the National Freedmen's Bank, chartered by Congress, located in New York. Mr. Booth, president of the American Tract Society, is its president; and Mr. M. T. Jewett, of New York, the vice-president and actuary, is traveling with us and is establishing branch banks. In this city he makes cashier Alfred Menefee, a colored man, who pays taxes on $40,000. Its investments, by the charter, are all to be in government bonds. The profits are to go to the depositors. Colored people ought to be encouraged to deposit in these banks, for this will stimulate economy, industry, enterprise, self-respect.

What can I say of Lookout Mountain, Missionary Ridge, and Chickamauga? Nothing worthy of their grandeur. By favor we are furnished with passes and a guide, and also with the company of chaplain Van Horne, now in charge of the post. As we ride laboriously up the ridge, which runs at an angle of forty degrees for half a mile, we realize the terrific character of the assault made by our men in the face of the rebel artillery and infantry above. Bullets and other mementos of the battle are easily found. The chaplain had had the pleasure of witnessing the whole movement of six miles' breadth: Hooker on the right, "fighting above the clouds" of Lookout; Sherman on the left and pushing up and along the ridge, and Thomas in the center, all converging upon the enemy. The ridge was named from the old mission of the American Board among the Indians. On the premises we found only the old mill, the old school-house, the old mission burying-ground, where we saw the monument of Secretary Worcester and the old missionary farmer, Mr. Vale, who came from New Jersey in 1819, and who had been a prisoner by turns in both armies. On the field of Chickamauga the chaplain made all very plain. The *débris* of battle was yet abundant — bayonets, scabbards, canteens, cartridge-boxes, hats, shoes, coats, etc. Trees cut down by shell were lying on the ground as though a hurricane had passed over. One such tree was two feet through at the point of cutting. We also witnessed the exhuming of bodies for removal to the National Cemetery at Chattanooga. A detail of two hundred colored soldiers in skirmish line five feet apart was sweeping the field, which is six miles long by three broad. They had already recovered one hundred and expect to find five hundred. We came upon them as they were at work at Bragg's headquarters. Upon a shallow trench which they were emptying of five bodies, we saw a young peach-tree growing, four feet high, sprouted from a pit that had been dropped in, the tree taking into itself the flesh and bones of the fallen heroes. And so, out of these thousands of graves are growing the trees of freedom, nationality, peace, and goodwill. The cemetery is under the charge of chaplain Van Horne. Crawfish Spring, located on the site of a portion of the battle, is one of the sources of the Chickamauga. A wonderful subterranean river just there bursts out below the perpendicular rock in a stream that is a rod and a half wide and a foot and a half deep, with a current sufficient to run the mission mill a few miles below.

LETTER XXIX.

KNOXVILLE. — CHATTANOOGA. — BATTLE-FIELDS. — DESOLATION.

MEMPHIS, November 6, 1865.

WE found Knoxville a small city of three thousand, begirt with military works, still under the paralysis of war. The returned Union soldiers are taking their turn now in driving away their enemies. Glorious was the loyalty of these east Tennessee patriots, who had traveled over the mountains on foot and by night to enlist in the federal army without bounty. From Chattannooga to Atlanta is one continuous battle-field, grave-yard, and desolation. Almost every foot of the way was fought over. As the line of railway was the line of battle, it is nearly one series of fortifications. Such destruction of property I had not imagined. Lonely chimney-stacks mark the sites of once prosperous farms. Villages lie in *débris*. Atlanta, the second city in its power for the rebellion, was left, like Richmond and Charleston, in ruins. But Atlanta is rising, phœnix-like, out of the ashes. Eighty brick stores are coming to completion.

From Chattanooga to Memphis, three hundred and nine miles, is another line of desolation. Over it we had an experience of rough travel, making the break of sixteen miles by stage. Second-class cars with board seats were the best that we could get. In all the south there is not a sleeping-car, and we have not yet seen a first-class couch. Huntsville on the way is a beautiful village of five thousand people, undestroyed. In the midst of the city a fountain bursts forth, a river indeed, which supplies the population. Recently a colored sister, coming up from immersion in its waters, shouted out: "Bless the Lord! Free from sin, free from slavery. Glory to God and General Grant!" Here Rev. Dr. F. A. Ross has just preached a sermon on "The Society of Huntsville, Past, Present, and Future." The past was paradise for purity; the present, transitional; and the future, full of temptations from fast men and fast women from the north. Here I see the slave-pen and the slave-jail. My friend said that colored people had told him that they had seen blood an inch deep upon its floor from the scourgings given for alleged offences to the servants of the pure and refined people of Huntsville, by the constable, at a dollar a head. Here, also, we see in the school for negroes a son of Senator Clemens, of Alabama. Alas, for the lost purity of Dr. Ross's paradise! Of seven hundred men who went into the war from here only one hundred and fifty can be accounted for alive. Three generals are among their dead. All the church bells were taken down and cast into the Huntsville battery, which was captured before it had fired a gun. It was here in the court-house that L. P. Walker, lately of the confederate cabinet, declared that he would wipe up with his handkerchief all the blood that would be spilled by the craven Yankees.

In Memphis we find our Union church in a prosperous condition. It was communion Sabbath. At the table Dr. Warren presented salutations, and exhorted to a life in Christ which should be the true leaven of Christianity. We had eight clergymen present, the pastor, the three travelers, Rev. E. O. Tade, freedmen's missionary, chaplains Hawley and Cherry, and Rev. A. L. Rankin, district secretary of the Boston Tract Society. Mr. Tade, with his own hands, aided by a brother and a black man, is building an American Missionary Association church for the freedmen.

LETTER XXX.

ON THE RIVER. — GENERAL HOWARD. — THE MISSISSIPPI LEGISLATURE.

VICKSBURG, November 13, 1865.

AFTER our three weeks of rough railroading, the four hundred miles of steam-boating to this city was a welcome respite. Helena was the only place on the west bank where the bluff came to the river-bank; and this is the first on the east bank, so that the town sites and strategic points are few and distinct. The everlasting winding through the everlasting flatness was attended with the monotony of desolation. Plantations, fenceless and grown up to weeds, were the unchanging scene. A pretentious "mansion," fronting the river, stands here and there with a dozen negro cabins in the rear, and with a former gin-house, identified by the chimney of its engine. But from the village in the rear the people are gone. I was struck with the temerity of the blockade running here, from the fact that the bend opposite throws a spit of land clear across the front of the city, so that all our boats had to pass twice under the guns of the rebels. The caves dug into the hillsides, to which many fled to avoid the shells of Grant, are still open. Only a half-dozen citizens were killed by these missiles. The shell holes in the Presbyterian church, one directly over the pulpit and the other over the center of the church, are still unclosed. We meet here a young man, who, as messenger through our lines between Pemberton inside and Johnson outside, was caught on the day before the surrender of this city. His message concerning a last desperate attempt to cut through he refused, under penalty of the halter, to reveal. But escaping his guard, he joined the army of Virginia and at the final surrender he again appeared before General Grant, who commended his former fidelity to a trust and gave him transportation home.

We fall in here with General Howard, on a tour of Bureau inspection, attended by his brother, Rev. Rowland B. Howard, and Rev. J. W. Alvord, the general school inspector, who also as secretary of the National Freedmen's Savings Bank, has established on the way branches at Washington, Richmond, Norfolk, Hampton, Wilmington, Newberne, Charleston, Beaufort, Savannah, Tallahassee, Mobile, Augusta, New Orleans, and Vicksburg. It is understood that Mr. Alvord is the father of this bank idea.

The branches on the coast have already received deposits to the amount of $175,000, and a total of $250,000.

We run out to Jackson with the general, where we hear his speech to the people, white and colored, not lowered in its tone from the high key of justice and philanthropy which I heard from him in Chicago before he started out, yet expressing such sympathy with the unfortunate on both sides, and imparting such instruction to the freedmen and such counsel to the whites as to disarm prejudice and to inspire a better feeling. All who heard it were greatly pleased. One southerner wished that every white man and every black man in the state of Mississippi had heard it.

During our two days' visit to the legislature the subject of laws for the freedmen was up in both houses, and the purpose, as expressed by one of the magnates, was to make their system of labor as safe as it was before. If a laborer quits his contract before its expiration, besides the forfeiture of back pay, he is arrested as a deserter, remanded by law, and compelled to pay the arrester five dollars and the costs of his arrest out of his wages. A law is proposed, making it a crime for a negro to enter the premises of a white man without permission — penalty, twenty dollars and twenty days' imprisonment. Juries are to be limited to white men, and black men are not to be allowed to testify against white men. Of course the government must put its foot on such legislation. These propositions to frame mischief into a law for the black man divulge the animus of the legislators. I do declare that I write this not in anger but in grief. There is a bright side and I like to look at it. Slavery is dead. There is more of quiet in the south than we had expected to find. We had feared that the confederate army would break up into guerrilla

squads and thus prolong the war. They came home and
now are the best disposed of all the people here. Magnanimity does become the victors. No man who sees the
desolation of this country can wish for any more of retribution. We are bound to live together. We are of one
blood and language. There are many noble qualities in
the southern character. We are yet to become an assimilated people, a missionary nation.

LETTER XXXI.

NATCHEZ. — COLORED SCHOOLS. — POPULATION AND MONU-
MENTS OF NEW ORLEANS.

NEW ORLEANS, November 18, 1865.

IT is one hundred miles from the mouth of the river up
to this city; four hundred thence to Vicksburg; four hundred thence to Memphis; thence four hundred to St.
Louis; and thence more than a thousand to the northern
line of our country. Over this distance the Father of
Waters now "goes unvexed to the sea." Natchez is a
beautiful city on a high bluff on the eastern bank, with
a population of eleven thousand, half of which is colored.
Having fallen like a ripe pear into the hands of Uncle
Sam, it has escaped the pounding of war. It has been
the home of aristocratic planters. We met there three
Congregational ministers: Rev. S. G. Wright, late superin-
tendent of the work of the American Missionary Association, but now to be chaplain of a colored regiment at
Winchester, Alabama, whither he takes two teachers;
Rev. P. Litts, his successor as superintendent, and Rev. G.
Hitchin, chaplain of a colored regiment here. The half-
dozen teachers under these two brethren had three hun-

dred children and a whole regiment of colored soldiers for their pupils.

Yesterday we gave to visiting the colored schools of this city, eight in number, brought in by General Banks, and named Lincoln, Fred Douglass, Banks, Conway, W. L. Garrison, General Howard, General Butler, and Charles Sumner. The schools are graded and are conducted on the best modern methods. The Fred Douglass school is in a building once used as a slave-market and still bearing in front the sign, which a coat of white paint and one of black could not efface, VIRGINIA NEGROES FOR SALE. Alas, Virginia! your occupation is gone. The janitor told us that negroes had been there whipped to death because they did not fix themselves up well to sell at auction. The colored people of the state, many of them creoles, are taxed upon an assessment of $16,000,000 for school purposes, and last year they paid $37,000 of this tax, all of which goes to the white schools. And yet they are petitioning the authorities to tax them again for their own children! Governor Wells promises to use his influence to have the legislature set apart the $37,000 to their own use. A school officer who has been over the state tells me that eighty per cent. of the colored pupils are tinctured with white blood. In no other place have I seen so much of the bleached material, shading out, as it often does, beyond recognition. There is also a mixture of dialect, as many of the negroes speak French or "Jumbo," a mongrel of French and English. French, Spanish, Indian, English, and African blood is strangely mixed — miscegenation indeed.

Before the war this city had a population of one hundred and eighty-five thousand. Now it is said to have twenty thousand more. Business is exceedingly brisk.

Northern enterprise and capital, as elsewhere in the south, are rushing in. The streets are paved with stone and are kept clean. In its business air, in its flatness, in its turnpiked suburban streets, it resembles Chicago. It is well supplied with street railways, some of whose cars are marked, "For Negroes." Reaching its right arm up through the center of the continent, and its left out upon the ocean, it is destined to grasp a mighty commerce. Its own relation to the Mississippi is an argument against a divided nation. Dr. Palmer is in his place again. His church is a magnificent structure on Jefferson Square; his congregation, the *élite* of the city. A college professor in Kentucky, who is also an influential elder in the Old Southern Church, told me that a delegation was sent from Richmond to secure the adhesion of Dr. Palmer to the Confederacy, the result of which was his famous sermon, which argued that it was the mission of the Church to conserve slavery. The elder also gave it as his opinion that, if Doctors Palmer and Thornwell had given their influence against the incipient treason, it could not have come to life. The three or four churches in this vicinity, transferred from the Methodist Episcopal South to the Methodist Episcopal Church, are just now, by the order of the President, passing back into the hands of the owners, so that Doctors Newman and Pyrn are thrown out of their places of worship. We here learn of Dr. Howard, who, having been a popular Baptist preacher in Chicago, came to this city, took up the southern side, and died a sutler in the rebel army. Rev. E. Andrus, of Michigan, who had been here in the hospital service for four years, is now to be the district secretary of the Boston Tract Society in this city. A house in Vicksburg had ordered an invoice from this society, and one of the proprietors told me that they had sold in two months one hundred and forty-seven dozen of Webster's spelling-books, and most of them to the negroes! Here in Jackson Square, gorgeously ornamented with shrubbery, floral bloom, and fruitage of orange, banana, and Japanese plum, is the equestrian statue of "Old Hickory," mounted upon a steed, whose base has inscribed upon it, "The Union must and shall be preserved." When the vandals began to chisel off these letters, General Butler proclaimed that the man doing it should be hanged. Here is also the Henry Clay monument, upon which General Butler had inscribed the words of the silver-tongued orator: "If I could be instrumental in eradicating this deepest stain, slavery, I would not exchange the proud satisfaction I should enjoy for all the triumphs ever decreed to the most successful conqueror." Here too I see our nation's emblem floating from the flagstaff on the Custom House, whence being hauled down, the perpetrator paid the forfeiture of his life!

LETTER XXXII.

GENERAL HOWARD AND THE SEA ISLAND NEGROES.

SAVANNAH, Ga., November 25, 1865.

I HAVE this report from Rev. J. W. Alvord, who was present when General Howard undertook his trying task at the Sea Islands. Although by order of General Sherman the lands had been parceled out and the freedmen had been promised the refusal of purchase for three years, and although they were making them homes, and gathering around them domestic comforts, rooting themselves into the soil, yet it had seemed best to President Johnson to pardon the original owners of the plantations, which must now be given up. It had been made General Howard's duty to effect the dispossession on terms satisfactory to both parties. The people upon the island Edisto are gathered *en masse*. Some of the old masters, who had not been on the premises for four years, have come down; among them, Judge Whateley, who said that his old slaves would be so glad to see him. The object is known; people are sullen under the apprehension of bad faith. The general states his instructions from the President; tells them that if men are pardoned they must have their land; appeals to their confidence as a fellow-Christian; but all are glum. Planters demand that the freedmen shall give up their lands and work for wages or quit the island. A committee goes out to consult. Meantime, what shall be done with the silent assembly whose fierceness flashes from their eyes like that of a tiger in a jungle? Judge Whateley talks. No response. A song is proposed. How shall we sing the Lord's song in a strange land? By-and-by an old man with elbows bowed on his knees and his face upon his hands, begins. One and another drops in until the vast assembly comes upon the mournful melody that runs as follows:—

> "While wandering to and fro,
> In this wide world of woe,
> Where streams of sorrow flow,
> > We'll camp a little while in the wilderness,
> > Then we're going home.
>
> When tears o'erflow mine eyes,
> Then to the mercy-seat
> I go my Lord to meet.
> > We'll camp a little while in the wilderness,
> > Then we're going home."

The effect is overwhelming; the hero of many battles cannot refrain from tears. The committee comes in, reports that they are willing to give up the lands, but that they wish either to lease or to buy the land, and they will not come so near the old relation as to be employed by their former masters. The assembly endorses by sullen silence or bursting sobs and groans. Meeting breaks up. The judge tries to beckon his late beloved people to him. They hold back. He gets one man by the hand. "Why, don't you know me, Jack?" After a vacant stare and one or two noes, he answers: "I used to know you." But of his hundred ex-slaves, only a half-dozen of the most forlorn and the raggedest of the women are drawn out to shake hands and to show any obsequiousness. The judge goes home, calls together his clients, whose hundred thousand acres he represents. The next day he reports that the planters will yield the point of employment and lease or sell the lands. What the final result may be is not known. Here is a scene for Carpenter's brush or Whittier's pen. Let us remember that this people, who are lifting up imploring hands to us, are not the barbarous Indians, who have faced us in warfare across the continent, and with whom we have broken faith; but a Christian race whose labor has enriched our country and whose blood has been poured out that our nation might live.

LETTER XXXIII.

LEGISLATURE FRAMING MISCHIEF INTO LAW FOR BLACK PEOPLE. — BLACK MEN'S HEROISM.

MONTGOMERY, Ala., December 4, 1865.

THANK providence! The fourth day of December has come. Loyal men in these parts have been praying, "Fly swift, ye wheels of time." And now the men who were elected along with Abraham Lincoln are met in Congress with the instruction of the recent canvass to execute the Testament of Freedom. We arrived at the Capitol just in time to witness the passage in both houses of the resolutions approving the amendment to the United States Constitution. They passed the House by a vote of seventy-five to fifteen; the Senate, by twenty-three to four. The legislature then expressed its interpretation of the amendment thus: "It does not confer upon Congress the power to legislate upon the political status of the freedmen in this state." And *The Advertiser* remarks: "If we can retain the power to make and administer laws in the states, what matters it if we have to pass the amendment and give the negro a political status?" And so just now the legislature is in the travail of negro legislation. These proposed bills provide that if a negro breaks his contract he forfeits his wages and becomes a vagrant, and may be tried for the same before a justice of the peace, who, if the master will not receive him back, shall hire him out for the rest of the year, and the proceeds go to a negro pauper fund — involuntary servitude restored! But there is no penalty upon the employer for his breach of the contract. A fine of $100 to $1,000 is to be imposed upon any man who sells or gives rations to or hires a freedman who has broken his contract, and in the same penalty every steamboat is forbidden to transport any such contract breaker. Moreover, to keep negroes from getting land to rent, or from squatting on wild land, the renter is made responsible for all the negro's taxes, rations, and clothing, and the owner of the wild land is held in the same way. What does this mean? It means, as a member said to one of our number in the lobby, "to keep the negroes down, to keep them from rising." When I meet the maimed and the sorrowing white people here, when I see their desolate land, my heart melts; but when I strike these legislatures, five of them in session, my blood boils.

But what shall be said of this wholesale killing and maiming of the negroes without cause? I have no heart to give more than specimens of reports that have come to me all along. At Jackson, Mississippi, General Chetlain, commander of that department, told me that within forty miles of that city, going out on an official trip, he found seven negroes killed. He also said that in two months within his district of nine counties there had been an average of one black man killed every day. Colonel Thomas, Assistant Commissioner of the Freedmen's Bureau, told me that there had been a daily average of two or three black men killed in that state by the citizens. At Mobile, Colonel Yerrington, officer of the Bureau, told me that there had been thirty-eight black men murdered in his district of six counties in three months. The official reports of killing, maiming, outraging, are simply dreadful.

Per contra to this framing of mischief into law and to this wholesale murder, take some instances of black men's heroism and magnanimity. When the other day the Mississippi steamers *Niagara* and *Post Boy* collided and the former was sinking in twenty feet of water, all was consternation. Ladies were running hither and thither for help. A colored deck-hand deliberately tied one end of a rope about his body and the other around a stick of wood, and then, throwing in the stick, jumped overboard, swimming to the end of the rope; he then turned over on his back and calmly called to two white ladies, strangers to him, one of them with a baby in her arms, to jump and catch hold of the stick. They responded to his solicitations, and plunged in and seized the stick. Striking for shore with his heavy burden, against a strong current, he drew them until they touched bottom and all were saved. But, to do this, he had to leave his trunk, with a good suit of clothes and $300 of money in it, to go to the bottom. An eye-witness on the boat told Mr. Alvord the story, and said that nothing was done by the captain or passengers either to re-imburse the black man or to compliment his heroism. Oh, no; he was only a "nigger." Take another. Captain Pease, Bureau Superintendent of Education in Louisiana, described to me the behavior of the colored troops at Port Hudson, where he was himself engaged. He said that four times they charged up those works and never wavered till the last time. He confirmed the story concerning eight or ten black men who lost their lives in trying to rescue General Paine or to give him a drink. Wounded, he lay behind a log, safe from the enemy's guns. When volunteers were called for to rescue him, a thousand offered, but he ordered them not to remove him, as that would call the enemy's fire and kill him. He lay there till he was brought off under cover of night. Put along with this the fact that the blacks did not rise in insurrection when the men were all away and it was in the negroes' power to destroy old men, women, and children. The people here expected it, and now wonder that it was not done. But let them go on with their cruel class legislation against those who have learned to use the sword and bayonet and the alphabet, and then see if there is not a war of races. And I can see no other purpose entertained by them but by black codes to keep the freedmen in a condition equivalent to slavery. It rests, then, with Congress to put this matter beyond a doubt.

Yesterday I went to the Presbyterian and Methodist

churches, hoping to hear some notice given of the national Thanksgiving service on next Thursday, as an honest expression of their love for President Johnson. But there was no such thing. Yet in the loyal Baptist and Methodist churches such notices were given. We also found their pulpits open to us with a genuine southern courtesy, as we have every-where found them. It has been a blessed realization of years of prayer and labor to be permitted to preach the gospel to these ransomed bondmen. Shall we turn our backs upon these who have fought for us and prayed for us and are still with us in prayer and in all the sympathy of their exuberant nature? We meet here General Wager Swayne in the fullness of service as Commissioner of the Freedmen's Bureau.

LETTER XXXIV.

THE CITY SHELLED AND BURNED. — COLORED PEOPLE'S BIG MEETINGS.

CHARLESTON, S. C., December 18, 1865.

WHAT can I say of this famous city so soon after that fine series of articles which appeared in *The Independent* last April, giving account of the flag-raising at Sumter? And yet even from them I had not realized the extent of destruction by shot and shell. It is the old nest of treason whose brood has been destroyed, and now the bird of liberty is building here her home. The geography of the harbor, with its cordon of forts, had been so accurately photographed upon my mind by this four years' process that I should have known my whereabouts if I had been transported to it blindfold. There has as yet been no re-building, but the remaining stores and dwellings are full and the rents are high. The city was more completely prostrated than any that I have yet seen. Here we find in the Bureau General Saxton, whose name has been so honorably associated with the freeing, arming, and elevating of the bondmen. These colored people excel, I find, in the magnetic power of their big meetings. The editor of *The Independent* remembers the mass of humanity animated with high emotion, before which he stood in Zion Church in this city. The same house was crowded on Thanksgiving day, and the service was continued from 10.30 A.M. to 3 P.M. The exercises consisted of exultant songs, prayers, and addresses of gratitude. An eye-witness has described three meetings to me, held last summer by Rev. M. French, chaplain, and General Wild. The first was a Fourth of July celebration in Augusta, Ga., where a procession moved through the streets led by a colored regiment, and then, ten thousand strong, listened to an oration by James Lynch, a colored man, whose address I have read in pamphlet form and admired for its good sense and eloquence. Two days after they held a freedmen's meeting at Edgefield, S. C., in a beautiful grove surrounding the academy. Within a few rods lay the remains of Preston S. Brooks, "the bully," the assassin of Sumner, while his own slaves and those of his neighbors, to the number of three thousand, lift up their voices in loud acclaim, "We are free! we are free!" When it was announced that the government will defend and maintain that freedom, the response was like the sound of many waters. The next mass-meeting was held in Washington, Ga., the home of Senator Toombs, of Bunker Hill notoriety, and in a grove adjoining his beautiful homestead. At that time Toombs was a fugitive in the swamps not twenty miles away, hunted as a criminal, while the freedmen were singing, —

> "Blow ye the trumpet, blow!
> The year of jubilee is come!
> Return, ye ransomed bondmen, home!"

The whole scene was bearing a transfiguration glow. This Washington was also the place where Jeff Davis had lost heart, dismissed his body-guard, and started off in disguise, a fugitive from justice.

In spite of the oppression yet abiding upon this people, it is interesting to observe the aspiration and the endeavor to come up by self-development out of the ignorance which slavery has enforced. They have seized upon the great power of the age, the newspaper. At New Orleans we found *The Tribune*, a daily, owned and edited by colored men; at Mobile, *The Nationalist*, a weekly; at Augusta, *The Colored American;* at Beaufort, *The New South;* at Nashville, *The Colored Tennesseean*. The *Religious Recorder* is the organ of the African Methodist Episcopal Church, published in Philadelphia. And now *The Leader* appears in this city, and it lies before me as I write in the Charleston hotel. And now the number of newspapers which negroes own and manage is one hundred and five.

At Savannah we found six teachers from the American Missionary Association, with three hundred children and over a hundred women as pupils. Rev. J. W. Alvord, who accompanied the army of General Sherman when it entered that city, immediately opened these schools for the colored people. In Charleston we find a school of ten hundred and fifty scholars under Rev. F. L. Cardoza, with fifteen teachers from the American Missionary Association, and six from the Freedmen's Commission.

At Beaufort lives Robert Small, captain of *The Planter*, which he now runs as the head-quarters' boat. The day we were there he said that he had intended to deposit nine hundred dollars in the Freedmen's Bank, but as he had found a farm for sale by a man who had bought it at a United States tax sale, he invested it in that piece of real estate. Who knows but that the government will next break its faith in regard to these tax titles? Small had been a slave in Charleston; had been hired out by his master as assistant pilot of *The Planter;* having learned the ropes and the signals, he formed the plan of capturing a prize. He opened the plan to a few trusty ones of the crew, got his family upon another boat, watched the time when the white captain, the mate, and the pilot were ashore, and when the officers of the other boat were all on land; then got rid of the untrusty ones in the crew, made steam at two o'clock in the morning, with the harbor guard on the dock, steamed up to the other boat, took on his family and the trusty ones of the other crew; then down past Sumter, raising the signals, which were answered "all right"; and then steering for the United States fleet and for that fame which will be perpetuated in the history of the nation saved.

LETTER XXXV.

EMANCIPATION CELEBRATED BY EX-SLAVES.

RICHMOND, Va., New Year's Day, 1866.
"MINE eyes have seen the glory of the coming of the Lord." I have been looking forward to this time, thinking that "I must by all means keep this feast that cometh at" Richmond. And here I am at the heart of the late slave-holders' confederacy, enjoying the freedmen's celebration of the Proclamation of Emancipation. I can not

realize that this imposing ceremony symbolizes the fixed fact of freedom. The service was held in the African Baptist church, where, as it is the largest house in the city, on the seventh of last month, the magnates of the rebellion tried to fire anew the southern heart. The house is beautifully festooned with evergreens, while across one of the galleries the green is intertwined with significant crape and white. The only motto is upon the wall above the pulpit: "This is the Lord's doing; it is marvelous in our eyes." I never saw humanity so closely packed before. There must have been three thousand people in the house, while at the twenty-five open doors and windows stood vast crowds for two and a half hours in the rain, multitudes going away for lack of hearing-room. Robert Johnson, a colored man, presided with dignity, introducing each of the five colored speakers with brief and pertinent remarks. Mr. James Holmes offered a prayer of thanksgiving.

Of course I can not give you a full report of the addresses. They were all made with a manly elocution and with no more imperfectness of language than you will hear where half a dozen country politicians harangue the people from the stump. In oratory as a fine art I think that this people are bound to attain eminence. All of them made a devout reference of all these blessings to God as the Author, and to Abraham Lincoln as the instrument. The memory of that man is embalmed in the hearts of these people. Next to him are the soldiers. All exhorted to behave better on this day than on any other; all urged industry, enterprise, education, patience. One man contrasted this New Year's with the last one. One said that he had been thrown into Richmond jail, and then sold and sent handcuffed to New Orleans, leaving his children, whom he has never seen since, and all because his father-in-law and his mother-in-law had run away to Massachusetts and he had received a letter from them. One told of an old colored man who had once waited on Abraham Lincoln, who told him that if he ever came to be President he would do all he could to set them free. Another said the day the Yankees came in was like the day of conversion: both times we shouted; we were new men both times. A gray-haired man said he was too young to speak, for he was only born on the third of last April. "But where to-day is the auction-block that stood down there *worn smooth?* Where is its auctioneer? He was seen the other day peddling papers." One man recited with magnetic effect the song of Whittier: —

> "Oh, praise and t'anks! de Lord he come
> To set the people free.
> Ole massa t'ink it day of doom,
> But we of jubilee.
> The yam will grow,
> The cotton blow,
> We'll hab de rice an' corn;
> Oh, neber you fear
> If neber you hear
> The driver blow his horn."

The fine band of the twenty-fourth Massachusetts, with twenty pieces, by order of Major-General Terry, was present, and it did seem as if all the good people in the old Bay State were laughing and shouting through those brazen throats. A banquet had been prepared for these brave men of the horn. Indeed, Massachusetts, in all her service, seemed to stand among the states as Abraham Lincoln among men.

Yesterday I had the honor of preaching in this African church to a congregation of twelve hundred. There is a tradition here that Lowell Mason, when here twelve years ago, remarked that he knew the only two choirs in Christendom that kept perfect time — that at Munich and this at Richmond. Professor Hickok recently preached in this church from the text, "The desire of all nations shall come;" and, as it was said, was carried away with his subject and his audience. These people are now drawing off from all the old white churches, both because they are no longer wanted there and because they prefer to be by themselves. They now want ecclesiastical as well as civil freedom. The presbytery in this city says that they have lost the confidence of the colored people. The synod of South Carolina mourns the same thing. All encouragement ought to be given to the southern churches in their efforts for the good of the blacks. But the fact is that they are now thrown mostly upon the north for sympathy and aid.

LETTER XXXVI.

GENERAL THOMAS. — GENERAL FISK. — THE VIRGINIA LEGISLATURE.

WASHINGTON, D. C., January 8, 1866.

ON my way to this city I had the pleasure of the company of Major-General George H. Thomas and Brigadier-General Clinton B. Fisk, both of whom, as well as myself, had been summoned to appear before the Congressional Committee on Reconstruction. That grand old warrior, a native Virginian, remarked that the problem of social reconstruction, the hardest yet to be accomplished, was to be solved only by sending down missionaries who should set up a better style of things. The Freedmen's Commissioner has just come from the uneasy state of

Kentucky, which by rejecting the constitutional amendment has tried to open the grave of slavery and to re-animate the defunct carcass. Before New Year's the general had received three thousand letters bewailing the impending "insurrection." He had also had instructions from President Johnson to go down into north Alabama to ferret out a reported plot for insurrection there. Taking some of his aids, all in citizen's dress, he came to the infested district and traced up the matter to the reputed head-center, an old colored shoemaker, who was found pounding upon his last. Working up gradually to the subject, the general at last plumply charged the man of the shoe-knife with preaching insurrection. It was denied. "Well, what did you do then?" "Why, bless you, massa, I was only preaching about the *resurrection!*"

While at Richmond, coming in from a call on the loyal Van Lew family and a visit to St. John's Church, where Patrick Henry, before the Virginia House of Delegates, had made that famous speech, "Give me liberty, or give me death," and passing, in the square, the equestrian statue of Washington, and in the rotunda the bust of Lafayette, set there in 1781, and the statue of Washington, set up in 1788, and then entering the halls of legislation, where were venerable men, men of the old school, I tried to forget the last five years and to feel a real respect to the "F. F. V.'s"; but almost the first topic that came up was a bill to prevent all negroes not now in the state from settling within its bounds! Besides the injustice of this measure, besides the folly of barring out that very labor by which Virginia can be made a power again, it is a piece of great ingratitude. For many years twenty thousand native Virginians have been sold away, making an income of twenty millions to the state, and now these scattered ones are to be forbidden by law to return to their native land. Oh, such prayers as I have heard among these people for scattered friends! When I attended the African church in that city, several letters were read from the pulpit, inquiring for loved ones left behind. Surely our national Constitution, which now means liberty, will enforce its decree, that in the several states the rights of all the citizens shall be the same as in their respective states. Dr. Read had just returned from the north with $11,000 to re-build his burned church, and he is going back to get $10,000 more; yet while the house was burning, one of the members, as told me by other members, expressed thanks that it was going up to heaven a pure offering, before the foot of a Yankee had polluted it!

Here I am at the national capital after a pilgrimage of six thousand miles, having girdled the late confederacy in a trip undisturbed by accident or rudeness. This last item of testimony I desire to emphasize. I have heard and reported the rough things, while I have sought to note the encouragements. This heat will pass off. The people of the north and of the south will come to know each other better and so to respect each other more. No man can see this desolation of war and desire to see any further visitation of retribution. We are brethren, though alienated for a time. We have the glory of our history as a common inheritance. We are of the same English blood and traditions. We are now to build up our common country upon the basis of freedom and national unity. We must be forbearing. We are proud of the prowess of the south. We must respect their heroic endurance for the sake of their convictions. The victors must be generous.

PERIOD V.

AFTER THE WAR. — TO THE FIRE, 1866-71.

Soldiers from Congregational Churches in the West. — "Blue Laws" of South Carolina. — Iowa Quarter-Centennial. — Chicago Christian Commission. — Roll of Boston Council: Analysis of it. — Illinois Responds to President Johnson. — Four Western War Books. — Abraham Lincoln, "Surveyor." — Grinnell. — Quarter-Millennial of Plymouth Rock.

LETTER XXXVII.

SOLDIERS FROM CONGREGATIONAL CHURCHES. — MINISTERS LOCATED SOUTH. — "BLUE LAWS" IN SOUTH CAROLINA.

CHICAGO, March 20, 1866.

IN order to give some view of the relation of home evangelism to patriotism, a circular was sent to the Congregational churches of the north-west, inquiring the number of soldiers sent into the army from their membership and congregations. Of course the results are imperfect. Of the 982 churches in the ten states, returns have been received from 502. These have reported 2,087 church members, or one in four of their male membership, including old men, invalids, and boys. From their congregations went 6,121, in all, 8,208, which is an average of sixteen from each congregation. If the 480 churches not reported have sent in the same proportion, they will have furnished 1,834 church members and 6,836 of the congregation — in all, 8,670. These will make a total of 3,921 from all the churches, and a grand total of 16,878, or a Division of

Western Ironsides. The reported churches sent 158 officers; they sent 173 sons of ministers. The reported churches have lost by death in the army from their congregations 1,129, or an average of three from each. The whole number of deaths would readily reach 3,000, three regiments of men, a great sacrifice indeed. The reported churches mention 189 conversions among the soldiers in the field and 65 young soldiers turning toward the ministry.

To our delight we find little demoralization among the returned soldiers. They went out not as mercenaries, but as patriots; and as soon as their work was done they were anxious to return to civic life. The report shows 1,331 of the church members "returned with character untarnished." This, when you take out the number killed and the number yet in the army, when the circular went forth, leaves but a small margin for demoralized men. Indeed, many of the reports mark an improvement of morals; thus: "Worst cases come home improved"; "Our young men have for the most part evidently improved in character by the service"; "Nearly all who returned are improved in character"; "It is not known that any have returned with character tarnished"; "Some have improved in piety"; "Morals of all improved"; "All but two of the ten church members [Ottawa, First Church] promoted for good conduct; one kept up prayer-meetings all the way through"; "All seem as good as when they went out." It appears that in a great many churches all the members liable to military duty were in the service. In some, all the male members went out. Sergeant J. E. Griffith, during the assault on Vicksburg, entered one of the enemy's forts with a dozen men who were all killed but himself. He alone marched several prisoners back to camp. He has been sent to West Point by General Grant. Dr.

Baldwin's College Report for 1865 says that Wabash sent 275 soldiers; Iowa, 65; Oberlin, 700, of whom 100 fell; of the 88 alumni of Beloit, 33 were in the army. Of the twenty classes of Marietta, each had its representative in the war.

Looking over my notes I find that at Charleston I came across Ransom's History of South Carolina, 1808. Much has been said of the "blue laws" of New England. Ransom says: "The first two acts which have been found in the records of the clerk's office enjoined the observance of the Lord's day and prohibited idleness, drunkenness, and swearing." As to joining Church and State, he says: "In 1698 the legislature settled a maintenance on a minister of the Church of England in Charleston." He also says that in 1704, when there was only one Church of England to four churches of dissenters, a legislature was secured which made a law that required all persons chosen members of the Commons, House of Assembly, to conform to the religious worship of the Church of England, and to receive the sacrament of the Lord's Supper according to the rites and usages of that Church. The taxing of non-conformists to support the state Church went on for seventy years until the Revolution. In 1773 Alexander Garden, whom the Bishop of London had sent to be commissary of North and South Carolina and Georgia, suspended from the ministry, after a short trial, George Whitefield for the offence of not always using the prayer-book. While preaching in St. Phillips Church in Charleston his great soul overflowed the set form of prayer, and for this he was forbidden to officiate as an Episcopal minister. He then drew off and went to preaching in the church of the dissenters, called the "white-meeting," but in these last years called the Circular Church. Mr. Ransom also states that the churchmen settled mostly along the coast, while the dissenters went into the north and the west parts of the state. This tallies with the fact that in the Revolution Toryism prevailed on the coast and patriotism in the north and the west.

LETTER XXXVIII.

IOWA QUARTER-CENTENNIAL. — CHICAGO CHRISTIAN COMMISSION. — DR. TARBOX'S ANALYSIS OF ROLL OF BOSTON COUNCIL.

CHICAGO, June 12, 1866.

THE deliverances of our state associations this season have had the patriotic ring. It is demanded that emancipation be followed by the suffrage and the securing of civil rights. The resistance of Congress to the usurpation of President Johnson is approved. Illinois declares that to remit the emancipated to the disloyal states will be to expose us to the retribution of new wars and pecuniary losses and divisions and bloodshed.

July 10, 1866.

A notable occasion in this city, yesterday, was a reunion of the army committee of the Young Men's Christian Association, complimentary to Rev. and Mrs. Jeremiah Porter, who had just returned from their service among the soldiers at Brownsville, Texas. The gathering was at the Sherman House, where were assembled forty or fifty of the clergy and prominent citizens of Chicago. Mr. J. V. Farwell introduced Mr. Porter as the first man who came to Chicago to preach (1833), the first to go into the army and the last to come out. This branch of the Christian Commission has raised and expended for the good of the soldiers

$137,658. The Young Men's Christian Association, under its president, Mr. D. L. Moody, is moving to build a hall that will seat three thousand, to be called Farwell Hall. The stock already raised amounts to $103,800.

An analysis of Dr. Increase Tarbox's catalogue of the names of the members of the Boston Council, with their places of residence and of birth, and with the birth-places of their parents, reveals some curious facts. Of the five hundred and sixteen members, only ten ministers and three laymen were born in the west. Among us western boys were Fred W. Beecher, J. M. Sturtevant, Jr., and that Nestor of the Council, Dr. Leonard Bacon, who was born in Detroit. Sixty-three were born in the Middle States; but the parents of almost every one of these were born in New England. Fourteen delegates were born in Great Britain; one in France; five in the south, among them Dr. Blagden and Reverends R. C. Dunn and M. W. Fairfield. So that four hundred and twenty-one persons were born in New England, while most of the others were of that parentage. And yet the Council represented twenty-five states and territories, reaching across to the Pacific. And this is the New England zone.

I have more authority for Thomas Jefferson's remark that the autonomy of the churches would be the best plan of government for the American colonies. This is found in Belcher's "Religious Denominations." Rev. Father Keeler, of Kokomo, Ind., informs me that twenty-three years ago, at a council, he met Rev. Mr. Brice, who had been a pastor at Richmond, Virginia, and referring to this statement by Belcher, Mr. Brice told him that Mr. Jefferson had also attended on his ministry in Richmond and had made the same remark to him.

LETTER XXXIX.

PILGRIM'S REST.

CHICAGO, October 16, 1866.

I WRITE this letter from Pilgrim's Rest, his new home on the Lake Shore, peering out from the Douglas Grove. President Hitchcock once closed an address in this city by wondering whether the people of Chicago appreciated the glory of the scenery around them. That morning he had climbed to the lookout of the Tremont House and observed the floating ice-field piled on the edge of the lake in grotesque masses, which shimmered in the rising sun. And this is but one element in the grandeur of this great lake, which affords us perpetual and ever-variant beauty. In repose, how calm and restful! Shadowed by clouds, how kaleidoscopic its colors! Kissing the shore in gentle undulations, how it soothes and lulls to sleep! Aroused in storm, jarring the shore and sprinkling it with spray, how grand! Making its surface a pavement of sapphire, as it sends forth the sun to present us his morning salutations, and plating its broad expanse with silver as the moon comes up to greet our evening chit-chat, how glorious! You never tire of this acquaintance; it grows upon you in the sense of companionship. Though hidden in the forest, with this for your only neighbor, you are not lonely. Then from this Rest I look out on the great Crib, standing in its dignity two miles from the shore, and making haste to open its fountains of pure water for the two hundred thousand people who wait patiently upon this great enterprise. Neither storms nor floating ice-batteries have availed to disturb its repose. Its steam-works are smoking day and night in tunneling toward the shore, and by-

and-by it is to mount the friendly light-house for the night-bestead and tempest-driven mariner. I have been out in the tunnel a mile from the shore. I could hear the splashing of steamboats overhead. Next to this is the old harbor light, at the end of the great pier; then comes the river's mouth, at which the birds of commerce are seen constantly going in and out; then the great central depot, the bee-hive of busy locomotives; then the frontage of the magnificent Michigan Avenue, — all this in view is a grand panorama. From this point I have frequently seen twenty-five or thirty vessels starting out upon their voyage. After the recent storm had raised its embargo of a day, I counted at one time one hundred and eighteen vessels that were just spreading their sails outside the harbor, presenting a sweep of four miles of canvas. From this point, looking east, with the sun in the west, by that wondrous mirage, I have seen the opposite shore, forty miles away, lifted into distinctness for a long distance. There was the water washing the sand-bank, which rises to a considerable height, and there were the crowning evergreens distinctly visible. From the top of his shot tower Mr. Blatchford says that by this mirage he has seen Michigan City over there, even as Bunyan's Pilgrim saw afar off the Celestial City. So some hour of unearthly experience or some season of bereavement lifts up the hither coast of eternity, revealing its shining shore, its City of the great King and its heavenly inhabitants, thus bringing near the future world and convincing us of its reality.

LETTER XL.

AMERICAN MISSIONARY ASSOCIATION ANNIVERSARY. — ILLINOIS' RESPONSE TO PRESIDENT JOHNSON.

CHICAGO, November 16, 1866.

At the twentieth anniversary of the American Missionary Association, held in Galesburg, Ill., last week, it was found that the $250,000 proffered by the Boston Council had been raised to $253,045 in cash, with clothing in value to carry it up to $358,486. Well done! The number of workers among the freedmen the last year was three hundred and fifty-three, of whom two hundred and sixty-four were women, and forty-one ministers. The Association resolved to try to raise this year $400,000. And so this little, despised, testifying organization has become a national potency.

Illinois responds to Andrew Johnson's visit to lay the corner-stone of the Douglas Monument by a majority of fifty thousand against him. Even Egypt cuts loose from him. Hon. B. C. Cook, who has been reëlected to Congress by a large majority, told upon the stump this story to make the blood of men boil: John Gifford, of Lisbon, in his district, wounded at Chickamauga, lay on the field six days and nights without food or water, was then taken up by the rebels, had his leg amputated, was sent to Andersonville for five months, and came home with a shattered constitution. On Mr. Cook's recommendation he was made postmaster in his own town, and then he was turned out by Andrew Johnson to make room for a copperhead! Of such an one, as our A. J. Junius says: "Truly, my lord, you may well be weary of the circuit you have taken; for you have now fairly traveled through every sign in the political zodiac, from the scorpion, in which you stung" such a mangled soldier!

LETTER XLI.

FOUR WESTERN WAR BOOKS.

CHICAGO, April 20, 1867.

THE west is just now presenting to the public four large books upon the war. One is "Wisconsin in the War of the Rebellion," a portly octavo of eleven hundred and eighty pages, from the pen of Rev. W. D. Love, D.D. The work contains a history of each of the seventy-three separate military organizations which Wisconsin sent to the war, an account of one hundred battles and expeditions, biographical notices of two hundred officers and privates, a classified list of the eleven thousand Wisconsin dead, twenty-five steel-plate portraits, and seven diagrams. The state may well be proud of its major-generals, Washburn, Schurtz, Hamilton, Cutler, Ruger, Saloman; its brigadiers, Paine, Starkweather, Fairchild, Allen, Hobart, Fallows. The loss of Governor Harvey by drowning while in the service of the soldiers was a part of the sacrifice. Horatio K. Foote, son of Rev. Hiram Foote, a lad of but eighteen, was chief of scouts in the first cavalry. He held receipts for more than twenty prisoners, captured by his own unaided prowess, while as a shot he "never wasted a cartridge." Suffering the horrors of Andersonville and Florence, he died in the prison of the latter, giving up his life rather than enlist in the rebel army, as he was solicited to do. "Lincoln and Slavery," an octavo of seven hundred and thirty-five pages, is another of these books. It is from the pen of Hon. Isaac N. Arnold, late member of Congress from this district. It is an effort properly to associate the greatest event of modern history, the overthrow of American slavery, with the second man of our nation. Upon the life of Mr. Lincoln the facts of this great accomplishment are strung in harmony and in brilliancy. He has set the picture of emancipation in the frame of the emancipator's life. The story of the "Patriotism of Illinois" has been told by Rev. T. M. Eddy. D.D., editor of *The Northwestern Christian Advocate* of this city, in his two octavo volumes. The work is wonderfully well done. We are proud that Illinois gave the nation its commander-in-chief and its general; that we sent a quarter of a million of soldiers to the war; that without authority from Washington we had taken Cairo, that strategic point, before the guns that silenced Sumter were cool; that we kept ahead of our quota on every call; that drafting was scarcely resorted to; and that by increasing majorities the voters of the state have endorsed the action of the boys in blue. Among the leaders Illinois counts Grant, Logan, McClernand, Palmer, Hurlbut, Oglesby, Wallace, Ransom, Chetlain, Brayman, Mulligan, Bross, and Yates. "Our Branch and its Tributaries" is an octavo history of the work of the north-western branch of the United States Sanitary Commission, by Mrs. Sarah Edwards Henshaw, whose middle name connects her by lineal descent with the great theologian of America. Upon the skeleton of statistics the authoress has put flesh and nerve and color and expression. We have had books upon the women of the war, but those gave us only the work of a few individuals. Here we find the mass of the loyal women of the north-west in their respective communities, working away in their homes, for four years in their labor of love, preparing articles of comfort, necessity, and delicacy, tiring not amid disheartening influences and triumphing all the more gloriously because their field of action was so much to the rear. The total receipts of our Branch were $411,027.35.

LETTER XLII.

A MUD RIDE. — ABRAHAM LINCOLN.

CHICAGO, February 22, 1869.

I HAVE been to Aledo, Illinois, to prepare the way for a new church. The time for the council was set after the expected arrival of trains on the branch of the Chicago, Burlington, and Quincy from Galva. But when that time came the road was not through by a gap of thirteen miles. On Saturday at noon the train leaves me at Windsor. No one has come to take me on. It is three miles to the end of the track, where a rig may be awaiting me. A hand-car is secured by a personal friend, against orders to the contrary, and is driven by six leisure men (for track laying is under the embargo of mud), who soon dump me in the middle of a plowed field. I find no messenger. It is five miles to Viola, where I am to preach in the morning before going on eight miles to preach at night in Aledo. Three or four countrymen decline furnishing a conveyance. No man for money will go through that mud and rain. And so, entering a farm-house, I throw aside my impedimenta, traveling-shawl, and carpet-bag. I start off with umbrella spread to the storm. Now on ordinary roads a walk of five miles would not be bad. But such mud, so deep, so thick, so heavy in loading the feet! There is no going around it. As I plod along, slipping, and sticking, and stalling, and soaking, "one of those wicked ones" gets behind this Pilgrim, and steps up softly, and whispering, suggests many grievous things, thus: "Ah, sorry, weary Pilgrim, all this, and then to be 'nothing but an agent'; you might have a loving parish, as once you had; you might have your study, with all its mental stimulus and its royal joy; you might be with your family, who in your absence have suffered from burglary and sickness and loneliness; let some man take this work who is not acceptable as a pastor, or one who has no wife or children to long for him; this plodding and preaching in school-houses and little sanctuaries, this universal scatteration, this continual dealing with the littlest, weakest churches, is unworthy of you; and after all, you are only an 'agent,' who is supposed to be a clerical mendicant." Just then the Master spoke out: "How is this? I was once myself an itinerant preacher and I went on foot; the disciple is not above his Master, nor the servant above his lord. My servant Paul, in his apostleship, was but a planter and trainer of churches." And then I saw that the Pilgrim, first ashamed of himself, and then cheered by so gracious presence, became light of foot and the walk of three hours for five miles seemed short indeed.

After the morning service a man arrived from Aledo. His bright span before a buggy, at the utmost of their ability, got us over that eight miles of mud in just three hours. But the house is full, and the people are waiting to hear the Word. On Monday morning a hack starts from Viola to bring the members of the council from the end of the rail track, and a four-horse, double-seated buggy starts from Aledo to connect at the middle station. Four o'clock, the hour of the council, comes, but its members do not. Seven o'clock; the lone preacher is just rising to go along with the service of institution when, to his great joy, in come Dr. Edward Beecher, Rev. Mr. Waldo, and a delegate, just alighted from the vehicle, chilled by the sharp west wind which they have faced all the way, weary and hungry withal. Soon they are thawed out. The council is put through. Dr. Beecher gives us a grand discourse, and the brotherhood, with a deacon ordained by prayer and the laying on of hands, is pronounced a duly instituted church of Jesus Christ. On Tuesday, back to Viola in three hours. But it will be impossible for the relief of the horses to reach the train in time, and so we settle down in the tavern and give out a notice for a temperance meeting at night. House full, three flaming speeches. Wednesday morning, four horses, eight miles, three hours, and we are drawn up out of the Slough of Despond. But we are back to Galva too late for the trains east or west, and so the pastors lose their prayer-meetings, and Pilgrim does not reach his Rest until morning. You Boston pastors, think of your former associate, Dr. Beecher, thus drawn through the mud to set up a little church! Do you pity him? It was his joy. It brought to mind an earlier trip. President Beecher and Professor Sturtevant were coming up to Chicago, two hundred and twenty-five miles, in a one-horse buggy on a mission. Driving into the Mackinaw the forward axle drops down from the box, and away to the other side go the horse and fore-wheels, while the doctors jump into the stream up to their shoulders to catch their luggage, and the buggy goes tumbling down stream. Mr. Beecher, with a hooked pole, goes a-fishing — he says he was with his father upon that traditional fishing excursion — for the truant buggy, and, getting a good hold, he pulls it ashore. Some man brings back the horse and cart, all is made fast, and now they go over safely, and turn in at the nearest cabin, and open and dry their wardrobe. My own experience of that mud was awarded by a find in Aledo. Within an ancient book at the recorder's office in that place I found the original plot of the town of New Boston, made in 1836, and bearing this certificate: —

I do certify that the above is an accurate plot of the town of New Boston as surveyed by me.

A. LINCOLN,
For Peter Butler, surveyor of the Co. of Warren and the attached parts thereof.

Afterward this same deputy surveyor became the Surveyor General for the United States. There having been a contest for a hundred years as to the line known as Mason and Dixon's, this high official (as when two farmers fall out in the same way) determined to run the line for himself. And instead of trying to confirm the old survey he starts at the coast and runs out to sea as far as his jurisdiction extends, and then keeps out from land around the point of Florida, through the Gulf, and up the coast of the Pacific. He then issues a proclamation, making that his Mason and Dixon's line, and decreeing freedom over all the inside domain.

LETTER XLIII.

CATHOLIC MISSION. — PRAIRIE EVANGELISM. — FOREIGN MISSIONARIES.

SAINT JOSEPH, Mich., August 4, 1869.

BLESSED saint! patron of peaches and strawberries. Two hundred thousand bushels of peaches, with other fruits to match in quantity, sent to market from this region the last year, to reach an income of three quarters of a million dollars! Two hundred years ago, in 1669, Father Allouez, who in 1666 had founded a mission at the falls of the Saint Mary among the Indians, discovered this place. Four years later Allouez and Marquette made a circuit of Lake Michigan in canoes, discovering and naming the rivers and bays. The river emptying here they called the Saint Joseph. In 1679 La Salle came to Mackinaw and thence around Lake Michigan to this point, where he built a fort of hewn logs, forty by eighty feet, clearing away the timber for two musket shots, for readier protection against the Indians. In 1700 the Jesuits founded a mission here upon a spot now known as the Indian Orchard, some of whose apple-trees yet remain. In 1720 Charlevoix visited the mission. In 1762 Pontiac, who had devised a plan for taking all the French forts west of Niagara, captured this one. In 1822 Rev. Isaac McCoy, under the Baptist Board, established a mission among the Indians up the river as far as where Niles now is. It was not until 1829 that a white settlement was begun at Saint Joseph. In 1804 the United States government desired to build a fort at this place. The Indians, not yet having ceded this tract, refused to have it located here. Then, as an alternative, the fort was located across the lake at the mouth of a vastly inferior river, where the town of Chicago afterward came to be built. Captain Napier, who has sailed these lakes for forty years, tells me that when he first began to visit this port it was quite superior in its business importance to the one over at Fort Dearborn.

GRINNELL, Iowa.

Imagine yourself set down in a sea of prairie, looking " as if the ocean, in his mildest swell, had remained fixed and motionless forever." The horizon all the way around shuts down on the green waves, except that in the southwest there appears the *terra firma* of a grove. No mark of human life is in sight, only as that speck in the edge of the woods may indicate a prairie schooner or a squatter's cabin. But now, as you look and wonder, an object looms up in the east. It turns out to be the vehicle of a young city pastor from New York, to whom Horace Greeley had originally said: "Go west, young man, and grow up with the country." He comes up to yon crowning center, and, taking in the sweep, proclaims himself monarch of all he surveys. He lays his title upon six thousand acres. He decrees a college there, and for himself a seat in Congress. All this is back in the mysterious past, in the year of our Lord one thousand eight hundred and fifty-four.

Again, at midnight, you are set down at that same center of the horizon. As day comes on and you look out, behold! the sea has become dry land. You observe that since your last visit little groves have been dotted in over the wide expanse, which seems also to have been cleft asunder by the plowing of a highway. Presently over this track comes thundering along a train marked "Pacific," and by its side runs a cable, not trans-oceanic, but trans-continental. And so, without farther reckoning, you find that you are on the commercial equator and a little past the meridian of the nineteenth century. Was it strange that the mid-century had centered its civilization at that conjuncture? You find a city of two thousand, whose mayor, Henry G. Little, must have little to do, since there has never yet been a lawsuit among his people, since liquor has never been sold nor a drunken man seen within his domain, and since there has never been a fire or a cyclone within his corporation. You find steam mills and elevators, a first-class hotel, brick blocks, a park of twenty acres, well-shaded, churches, the veritable college that was fore-ordained and is now in the glow of commencement, and all surrounded with thrifty farms. And now where do you find yourself to be? Why, at the place which bears the name of its founder, that little man who first planted his buoy upon the ocean prairie, who seems yet to be a factotum in all its affairs, and who has already occupied and honored his seat in Congress, the Rev. and Hon. J. B. Grinnell.

CHICAGO, September 28, 1869.

This sending away of foreign missionaries is coming to be a reality to us in the west. Heretofore they have been sent from your coast eastward. We have read of your farewell meetings. We have imagined the scenes. Even when we felt our first missionary thrill, upon the occasion of ordaining five of our seminary men for the field abroad, we did not add to this the experience of a good-by meeting. They too sailed from your shores. But now the course of missionary journeying is changed in part. It seemed a strange event that seven missionaries, starting for China, were coming this way. Yet they were now taking the direct course. We welcomed them. It did us good to see them. We sent them along with our blessing. Their passing by us was the preaching of a missionary sermon, which was extended across the continent, as they traversed this highway of the Lord cast up for the messengers of his Word. A first-class caterer to missionary occasions is Secretary Humphrey, here at the halfway place. It was a union meeting. The veteran missionary, Dr. Scudder, from his advanced position on the Pacific, had come to receive and cheer along this apostolic company. His eloquence and his personal knowledge of the foreign work served the cause grandly.

The names of the missionaries are Rev. and Mrs. D. Z. Sheffield, Rev. and Mrs. J. L. Whiting, Rev. and Mrs. D. C. McCoy, and Miss Mary Thompson. Ohio, Illinois, Wisconsin, and Iowa were represented in this sacred number. And so the west is falling into line. Six others are soon to follow, destined to the same field.

LETTER XLIV.

THE CELEBRATION OF THE TWO HUNDRED AND FIFTIETH YEAR OF THE PLYMOUTH ROCK LANDING.

CHICAGO, April 30, 1870.

WE are proud to have the Pilgrim reunion brought to our western home. We feel much as a well-to-do son who receives to his own home his honored parents, and who, from filial affection and reverence, delights to do all in his power to make them happy. Five hundred delegates, coming from Maine and from California, and from all the region between, have been entertained, and as many as four hundred have been received into the homes of personal friends. Dr. Edward Beecher served as temporary chairman, and B. W. Tompkins as the permanent. Dr. Leonard Bacon made an instructive opening address upon the difference between the Puritans and the Pilgrims: the former held to a reformation inside of a state church; the latter were "separatists," and held to coming out from the corrupt churches and making pure organizations on the scriptural model. The latter, few at first, despised and persecuted even unto death, proved victorious in the end. In New England the Puritans fell in with the ideas of the Pilgrims. We are met here to-day from the breadth of a continent to commemorate the saintly virtues of these heroic servants of God. Before us here is a photograph of the members of the Boston National Council when they stood around the forefathers' rock. One of the moments of my life which stands out clearest and brightest in my memory is the time when we, a thousand of us nearly, gathered from every state between the Atlantic and the Pacific, sat upon Burial Hill, proud of the declaration of our faith, transmitted to us by the men who were buried there.

Dr. T. M. Post delivered a beautiful and eloquent address upon "The Occasion and the Situation." The one thing that the Convention did as to measures was to initiate the permanent Triennial National Council. Dr. H. M. Dexter made report of the plans and of the methods of the Jubilee Executive Committee appointed at New York for increasing the interest of young and old in this work by circulating memoranda of historical facts concerning the Pilgrims, by the use of books of memorial record, and by the sale of memorial medals to children and others. An interesting letter was read from the Church of the Pilgrimage at Plymouth, Mass. The following action was also taken:—

Resolved, That the triumph of ideas and principles of the fathers in the late civil contest, emancipating and enfranchising four millions of blacks, and giving nearly equally important disenthrallment to eight millions of whites, imposes a vast responsibility and offers a grand opportunity for the dissemination of the religion of the Pilgrims; and in this memorial year of their landing on these shores we pledge ourselves to renewed effort to preach the gospel and plant its institutions in the south.

The Pilgrim Celebration, the Triennial, and the Anniversary were held here the same week and by the same people, largely; but they had no other relation to each other than that of contiguity, comity, and co-working. The seminary graduated fourteen young men and had eloquent addresses from President E. O. Haven and Rev. Joseph P. Thompson, D.D., and inaugurated Dr. J. T. Hyde as professor of pastoral theology and special studies. The Triennial received reports of the three past years of the seminary's operations, elected directors for the same, and participated in the exercises of the Anniversary. The treasurer, Dr. G. S. F. Savage, reported the net assets as $254,036. The whole week was a grand tripartite occasion, three in form, one in essence. An adjunct of the week was a conference of the secretaries of the Home Missionary Society, coming from Maine and California. Dr. J. H. Warren, who had been forty days in going out to California, had come back in six, and by rail, as he had promised on going out.

PERIOD VI.

FROM THE FIRE TO THE CENTENNIAL, 1871-76.

The Chicago Fire. — National Council. — Tour in Connecticut. — The Ohio an Ancient Highway. — An Exploration of Colorado. — Among the Dakotas. — The Boston Fire. — Philo Carpenter. — Lake Superior. — Lone Star State. — The Woods of Northern Michigan.

LETTER XLV.

THE CHICAGO FIRE.

CHICAGO, October 12, 1871.

DESOLATION, desolation! A broad swath mowed down on the west side. On the South Side the business heart of the city eaten out. The north side literally swept away, only one house having been spared. The north division, a city of itself of seventy-five thousand, with water-works, gas-works, homes, business places, a dozen stone sanctuaries and many wooden, but all swept away. On the South Side a half-dozen of the best churches in the city gone. The New England Church and that of her daughter, the Lincoln Park Church, are lost, and not a family of these churches is left with a home. During the fire thousands gathered on the lake shore to escape the flying fire, and many of these had to sprinkle themselves to keep off the flames. Even in the midst of such terror the ludicrous would appear. A burly Irishman, espying a judge who was wetting himself down to keep from catching fire, drew himself up before "his honor," and spoke his mind, thus: "And, Joodge, it was a joodgmint from hiven upon ye, for ye did n't joodge right!" Many thousands lay out on the prairie over-night. On that same Monday night, by the light reflected from the heavens, I could read the door-plate of our home at Oak Park, nine miles westward. On the train that brought home some of the friends that had been on to the American Board, there were persons who represented two and a half millions of loss. One of these, whose wealth was only moderate, said that the seven or eight thousand that he had given away the last year had all been saved. On Monday, as I fell in with Mr. T. B. Bryan, of the "Fidelity Safe," he and I tried to work our way into it, adjoining the old Sherman House; but it was impossible for us to reach the place, because of the heat. He told me afterwards that when he did come to open that treasure house in the presence of his patrons, he saw upon those hot, tumbled bricks such dancing as he had never seen in Paris, when the men came to find that these deposits, all they had left, were safe! The heat! Why, it melted down iron, glass, brick, stone, into a conglomerate, and Mrs. Pilgrim has a ton of that material piled up as a monument. The Academy of Science stood entirely detached. Its iron doors and shutters were closed. I saw it burn. It was a back fire, going against the wind. And yet such was the superambient heat that through the shutters and walls it set fire to the inside material, whose flames burst through the iron doors outward. The total loss is estimated at $300,000,000.

October 18, 1871.

How grand this testimonial of charity! Two millions, six hundred and sixty dollars already received in cash, besides the hundreds and hundreds of car-loads of clothing and provisions. It comes from every part of the land. It comes from over the ocean. It is all needed; all worthily conferred. It will be wisely disbursed. Two-thirds of the business capital of the city was consumed. Dr. E. F. Williams, up among the Indians of the northwest, heard in a few hours of the burning. A citizen just home from Europe told me that seven hundred miles out he had heard of it from a pilot whom they had picked up on the coast. The pastor of the New England Church, hunting in the *débris* for a memento, found a piece of a black and charred leaf of a pulpit hymn-book and on it read : —

> Daughter of Zion ! awake from the dust,
>   Exalt thy fallen head ;
> Re-build thy walls ; thy bounds enlarge,
>   And send thy heralds forth.
> Say to the South, "Give up thy charge,
>   And keep not back, O North."

The hymn was sung at their first re-opening of service.

LETTER XLVI.

THE NATIONAL COUNCIL.

OBERLIN, Ohio, November 21, 1871.

THIS is the first in the series of National Triennial Councils now established. It has been in session for six days. It has had three hundred members. It received reports from the national societies and theological seminaries. It burnished its constitution theologically. It heard the jubilee singers, to be moved by them to tears. It gave the New England Church of Chicago the right hand of material fellowship. It received President Finney, and, by request, heard from him on the subject of Enduement with Power, only to invite him to preach to the body on the same topic, on both of which occasions its members were deeply moved. It assisted in laying the corner-stone of Council Hall for the theological department of Oberlin College, at which service the moderator, Rev. W. I. Budington, D.D., made the speech of the week when he said: "We stand on the grave of buried prejudice." It heard from Dr. H. Q. Butterfield, secretary of the college society, the speech of his life, and from Rev. Joseph E. Roy, a paper on Home Missions. It denounced caste as in connection with our northern churches, schools, and colleges, and at the south also, as the great hindrance to the harmonious organization of society there. After the address of Secretary Strieby, it re-indorsed the American Missionary Association as raised up and signally adapted to take the foremost place in the accomplishment of the education and the moral elevation of the freedmen; recommended that four hundred thousand dollars should be annually contributed by our churches for this purpose; and commended its seven colleges and theological schools to the special consideration of benevolent men in reference to needed buildings and endowments. It gave special approbation to the work of the Home Missionary Society and of the Congregational Union and the College Society.

LETTER XLVII.

AFTER THE FIRE.

CHICAGO, January 8, 1872.

IT is now three months since the fire. The grain heaps of two elevators are yet smouldering and flaming, notwithstanding the floods of water that have been poured on and the cargoes of wheat that have been raked out and shipped. Two thousand wooden shanties and houses have gone up, and three hundred one, two, and three story brick buildings. Thus far the trowel has not ceased its click for more than five days on account of the cold. On one wall, up high, I counted five furnace fires burning for the warming of fingers and toes. One of our oldest architects publishes a statement that of the sixteen miles of available building front in the burnt district of the south side, nine and a half miles, previous to the fire, had been occupied by offices, manufactories, banks, hotels, and stores; and six and a half miles by dwellings, churches, school-houses, and other public buildings. There were nearly three miles of five and six story cut-stone and iron buildings, many of them of the most costly character, equal in architectural appearance to any buildings on the continent. He is confident that three miles of front will be re-built this year within this district for commercial purposes, and that the new will equal the old. The nineteen national banks are justifying the assurance given by the United States comptroller after inspection as to their soundness.

February 27, 1872.

A report of the Chicago Relief and Aid Society brings out a total of $3,335,700, with a balance on hand of $1,314,269. This, besides all the scores of railway trains of provisions and clothing. Thanks to God for this world-wide uprising of charity! The people of twenty-two nationalities have been the recipients of this bounty.

LETTER XLVIII.

A MISSIONARY TOUR.

CONNECTICUT, April 30, 1872.

WE are going over this state in a two months' series of missionary conventions. Our seven national societies are represented. We have Rev. Doctors Langworthy, Tarbox, Strieby, Barrows, Cushing, Butterfield, and missionary Tyler from South Africa, and all led by Secretary W. H. Moore. At the west I am always wondering where the Yankees out there ever came from. Here, as I learn of their migrating, I wonder where they all go to. Connecticut, as if yet claiming sovereignty over her belt across the land, still persists in bringing her representatives from those parts into all legislative bodies. In 1821, of 126 members in the New York Constitutional Convention, 32 were from Connecticut. A few years ago she had 15 members in the New York legislature. In Congress one time, Hillhouse found that 47 members, or one fifth of the whole, were from this state. Calhoun once admitted that the members from this state, together with the graduates of Yale, lacked only five of a majority. De Tocqueville's observing eye detected this representation in Congress from Connecticut. At a Fourth of July celebration in Paris, where he was the only foreign guest, he said: "Von day I was in the House Representative; I held in my hand one map of the confederation. Dere was one leetle yellow spot dat dey call Connect-de-coot. I found by the Constitution he was entitled to six of his boys to represent him on dat floor. But ven I make the acquaintance *personnelle* with the member, I find that more than t'irty of the representative on that floor was born in

Connect-de-coot. And den ven I was in de gallery of de house of de Senate, I find dat de Constitution permit this state to send two of his boys to represent him in dat legislature. But vonce more, ven I make the acquaintance *personnelle* of the senator, I find nine of the senator was born in Connect-de-coot. And now for my grand sentiment : Connect-de-coot, de leetle yellow spot dat make de clock-peddler, de school-master, and de senator ; de first give you time, de second tell you what to do with him, the t'ird make your law and civilization."

In ecclesiastical matters at the west, starting after the first two tiers of counties on the east side of New York, the case is about the same. New Jersey, at the time of its settlement, might as well have been called New Connecticut, as was the Western Reserve. As early as 1661 colonists from Guilford, Milford, New Haven, and Brandford, having negotiated with their high mightinesses of New Amsterdam, had made settlements at Woodbridge, Newark, and Elizabeth, transferring all their ideas of church, town, and ministry, setting up Congregational churches in each town. Recently spending a Sabbath over there at Connecticut Farms, the ancestral home of my mother, I found such records as these : In their treaty with New Amsterdam they stipulated for "the right to gather a church in the Congregational way such as we have enjoyed in New England about twenty years past." Their pastors were called from New England and installed by councils from that quarter. Rev. James Davenport was in the line of pastors at Connecticut Farms. Yankee-like, they must have their own college, and so, at Elizabeth Town, under Pastor Jonathan Dickinson, was set up the institution which is now Princeton College. Now I see how natural it was for Jonathan Edwards to become president of that college, and how natural for Absalom Peters, Jeremiah Porter, and many others to go from New England to Princeton. Then Connecticut claims her score or more of college presidents out west, and many scores of college professors. Our "Illinois Band," which did so much to give character to our state, was made up of Connecticut men. Yale is claimed as the model of most of our western colleges.

Then look at the men of mark that have gone out from these hills and valleys. Here were born Samuel J. Mills and President Humphrey, and David Brainerd and Nathaniel W. Taylor, and Asahel Nettleton and Titus Coan. Then Guilford and her seven daughters have raised up one hundred ministers. Waterbury has contributed $100,000, has grown into seven churches and raised up thirteen ministers, and so on.

LETTER XLIX.

THE OHIO AN ANCIENT HIGHWAY.

HUNTINGTON, W. Va., June 3, 1872.

STEAMING up the Ohio from Cincinnati I am reminded that it is an ancient highway of the nation. Before railroads or wagon-roads or bridle-paths had shot into the north-west territory, emigration floated down this stream, lodging along these beautiful bottoms and turning around into and up the affluents beyond. Thus drifted down the first colony, that of Marietta, in 1788; then another which rounded up into the Wabash to make Edwards County, in Illinois, a center of Puritan influence; then that band of young men from Yale, bearing the precious seed-corn of Illinois College, of its supporting churches, and of not a few of our state institutions; then the colony that swung up the Mississippi and the Illinois, and then tied up its flat-boat to plunge off into the prairie to develop the city and college of Galesburg. The rivers afford the first line of settlement; so Illinois was settled on the west side long before it was on the east side; and so Iowa was first occupied on its east water front, and then on its west water front, its grand interior having been left to the explorations of the iron horse. So it is now along the upper Missouri, the Columbia, and all the other frontier rivers. It was on his way up this Ohio, eastward bound, in 1844, that Theron Baldwin conceived the idea which bore such fruitage within his life, that of the College Society, that is now going on to bless the rising states of the deep interior.

And here I am for the first time in West Virginia, which revives associations of the war. The Big Sandy, the Guyandotte, the Kanawha, are familiar names. At Guyandotte was raised the first rebel flag along the river. Out at Charleston, the capital, was fought a battle in that series of chasings up and down the Kanawha of Generals Cox and Wise. Now life is thumping under the ribs of this new Virginia, as northern capital and enterprise are taking hold of her resources. The Chesapeake and the Ohio Railroad, coming from the mouth of the bay across the state, over the Blue Ridge and the Alleghanies, to the river, is waking up her sleeping energies. Here in this new town on the river, taking the name of the president of the road, we have just been organizing a church which is to build a ten thousand dollar church edifice.

LETTER L.

AN EXPLORATION OF COLORADO.

DENVER, Colo., July 15, 1872.

"FIRST VIEW" is the name of a station one hundred and fifty-nine miles east of Denver, where, in clear weather, the first glimpse of the mountains is secured. And my first view was a grand one, taking in the snowy range, Pike's Peak at the south and Long's Peak at the north. What a relief to the monotony of the plains! I am just in time to take the first excursion out on the narrow gauge, Denver and Rio Grande, fifty miles to the Divide. We leave Denver at twenty-five hundred feet above the sea and rise up two thousand more, and above that I climb another thousand feet and forget my weariness in the exhilaration of the scene. The egg has been set on end. The narrow gauge is a success, as is proved by this first one built in our country.

Colorado is destined to become a noble state. It has the backbone of grandeur and wealth running through the middle of it. Its tumbling streams carry down fatness from the mountains for the valleys and the nearer plains on both sides of the snowy range. Its mines will always be a source of attraction. The ores of gold and silver and lead are here in abundance. Colorado adds her millions to the wealth of the nation. The miners, under a rough exterior, are a splendid set of men. When they washed out the pure gold in pans or sluices, anybody could do that. But now the process requires scientific skill. I saw their generosity illustrated at Georgetown by the raising of a purse of $700 to aid an old miner, who was becoming blind, to go east for treatment. I have to give it up that the soil of these valleys and plains is rich, and the bunch-grass on them, too. The herds of cattle every-where seen are fat and sleek. They even live on this grass, as cured hay, all winter. The milk and butter are rich. The beef and mutton made by grazing are sweet and juicy. Vegetables and small fruits grow to a fine size and richness. The wheat is equal to that of California. But all of this implies irrigation. Yet providence and science have made this a success. In winter the abundance of rain is stored upon the mountains in drifts of forty feet of snow. By the warmth of the growing season these snows are melted and brought down the cañons and creeks in boiling streams, much larger than I had supposed. The South Platte and the Arkansas rivers, the Clear, the Boulder, the St. Vrain, and the Cache La Poudre creeks come forth from the mountains in streams each as large as our Illinois and Fox, and with ten times the current. Then in the summer, as the parched earth and people below seem to be mocked by the succession of showers that fall along the ranges almost daily, these are yet gathered up and sent forth with the snow floods for the needs of irrigation. Then the fall from the mountains out upon the plains is so prodigious that you can raise your canals and ditches so high that, to an unaccustomed eye, it seems all the time as though they were making water run up-hill. They even claim that this method of providence is better than that which sprinkles the water over the fields in showers, as it brings the wetting when it is needed and no more than is needed, saves the wages of rainy days and gives a dry harvest. But Moses did not quite think so, for he says: "The land whither thou goest, is not as the land of Egypt, where thou sowedst thy seed, and wateredst it with thy foot [turning the rills with the foot] as a garden of herbs, but is a land that drinketh water of the rain of heaven." But surely these irrigated plains, stretching from Pueblo to Greeley, are the land of Goshen. The climate of dryness and of sunshine is truly delightful. My brother, who has been breathing this air for a dozen years, says that it is to the lungs as is the difference between hard and soft water to the hands.

I have been upon those famous six-in-hand stage-coaches, and from Central City over to Georgetown, by special favor, on the box by the side of the driver. We are now at the top of the Virginia Cañon. The driver has been whiling away his time. "Drove four years by the side of Hank, Mr. Greeley's famous friend. Poor fellow: he got to drinking and the company had to discharge him." But now it is three miles down to the bottom, where the charming Idaho Springs nestle in the valley. It is two thousand feet of descent. Time, twenty minutes. Don't cringe at those tremendous cracks of the whip. Do you see that steep pitch, that sidling place, that sharp curve around a great rock, that narrow road-bed? Do you look straight down from the box into the yawning gulf? Do you see how the steeds seem to share in the driver's enthusiasm? Surely it is a *descensus avernus*, and we are glad when we are down.

LETTER LI.

AMONG THE DAKOTAS.

SANTEE AGENCY, July 25, 1872.

IN the year 1835 the Rev. Messrs. S. R. Riggs, T. S. Williamson, and J. D. Stevens, with their wives and their assistants, began work among the Indians where were to arise Minneapolis, St. Paul, St. Peter, Shakopee, and Lac Qui Parle. In time the barbarous language was reduced to written and printed form; elementary books were issued; the Bible translated in part; and hymn-books and works of devotion, like that of Bunyan, were produced in the native tongue. Schools were set up, churches were gathered, and the process of Christianization was well under way. Then in 1862 came the agony and the spasm of the massacre, in retaliation for culminating outrages. The Christian Dakotas were the means of saving the missionaries from the fury of their heathen brethren. Into prison in the up country and at Davenport the devoted missionaries followed the arrested men, teaching them reading and writing, and preaching to them repentance. A wondrous revival ensued which led a couple of hundred of the savages to Christ. The entire nation having been removed by the government from Minnesota, these apostolic men again undertook to set up the Christianizing work in several of the reserves in Dakota to which the people had been assigned. Dr. Riggs took his station at Good-will in the Sisseton Reserve. Dr. Williamson took up his home at St. Peter for the prosecution of his work of translating the Bible. His son, Rev. John P. Williamson, took up a station at the Yankton Reservation; and Rev. A. L. Riggs, a son of the other pioneer, settled upon this

Santee Reservation; while Rev. Thos. L. Riggs, another son just leaving the Chicago Seminary, where his brother had graduated several years ago, located with another branch of the same tribe at Fort Sully on the Missouri, two hundred and forty-five miles above, three hundred and fifty by the water-course.

I am delighted with my visit to this Santee Agency. It is thirty miles up the river from Yankton and on its south bank, a reserve of twelve by fifteen miles. Here are a thousand people in two hundred and fifty families, which are generally quartered in their own cabins on their own allotted land. They are making small farms. They don citizen's dress. They are learning to work. I find that they are respected by the white people on the other side of the river. Mr. Riggs has now a house for the missionary family and a house used both for church and school purposes. The church numbers two hundred and twenty-five members; and the school, one hundred and eighteen pupils, with a night school of one hundred and thirteen members, and a Sunday-school of one hundred and thirty-six scholars. I find Mr. Riggs superintending the cutting and hauling of two hundred saw-logs to be sawed by the government mill for an out-station chapel and a girls' industrial school building. The Indians do the work for wages. That is the way that the missionary takes his vacation in dog-days, down in the bottoms of the Missouri. The purpose is to build up here a grand industrial and normal training-school for raising up native teachers and preachers for the wild Indians.

There are eight churches in the mission, five near Dr. Riggs, one at Flandreau, one on the Yankton Reserve, and one here at Santee. These have seven hundred members and are under seven native pastors. Three thousand have embraced civilized life, and ten thousand have had the influence of civilization brought to bear upon them. They have a newspaper in the Dakota, *The Iapi Oaye.* They have just had their yearly meeting. Last Sunday night, at Yankton, I heard Rev. Joseph Ward report that meeting to his people, as he had been up there. He said that he had once thought that the only good Indian was a dead one, but now he thought otherwise, and he wished to do all he could to help that people. To reach that meeting, Thomas Riggs, attended by one soldier from Fort Sully and an Indian guide, made the three hundred and forty miles on pony back by the ninth hour of the fifth day, carrying rations and swimming the Dakota or the James river three times. Twice they traveled fifty miles without finding water for man or beast. Honored men, greatly honored, are these fathers and sons.

LETTER LII.

THE BOSTON FIRE. — DEACON PHILO CARPENTER.

CHICAGO, November 18, 1872.

CHICAGO to Boston in the fellowship of fire! We know what it is; we give you a genuine sympathy. The telegraph has told you how quick it was. The excitement here was next to our own calamity. We rejoice that yours was not greater still. We are proud of the pluck and self-reliance of your people. We stand aghast when such buildings as yours are burned, kindled in granite. The heart of our city was built of iron and stone and brick, but it had a wooden kindling on the west side.

I have just had from Deacon Philo Carpenter an account of his coming to Chicago. Born at Savoy, in Berkshire

County, in 1805, educated in the common school of Adams, entering the Christian life under Dr. Beman at Troy, N. Y., where he had learned the drug business, impelled by the spirit of that revival to go west and do good, and learning from a western rover of the little town of Chicago, in the summer of 1832 he pushed through the canal and the lakes to Detroit; thence by mail-wagon to Niles; thence, as the mail went on to Chicago, one hundred miles on pony back, down the Saint Joseph on a flat-boat to the town of that name at its mouth; thence (as the little sail-boat that ran over the lakes did not dare go, on account of the cholera prevailing at Chicago) around the head of the lake in a canoe towed with a rope of elm bark by a couple of Indians. Coming to the mouth of the Calumet, the Indians did not wish to go farther, fearing the pestilence; but, persuaded to go on, they came to a peremptory halt when they reached the place of Mr. Ellis, which was four miles outside of town, within sight of the flag of Fort Dearborn. But this settler, Mr. Ellis, being himself a man from Berkshire, in his own ox-wagon brought the new-comer on to Chicago. It was now August. He found a village of a couple of hundred of whites and half-breeds, and a few companies in the fort, which kept its trench open for burial of cholera-stricken soldiers. In a batch brought out for interment he saw one who came to life just as he was about to be laid in, and so one more was saved for service, when all were needed, for General Scott was here directing the Black Hawk War. On the night of his arrival he happened into the first prayer-meeting of Chicago, a Methodist brother and a military officer joining him. On the next Sunday he started the first Sunday-school of the place, and this was kept up to become the Sunday-school of the First Presbyterian Church, which was gathered the next year (1833) by Rev. Jeremiah Porter. During that intervening winter a public service was maintained by reading sermons, and he, the first druggist of Chicago, was the reader. He wrote and circulated the first total abstinence pledge in the community.[1]

LETTER LIII.

AT THE HEAD OF LAKE SUPERIOR. — BISMARCK.

DULUTH, Minn., October 6, 1873.

SEVENTEEN years ago, 1856, I came up by the steamer *Lady Elgin* from Chicago to Superior City in company with her proprietor, Gordon S. Hubbard, William Bross, of *The Tribune*, and Rev. George W. Perkins, for a summer vacation. Taking a tug at that baby city, we came up the bay and had a picnic on some of these heights, not dreaming that here was to come up a rival to that ambitious point that shivered on the brink between the lake and the tamarack swamp. We then longed for a public conveyance to Saint Paul, that we might go back by way of the Mississippi, and were tempted to try the trail. But coming this time from the meeting of the American Board at Minneapolis, over the railroad through

---

[1] While I have been copying this letter (August 14, 1886) Deacon Carpenter's remains are awaiting interment. "A good man and a just." "And he died in a good old age, full of days, riches, and honor." He had pioneered and maintained the reforms of temperance, anti-slavery, and of opposition to secret, oath-bound societies, giving to the latter, including a business house and donations to Wheaton College, as much as fifty thousand dollars. He has been one of the founders of the Chicago Theological Seminary, giving it more than fifty thousand dollars. For many years he was a member of the Chicago Board of Education, of which he was a part of the time vice-president. He had years ago deeded to our three missionary societies three stone-front houses, which now become available. His will, besides providing for legacies to the amount of $30,000, makes the Chicago Seminary the residuary legatee, and this will probably bring in $75,000 more.

the dense swamps and rough uplands, I was content with having waited for the wagon.

Duluth is finely situated upon an acclivity that runs back a mile, sloping sunnily toward the south, fronting the bay and looking down the lake. The Minnesota Point, cut through, furnishes a passage-way to the finest kind of a harbor. Back are the Dalles of the St. Louis River, with its series of cataracts for mill-power, and the railroad following the stream to find its way through and to afford transportation facilities. The Northern Pacific, having its terminus here, must soon find a rail communication around the head of the lake and so on to the east. At the head of Lake Superior navigation, Duluth must become a second Chicago.

I have just been over the road to Bismarck. What of the country? Out to Brainerd on the Mississippi, one hundred and fifteen miles, it is a tamarack swamp, dreary enough. And yet here are the wood and timber for lumber to supply the prairies beyond. For sixty miles on the other side of the river it is indifferent. Then you come for seventy-five miles to beautiful farming country, with undulating prairie, grove, and lake in delightful interspersion. Then comes the flat forty-mile-wide valley of the Red River of the north. Then from the Red it is two hundred miles of high rolling prairie until you come to the Missouri, where now the steamers take their start with garrison and commercial freight for the many hundreds of miles up to Fort Benton. Opposite Bismarck I visit Fort Abraham Lincoln and find General Custer just in with his army from a campaign of chastising the Indians. I was much drawn to the general for his gentle and modest way. From Bismarck I wish to reach southern Dakota, to attend its association at Vermillion on the Missouri. It is nine hundred miles down the river by its course, and the boats are uncertain and slow. And so back I go, by way of Duluth, Saint Paul, and Sioux City, to meet the brethren of the new territory. While up in this country I learn of the slanderous black-mailing charge against the Indian commissioner, Rev. E. P. Smith, for official service while Indian agent at Leach Lake. He had prevented the ring men from swindling the Indians in a lumber deal; and this is the way they treat every official that stands between them and the objects of their rapacity. I fear that these white savages will weary the life out of him.

LETTER LIV.

THE LONE STAR STATE.

DALLAS, Texas, April 14, 1874.

"Go to Texas." As this was not an execration, but an official injunction, I cheerfully obeyed. And here I am. Across Illinois, Missouri, Kansas, and the Indian Territory; over the Mississippi, the Missouri, the Arkansas, and the Red; across this stretch of territory from the heart of the interior, one passes to reach the border of a state which yet stretches on to the gulf, with an area equal to four times that of New England. Crossing the territory for two hundred and fifty miles, the passengers had to come, as it were, in bond, for no white people are allowed to settle there. All along the railway, in spots, the Indians' settlements were to be seen; the Indians themselves clad in citizen's dress, in cabin homes; their farms fenced; their fields under the plow held by red hands and drawn by horses or mules. Their homes and farms looked less unthrifty than do most of those in our Egypt of Illinois. At one station they had shipped twenty carloads of cattle and as many of hogs since the opening of the road. At two or three stations I saw bales of cotton awaiting shipment. Just now the Cherokee superintendent of schools reports twenty-three hundred children in attendance, with the schools running nine months in the year, with twenty-two white teachers and forty native. They have also a ladies' high school, taught by a Mount Holyoke teacher. The annual cost to the government, as for the thirty years past, is $35,000.

Texas, like Kansas, is a state with a history. She gained her independence from Mexico in 1836. Her defence of the Fortress of Alamo in San Antonio, where Davy Crockett and Bowie and Travis lost their lives, and not a man remained to tell the story, was her Thermopylæ; and her final battle of San Jacinto was one of those which determine nationalities. Her annexation to the United States, in the interests of slavery, was after another battle, one of moral forces, and her complications with Mexico brought on another war. But as a result, by the overruling of providence, that vast region of California, Arizona, New Mexico, and Texas was transferred from Romish to Protestant control, and then at last consecrated to freedom.

I am delighted to find the provision made by Texas for public schools. Coming in as a sovereign state, possessing her own vast domain, she makes a yet more liberal appropriation for this purpose than does the United States in the territories. She set apart four leagues of land, 17,712 acres, for each county, and in making land grants to new railroads she gave the alternate section to the same fund. For a state university she set aside fifty leagues, 221,400 acres. In all she has thus devoted three million acres. Then of the $10,000,000 for which she sold New Mexico to the United States, she put $2,000,000 into her school fund. I once asked a Texas editor how it came that Texas had gone so far ahead of the other slave-holding states in making provision for education.

"Why, don't you know that Mr. Austin, one of the founders of the republic, was a New England man, and that most of his settlers were from the north?"

Yet in Texas, of persons over ten years of age, 70,895 whites and 150,617 blacks, one fourth of the population can neither read nor write! We have just organized churches at Paris and Sherman and have prospected for one in this rising city of Dallas.

LETTER LV.

NORTHERN MICHIGAN.

GRAND TRAVERSE BAY, January 15, 1875.

SIXTEEN years ago, 1858, I took my vacation at this old mission. A sermon which I had just touched off in my Plymouth pulpit, upon the occasion of the sputtering of the original Atlantic cable, was fired again on the next Sabbath up here in the woods, we all being unconscious of what the outside world knew, that the first oceanic telegraph was a failure. But then it was quite the thing to be behind the times up here, for the excellent old Presbyterian Indian missionary was brisk in arguing with me that the Creator had made the fossils of the globe and had put them *in situ* for his own glory, and because the mail came only once a week upon an Indian's back through one hundred miles of forest. In all that north-west wildwoods I found only a single circuit-rider and two Indian mission churches, that at Northfield, under the American Missionary Association, and this one under the Presbyterian Board. In a year or so Superintendent Read coasted along this region and made a newspaper report, which seemed as romantic as though it were an account of an exploration of some part of the coast of South America. Then off he posted to Oberlin to get missionaries for the newly discovered field. LeRoy Warren, an ex-soldier, and Mr. Crum were found heroic enough for the undertaking; and now in these last six years the forty churches of his district have increased to sixty-seven, with two new conferences added. Providence seems to have preserved these woods of pine and beech and maple from the slashing of the early settler's axe as a grand timber lot for the prairies beyond. If they had come in here as they did into Ohio, their log-heap fires would have been far more destructive than these forest conflagrations have been. As it is now, you find Michigan lumber all over Illinois, Kansas, Colorado, and Texas.

PERIOD VII.

AN INTERVAL OF SILENCE.

The Centennial. — The Gilded Dead-fall. — Transfer South.

LETTER LVI.

AN INTERVAL OF SILENCE. — THE CENTENNIAL. — THE GILDED DEAD-FALL. — TRANSFER SOUTH.

It was a gladsome time that was in anticipation, a vacation of two months at the Centennial Exposition and on the sea-coast. But on the way the gilded dead-fall of the sleeping-berth came down on the top of my head. It produced congestion of the brain. After a week at Philadelphia under medical care, I was transferred to Clifton Springs. Here for a year and a half I submitted myself to the round of ordinances in that sanitarium. For much of the time my head felt as though it were in a crown of iron and this was tightening down upon it, while the people, as I dragged myself from one shade in the ample grounds to another, looked on me with a pitying eye, as if to say, "Poor doomed man!" But my thought was all the time: "I shall not die but live and declare the works of the Lord."

Advanced in convalescence I was advised by physicians for still farther benefit to make a transfer to the south; with this advice fell in the appointment as field superintendent of the American Missionary Association at the south.

As I am about to be shifted from the right to the left wing of our corps of the grand Home Missionary army, let me cast an admiring glance along and back over the history of its "march to the sea." At headquarters, men of wisdom and tenacity; along the line, comrades with absorbing devotion to the common cause. How this corps did sweep out over the Alleghanies. down into and across the valley! How, as it struck the barrier of the Rockies, it flanked that continental range, by way of the Isthmus and Cape Horn, and surprised the golden coast by a relentless occupation! A total exchequer of more than eight millions; a band of leaders kept mustered full from year to year a thousand men; thirty-five hundred spiritual garrisons set up and kept fully manned, — these are but slight indications of the grand campaign. And now all along the front there is the solid tread of marching men. And out beyond are the steady pickets and the restless scouts. How slight the fatality at headquarters for these more than half a hundred years!—Absalom Peters, Charles Hall, and Milton Badger, — their names a treasure in the land, a rally-cry to many a veteran on the field; and now the three men at the same place, Coe, Clapp, and Storrs, how enduring! On the staff we revere the memory of Kirby and Baldwin, and Kent and Clary, and Guernsey and Merrill. In parting, I must say that in these sixteen and a half years of communication with the secretaries, superintendents, and missionaries of the American Home Missionary Society, not one word has occurred to jar our personal friendship. But in this transfer it is a comfort to consider that it is all one cause after all; that on the left wing there is a dauntless courage of self-sacrifice;

that its course has been one of startling providential development; and that the terminus of both lines is the same. Indeed, I remind myself that this change is but a coming back to my original status, from which I went over to the right wing.

I am moved with affectionate regret upon leaving official relations to Secretaries D. B. Coe, A. H. Clapp, and H. M. Storrs. As the courts accumulate the wisdom of precedents and of experience, so do these representatives of their sphere of service. And does n't the breadth of their operations set out their natures into broader manhood, into richer fellow-feeling? Take this specimen from a letter I received from Dr. Clapp while I was shut up at Clifton Springs: "Did you ever see the old lion up to Central Park pacing his cage all day with only a lion's restlessness, looking never at the crowd around him, but sending that far-away gaze off through his prison bars, evidently thinking of the deserts and jungles where he used to roam at his own wild will? Something makes me think of that lion whenever I think of you. I don't believe any harder work could be found for you than to be shut up in that cage of enforced idleness. You try to make us think that you 've got so tamed and humbled that you take it patiently. And I 'll believe all of it that I can and pray that you may really 'attain' to it.

"You 'll say: 'Oh, yes, brother Clapp can preach patience and all that, but just put him in my place and see how he 'd bear it!' I 'd bear it like the gentle, submissive saint! You 've no idea of the prodigious capacity I have for laziness — if I could only get a chance! I don't want to have a chance, though, by having my few brains banged out through a darkey's carelessness. And now, my dear old fellow, when you get well, 'r' you going to do any better? That's the question. Are you going to set up your jammed head again against all the laws of nature? I know just how humbly you'd talk if I were to ask you the question in person; but what I want to know is, what are you going to do about it? Just the same as before? If you do, I'll hire a darkey as is a darkey to 'let suthin' drap' onto your head that'll fix it next time once for all! Do you hear that? And will you take warning? Doctors Coe and Storrs would send 'bushels of love' and good wishes of love if they were at hand just now."

When Dr. Clapp had his own pull-down a few years ago and I sent on this original letter to his wife, proposing that she get him to take his own medicine, he answered after a little: "Take warning from me and don't be so lazy; you see what it leads to." And did n't he go right off again to doing the work of two or three men? But then he seems to keep himself familiar with both sides of the equator of life. When I told him once that I had failed to reach a certain missionary by mail, he asked, "Where did you direct it?" To Oberlin. "Why, did n't you know that he had gone to heaven?" No, I did n't. "He has, but then he'll get it all the same, for that is the nearest post-office." The first time that I ever saw him was in 1853 at the Presbyterian General Assembly in Washington, where the sprightly, raven-haired representative from the General Convention of Vermont tickled the sides of the grave and reverend commissioners by reminding them that the exports of his state were men and women. And now a western editor calls him "that grizzly old soldier of the cross."

I am often inquired of how I came out in the legal case. The jury in the United States District Court at Chicago rendered a verdict of $10,000. The Pennsylvania company appealed to the United States Supreme Court. After four years more this case was reached and the decision of the court below affirmed, that it was the railway and not the Pullman company that was responsible; but upon a technicality it was remanded for a new trial. The Supreme Court said: "There was an error committed on the trial, to which exception was duly taken, but which does not seem to have been remedied by any portion of the charge appearing in the bill of exceptions. The plaintiff was permitted, against the objection of the defendant, to give the number and ages of his children—a son ten years old, and three daughters of the ages respectively of fourteen, seventeen, and twenty-one. . . . For this error alone the judgment is reversed and the cause remanded for a new trial. It is so ordered." My attorneys, in their argument, made no allusion to this testimony, and the error, if it were one, they thought had been cured in another part of the charge of the judge. As it would take four or five years to go through the process again, I was willing to consider the proposition of the company for a compromise. I said, Give me the principal, $10,000, without the interest, which would now be $2,000 more. We agreed upon $9,000. The necessary medical, traveling, and legal expense had amounted to $6,000. A prominent member of the jury, A. M. Poole, Esq., of Henry, Illinois, writes me: "All sympathy for you or your family was carefully and ruthlessly excluded from the computation by the jury and the case decided *quid pro quo* on a strict dollar and cent basis, the same as though you had been a bachelor with no kith nor kin dependent upon you."

PERIOD VIII.

IN THE SOUTH, 1878-79.

Atlanta. — Emancipation Day. — Talladega, Ala. — Chattanooga. — Mardi Gras and Washington's Birthday in New Orleans. — The Acadians in Louisiana. — San Antonio. — Corpus Christi. — Alabama Anniversary Week. — Hampton, Va. — Fisk University.

LETTER LVII.

ATLANTA AS A PLACE OF BUSINESS, OF EDUCATION, OF HEALTH.

ATLANTA, Ga., November 1, 1878.

FROM the "Garden City" to the "Gate City," which is the "Chicago of the south." The one set on fire by the lamp of a cow-shed, and the other, by the torch of war; both re-built by the same magic. This city, upon the foot-hills of the Appalachian range, is eleven hundred feet above the ocean, while the other is only six hundred. Kenesaw, with its association of "Hold the fort," the Stone Mountain, and the Lost Mountain are in full view. This elevation gives to the softness of the southern air the tonic of a more northern latitude. The city is healthy, and has never had an indigenous case of yellow fever. As we were removing to this city from Chicago, it was deemed advisable to avoid exposure to that epidemic at Chattanooga, and so came around by way of Washington. When the soldiers before the scourge had been transferred from New Orleans to Chattanooga and thence to this city, their baggage was left a whole day at the "car-shed" in the very center of the town, as if to do the best possible to import the plague. But it did not come. This being above the yellow fever line gives Atlanta the great advantage for manufacturing and for jobbing in a southern city. A pastor here, with a church of four hundred members, tells me that within his congregation he does not have more than two funerals a year; and that at one time he went for eighteen months without the death of a child in his parish. Atlanta has more northern people and capital and business houses than any other city in the south. It is fast making itself a center in the wholesale business. It is coming up in the line of manufactures, cotton mills, and such like. It has street railways running in all directions. It is lighted with gas and is supplied with hydrant water. The population is called thirty-five thousand.[1] After the war the capital was removed from Milledgeville to this city. Our legislature presents a wide-awake yet dignified appearance in both Houses. With the members all in one party it might seem difficult to get up the enthusiasm of debate; but on all questions, aside from the one of the solid south, they divide off, as is the nature of man to do, and go into discussion with a regular southern vim. In respect to Sabbath observance there abides in this section a good degree of virtuous conservatism. We have here three Presbyterian churches, three southern Methodist and two northern; of the last, one for colored and one for white people. The northern Methodists have here the Clark University for colored students. This is also the Episcopal See of Bishop Haven. He has given me a royal welcome.

I find the work of the American Missionary Association

[1] It is fifty thousand now (August, 1886).

here in good condition. The Atlanta University runs with about three hundred students, one half of whom are boarded in the institution. The site, which from its command of the city had been covered with confederate earth-works, is fine indeed, with the mountains in full view. What sort of men and women do I find in charge? Why, the president and two of his associates are graduates of Yale, one of Dartmouth, one of Harvard, and one of Lawrence University; while the other teachers, seven or eight ladies, are of personal and literary cultivation to match. These instructors are doing first-class work. The legislature, in recognition of the right of the colored people to a share of the fund for agricultural colleges, appropriates from year to year $8,000 to this institution, which thus serves as a state normal for the freedmen. The Storrs School, in the heart of the city, with six lady teachers, has each year about four hundred pupils. Hard by is the First Congregational Church with over one hundred and fifty members and a Sunday-school of over two hundred and fifty. Theirs is one of the most beautiful church edifices in the city. Built of brick, with a slate roof, with a tower and a bell in it, and with stained glass windows, it cost $5,200. All the work upon the building was done by colored men. Thanksgiving will be observed there and in the union church of the university. At the McPherson barracks, within the city limits, four companies entertain themselves with the drill and routine of camp life. Their morning and evening salutes and the floating flag are grateful symbols of our national union.

LETTER LVIII.

EMANCIPATION DAY.

ATLANTA, Ga., January 2, 1879.
THE salutation of a "Happy New Year" to these ex-bondmen takes on a new element of gladness every year as they celebrate Abraham Lincoln's edict of freedom. For ten years they have observed the day in the First Congregational Church. This time they thought to give the occasion more scope, and so, as citizens, they sought and obtained the use of their capitol. And there these dusky Americans gathered, with Jefferson and Franklin and Andrew Jackson and several other Georgia worthies looking down upon them from the walls. The chairman, a former student of these schools and now one of Uncle Sam's letter-carriers in this city, opens the service by a dignified and sententious address. The orator of the day is Richard R. Wright, principal of the high school at Cuthbert, Ga. His first speech was that one made to General Howard in the Storrs School, "Tell them that we are rising, sir,"— a speech that was honored by a poem of Whittier. After a tribute to the character and the work of the great emancipator, he went on to show some of the results of emancipation in the acquiring of education and of property. It was an eloquent address from one who could tell how sixteen years ago he was brought to this same city with his mother and put upon the auction block, and how he could yet hear the cry: "What do I hear for this nigger gal and boy?"

LETTER LIX.

TALLADEGA COLLEGE.

TALLADEGA, Ala., January 10, 1879.
BEAUTIFUL for situation. As the mountains are round about Jerusalem. Here upon these mountain slopes I have seen for the first time the sunset tints of orange, rose, and pink, deepening into purple and blue. The tonic and the softness of this climate make it delightful. The main building of the college, upon an ample campus, is that of an ante-bellum Baptist institution which was purchased by the Freedmen's Bureau after the war. A planter who had subscribed nine hundred dollars toward the erection of that building sent Ambrose Headen and other slaves to work it out as carpenters. Headen says that then he thought it hard so to work to educate his master's children while his own could have no chance. He is now a trustee of the college and his four children have been educated there, one as a minister and the others as teachers. A fellow-servant who had helped to make the brick for that old college is now a deacon of the new church in it; he has come to possess the plantation of his old master, to whom in genuine kindness he administers charity; and he is now himself a contractor for making brick and laying it up in the wall. During the war this building was used for a prison for federal soldiers, and so upon one of the panes of glass has since been found the etching, "Union prisoners." This institution magnifies the normal, theological, and the industrial lines of education. Prof. G. W. Andrews is doing a grand work in training young men for the ministry. The Winsted Farm, bought by friends in Winsted, Conn., is used for

teaching the better methods of agriculture. The first agricultural fair ever gotten up by the colored people of this country was held upon this college campus for four days of last November. It was a grand success. It drew together three thousand people, many of them white. The show of animals was fine. Instead of the white folks' horse-racing there were matches for spelling, speaking, and band playing, with prizes rendered. It had a surplus of one hundred and forty-three dollars. It was opened with prayer and closed with the doxology by a spontaneous outburst. Then the colored men straightened themselves up in conscious dignity.

The Shelby Iron Works are forty miles below. Its company is made up of northern and southern men. It runs two furnaces. It has put up a large two-story building for church and school purposes among their colored operatives. Its officers say that the school has increased the value of labor ten cents a day. This is only one of fifteen such furnaces as have been set up in northern Alabama since the war, largely with northern capital and northern brains.

LETTER LX.

ALL YE ARE BRETHREN.

CHATTANOOGA, Tenn., January 18, 1879.

THIS strategic city, which was so severely assaulted last fall by the yellow fever, is now the master of the situation. Its river, the Tennessee, is booming with a rise of thirty-eight feet. I note a wonderful progress since I was here thirteen years ago. Lookout Mountain, Missionary Ridge, and Chickamauga will tell their historic tale to future generations. The National Cemetery here will ever have its story to relate. This is the center of an immense iron interest, and the city must become one of the most important in the south. I meet here the Central South Association, four of whose churches are those of white people. About half of the ministerial members of the five southern associations are white men, and all churches are open to Christians, irrespective of color. And so these bodies are illustrating the Saviour's words: "All ye are brethren."

LETTER LXI.

THE SCHOOLS.

MEMPHIS, Tenn., January 20, 1879.

THE Mississippi, which has for a long time been blockading navigation by floating ice, is again clear. A good business was done in capturing the ice as it was hastening on to a more southern market. The dreadful effects of the yellow fever last fall are yet felt in many ways. But this is a noble city, well built, and commanding an extensive trade. By the census of 1870 it numbered 47,226; by the epidemic the population has been greatly reduced, but Memphis is bound to come up. Her new system of water-works and sewerage will be a protection in the future. The city has a fine public school system which gives the colored schools teachers of qualification and pay equal to those of the white schools. The Le Moyne Institute, with its Teachers' Home and an endowment of eleven thousand dollars, named for its founder, Dr. LeMoyne, of Pennsylvania, serves the purpose of a high school and normal school for the freed youth. Prof.

A. J. Steele, the principal, is training his girls in nursing and sewing, and intends to introduce cooking. He is also looking toward mechanical industries for boys.

LETTER LXII.

MARDI GRAS. — STATE SUNDAY-SCHOOL ASSOCIATION. — WASHINGTON'S BIRTHDAY.

NEW ORLEANS, February 25, 1879.

MARDI GRAS ("fat Tuesday"), the last day before Lent. No other people on the continent but these Franco-Americans could originate and keep up such a carnival. But here the spirit of it pervades the entire community. From a gallery I had a view of the whole pageant, "the history of the world" from the garden of Eden down to seventy-six, exhibited upon twenty-four cars, each one drawn by four or six horses. So much cost, and all just for the fun of the thing! Last night at the carnival dinner, given at the Saint Charles, General W. T. Sherman, being present, was made the Duke of Louisiana, in honor of his former citizenship in this state, having been, up to the war, a teacher at the military academy at Alexandria. Addressing him, the Lord High Chamberlain said: "We have all worn the gray, but it gives us the greatest pleasure to welcome you. We feel honored in paying honor to a soldier whose deeds have cast luster upon the military annals of the republic."

I fall in here also with the State Sunday-school convention. Aside from the essential merit of this movement, it is a grand process for promoting good feeling between the north and the south. Here is a common basis of union. Messrs. Peltz, of *The Sunday-School*

Times, Ralph Wells, of New York, and E. Payson Porter and B. F. Jacobs, of Chicago, by invitation, are present to aid in launching the new enterprise. They are each upon the platform three times with their set speeches, which are intensely practical in detail and fervid in delivery. Dr. B. M. Palmer, in his words of welcome, took down all the bars to coöperation in this work, and praised Mr. Moody for his line of service. Bishop Keener made an address on the claims of the Sunday-school upon Christians.

Rev. Dr. W. S. Alexander, the president of Straight University and pastor of our Central Church, who is a member of the executive committee of the city Sunday-school Association, was officially prominent in the convention. He and two colored pastors were made officers of the state body. By resolution, there was an earnest call for sympathy, prayer, and endeavor in behalf of the colored people. A colored delegate made a speech. Several colored schools were represented on the floor. Mr. W. R. Lyman, upon taking the chair of the body, turned to the colored delegation and said: "As a representative of the southern churches, I say that we intend to reach out our hand to your people and to do all we can for you. Your children must be trained for Christ." Mr. Lyman, in his paper on the religious history of the state, said that in the Natchez country, during the Spanish occupation, there was a law against the holding of Protestant religious worship and against the circulating and the reading of the Bible of the Protestants, and that the law was enforced.

The military display on Washington's birthday was the most brilliant of any I ever saw. The streets were full of loyal bunting, and the Stars and Stripes were carried by every battalion. The Union soldiers stationed here were in the lead of the militia. General Sherman, arriving later, was received by a committee of the Grand Army of the Republic.

LETTER LXIII.

THE ACADIANS. — SUGAR MAKING. — REVEREND DANIEL CLAY.

NEW IBERIA, La., March 1, 1879.

THIS is the region where settled the refugees from Nova Scotia, the Acadians. More than half of the white people of the town are their descendants, wonderfully mixed with American, Spanish, and African blood. Refusing to take the oath of allegiance to England, they naturally sought a French and Catholic province; but it was not long before this Louisiana was acquired by the Protestant, English-speaking republic which has also of late required of them the oath of allegiance. The black people say that the "'Cajans" were cruel with them. Surely the story of Evangeline was no mere romance. Louisiana ought to be loyal to the states of the Mississippi valley, for they have furnished her with land. Down here that mighty river in its geologic history has had to shift its course so as to dump its loads of mud for the forming of this delta, just as the coal-heaver changes the track of his wheel-barrow in unloading his cargo. Brother S. S. Ashley says that this part of the country was settled a thousand years before the Creator had gotten it ready. Yet it is the sugar-bush for North America. This deep, rich alluvium and the long hot summer make the sugar-cane. But the belt that is good for this culture is quite narrow, so that the best sugar-lands sell for forty or fifty dollars an acre. Coming up the Bayou Teche, the seventy-two miles to this town from Morgan City, I gained some idea of the extent of this business. For sixty miles the banks are lined with sugar plantations that reach back one or two miles to the irreclaimable swamp. About every half-mile you pass the sugar-mill with its village of negro shanties back of the mansion. Each plantation has a landing, and so we zigzag all the way up, putting off freight or the pilgrims returning from the Mardi Gras. These great plantations are changing hands a good deal. Many of the old planters are reduced to poverty. Northern men are buying up the premises. Here are half a dozen from Chicago. They are plowing deep and fertilizing. They get great crops. The tendency now, under free labor, is to break up the great plantations. Instead of every man having his mill, many will raise the cane and sell it to the sugar-maker. It is not profitable to manufacture on a small scale. The adulteration of the northern refiners is leading to the process of refining in making the sugar here. Last year nine refineries were put in here on the bayou at an immense expense. The old style makes the sugar in open kettles; the new boils the juice *in vacuo* and carries on the bleaching process before the sugar comes. This process avoids the using of chemicals to change the filthy brown into white. These plantations make, per year, from four to nine hundred hogsheads of twelve hundred pounds each. Two New Yorkers last year made fourteen hundred hogsheads. I am interested in the planting. The seed cane is preserved during the winter in piles covered with litter and dirt as we cover grape-vines. When planted, it is laid in trenches, two stalks together, in a continuous row, so that it is plowed only one way. One planting lasts three and four years, the old roots sprouting up in the spring. It is a tender growth. It is easily killed by the overflow of the water. It may be frosted. It may sour. Hence the rush and the drive of the sugar season. Night and day and Sundays the mills had to run in the old time, and the hands were allowed five hours for sleep. Now it takes one man to do the work of three under the old régime.

At Terre Bonne I enjoyed the hospitality of Rev. Daniel Clay, who is the pastor of the church there and the bishop of three others. He had given the land for the church site and had built the house, about 30x50, which was ceiled not with cedar but with yellow pine. He had built a plain parsonage. No aid from abroad. He is a man of decided influence and of universal respect. During the yellow fever plague he gathered up from his poor people ten barrels of corn-meal, two hogs, chickens, eggs, geese, and twenty-three dollars in cash, and carried it all to Thibodeaux, the parish seat of Terre Bonne. Nearing the dead-line, on which stood an armed guard, he unloaded his stuff just outside that line. He then retreated and the guard rolled it inside. The town committee then came and took off the spoil. No breath from the townsmen must touch the guard, and his, in turn, must not touch the benefactors. Once when Henry Clay, during a presidential campaign, came through this region speaking upon the stump, the slave who was put on the stage to turn the water was this one. It was only with his native eloquence and his personal experience that Daniel Clay could say to his people, as he did say after my sermon that had referred to the old times: "Yes, indeed, I cried, 'O Lord, how long, how long!' and the Lord said to me, 'Daniel, it won't be long; you shall yet sit under your own vine and fig-tree.' I believed it, I expected it." And now he does sit under his own vine and fig-tree. He is cultivating two hundred and fifty acres of the old plantation where he had served as a slave, and owns ten, for which he paid forty dollars an acre, and is working his own four mules and three horses. The four adjoining plantations of the family of his mistress have all gone into financial ruin. His wife is a French African Creole, the mother of his fourteen children, ten of whom survive to live about him, a family of rare respectability. His son Henry, who died at the age of twenty-one, was an eloquent man. Now, why might not the Lord say to this prophet in captivity, "Daniel, it won't be long," as he also said to the prophet of the Babylonian exile: "O Daniel, greatly beloved, the Lord will accomplish seventy years in the desolation of Jerusalem!" I saw the legal document by which the church was incorporated. In it Mr. Clay is recognized as its bishop, and three or four brethren as preachers. How did he ever come across that New Testament idea of elderships, a presbytery, and a bishop in a local church? It has been a surprise to me to find that his church and nearly all those of like faith in the south were set up on Roy's Manual. But Royville, a few miles from New Iberia, was not. It is a French Catholic town.

LETTER LXIV.

SAN ANTONIO AND THE TRIP TO "CORPUS."

Corpus Christi, Texas, March 22, 1879.
My course to this city was by way of Galveston, Houston, and San Antonio. This last is the ancient seat of Spanish Romanism, with its antique mission fortifications

yet standing in their frowning strength. Its early preemption secures two thirds of the present population, twenty-one thousand, to. the Romanists, who have three massive stone cathedrals, — one for the Germans, one for the Spanish, and one for the Americans, — and who have their nunnery and their Jesuit college, which are patronized not a little by American families. From San Antonio to this city it is two hundred miles by a zigzag line overland. On the way two churches are to be visited and appointments filled at the county seats, Helena and Goliad. The hack will take us fifty miles to the ranch of Hart, who has engaged to set passengers over to Helena twenty miles. Soon we find that one of the wheels of the new Concord coach is giving out. Then it is thirty-five miles in a Mexican lumber wagon. On retiring at Hart's, he warns us of fleas. He can not go over to Helena. He strikes out two and a half miles to find a conveyance, and fails. Another ranchman, coming along, thinks that Jones, eight miles away, will go. So over he drives. Jones can go, but his horses can not. Brown says, "Go on with my team." It is twenty miles. No dinner. At dark we arrive in Helena, with ponies tuckered out. But lo! the church is three and a half miles in the country, so we tie up at the tavern. In the morning we reach our colony of colored people. Mine host is a farmer with one hundred acres paid for and under cultivation in cotton and corn, with cattle and horses about him. His table fare is plain. He keeps up family worship. His oldest child is away at school. His neighbors, all colored folks, are doing tolerably well. They are happy in their church and school. Visiting that school, I find it among the live-oaks, with cactus and Spanish bayonets in bloom, and mocking-birds singing in the trees. I see ten or a dozen ponies picketed, on which some of the children, riding double, have come to school, some as far as five miles. The teacher is a graduate of Straight University, and she has the genius of a teacher and disciplinarian. She has also a night school with eleven adult members, among them mine host and his wife, who are learning to read and write. She also runs the Sunday-school, and is really the mistress of the community. And so the one educated girl is lifting up the whole neighborhood.

After our three days' meeting we strike next for Goliad, thirty-six miles onward. But the colored pastor has looked in vain for two days to find one of his strayed ponies. Another is borrowed. Ten miles out on the road we espy the strayed pony with a herd of horses. And so the dominie takes out one pony from the team, and after a two hours' chase brings in the captive. At noon, a lunch under a live-oak. A sermon at night in Goliad, where is also taught a school by another Straight graduate, from the household of Rev. Dr. Palmer, in New Orleans, her mother being his cook. A half-dozen families bear the name of Lott; and though there are lots of them, yet the women all repudiate the character of Lot's wife. Here at Goliad we see the Spanish mission where over three hundred Texan patriot prisoners were slaughtered by order of Santa Anna. We pass close to their graves.

Now for Corpus Christi, eighty miles in the two days before Sunday. We camp out, cooking our own coffee and meat, and sleeping, black and white together, in an open wagon with the stars for sentinels. We find here a church and school where Rev. A. Rowe had just put in several years of the best of work. As the crusaders contended for the sepulcher of the Sacred One, so for thirty years a legal war has been kept up between an old Spanish grant and a Texas warrant as to the possession of this "Corpus," and our pleasant sanctuary is the victim of this crusade.

P. S. — Leaving that city, as steamers could not get over the bar, I had to take a little sail-boat, by the "inside" route, to Indianola, and we had to beat all the way — one hundred and twenty miles — against a "norther," harsh and chilly, running around several times and taking forty-eight hours for the trip.

LETTER LXV.

ALABAMA ANNIVERSARY WEEK.

Montgomery, Ala., April 2, 1879.

This is our anniversary week for Alabama. The conference of churches, the theological institute, the Sabbath-school convention, and the Woman's Missionary Association are making this a festal time at the capital. This beautiful city is now in the bloom of our northern June. The missionaries are entertained in families which have come from the north. Formerly when hearing and reading of these rising southern associations and reading the reports of the same, I was inclined to think that they must be funny meetings, and that the accounts furnished the papers must be pretty well colored. Come and see. The church is a beautiful and commodious building, located not far from the state capitol. The congregation is well dressed and intelligent in appearance. The prevailing sable is relieved by the white of seven or eight preachers and of nine lady teachers and of a few citizens now and then dropping in. The singing is led by a choir and reed organ. In public worship there are voluntaries and responsive readings and the offering of the Lord's Prayer.

The association opens, organizes, proceeds with business, with essays and discussions, just as any such body would at the north, the southern men showing a wonderful aptitude in parliamentary proceeding. The missionaries and the native pastors mingle in the services just as though they were all of one color. Dr. Flavel Bascom, of Illinois, who has served the church here for four months gratuitously, by invitation preaches the opening sermon. His address of welcome is a gem. Rev. Dr. Petrie, of this city's Presbyterian church, and Judge Bruce, of the United States District Court, being present, are made honorary members and participate in some of the discussions. Nine young men from Professor Andrew's theological department at Talladega, are examined for licensure, which is cheerfully granted. It is wonderful how much theology their instructor does work into them. They seem to take to this science with readiness. While engaged in study at the college, they prosecute Sunday-school work in the country round about, and this has already grown into several churches. It is a beautiful sight, that of these educated, consecrated young men coming on to use the gospel for the elevation of their own people. One young man was ordained by council. The theological institute is a training in the same line. It takes a day, and so does the Sunday-school convention, with its routine of question-drawer, papers, discussions, and evening of short speeches and reports of the work. So these southern sisters, following their teachers, are having their Woman's Missionary Society. It is a vine resting upon the live-oak of the state association. It moves off with the glow and the order of such a meeting at the north. And so here were five days of consecutive service, each one packed full of interest and profit. It was a feast of fat things. All remained to the end. After the closing service the people to the number of one hundred waited on Dr. Bascom and his wife at the Teachers' Home, in a surprise party, which testified by music, refreshments, and good cheer their love for the departing friends.

LETTER LXVI.

THE HAMPTON INSTITUTE.

HAMPTON, Va., May 6, 1879.

THIS normal and industrial institute is a grand affair. It occupies the former site of the government hospitals. Adjoining its grounds is the national cemetery, kept with the utmost care. Here are the marble headstones of five thousand patriot martyrs. The monument in granite, built by Miss Dix, is one of imposing impression. Near by is also the Soldiers' Home, where Uncle Sam takes care of five hundred of his disabled boys, the building being that of one of the best of old-time colleges. Two miles down is Fortress Monroe and the famous Hygeian Hotel. Just over the bay at Portsmouth is the grand United States hospital for soldiers; and over there the navy yard of Norfolk. In full view from the institute windows is the site of the duel between the *Monitor* and the *Merrimac*. It is fitting that a freedmen's school should stand in the midst of these historic associations, especially so near to the spot where the first cargo of slaves was discharged the same year with the landing on Plymouth Rock. The chapel built for the use of the soldiers, and occupied now as a church by the congregation of officers, teachers, and students of the institute, sundry citizens also attending, is still allowed to remain standing within the stone walls of the cemetery. So truly is the freedmen's temple of liberty and education built upon the graves of hundreds of thousands of our patriot brothers.[1] The institute for its campus and farm owns one hundred and fifty acres. The grounds are tastily laid out. The buildings make a village as they are scattered around in the irregularity of nature. The scholars are nearly all of them boarders. The course of study embraces three years. Forty are to graduate this year. Fully three fourths will go out as Christians.

As soon as the first contrabands of General Butler came through our lines at this place, the American Missionary Association met them with bread and clothing in one hand and the spelling-book and the Testament in the other, setting up here the first of all the schools for this people. General S. C. Armstrong, who has been detailed by the Freedmen's Bureau to look after the mass of fugitive humanity gathered here, conceived the plan of this industrial institute, taking his ideal from a school which his father, a missionary in the Sandwich Islands, had there developed for the natives. The general has pushed the enterprise along to a grand accomplishment. The American Missionary Association, which had founded and supported the school in its earlier years, has now transferred it to its independent board of trustees. Virginia appropriated one fourth of its United States agricultural scrip to this school. This amounted to $95,000, $10,000 of which was allowed to be put into lands and buildings. The remainder is in the bonds of the state, which pays interest on the same toward the running expenses. So the Old Dominion has a share in this concern, sending

---

[1] Mr. E. B. Monroe, the president of the board of trustees, has since built a beautiful chapel in stone. He loveth our nation and has built us a synagogue.

each year its governor or some official to the anniversary to inspect the work done. Captain Henry Romeyn, who in the last fight with Chief Joseph, was left for dead on the field, with a bullet-hole bored through his lungs, has been detailed by the government for drill duty in this school. His training is manifest in the manliness of the boys. With ready skill he turns from military drill to devotional exercises, which he leads for the whole school in the use of the prayer-book. Dr. Mark Hopkins, that college Nestor, is here now with his family, spending a few weeks in the home of the General, who is an alumnus of Williams, and also a former member of the family of the president. The old gentleman, still in the fullness of strength, preaches often twice on the Sabbath. Even here upon a respite, he must have a room assigned to him for a study. May his seventy-four years yet have many more added! The Rev. John H. Dennison, a son-in-law of Dr. Hopkins, lately pastor of the First Congregational Church in New Britain, Connecticut, is now pastor of this new institute church. Governor Smith, of New Hampshire, is here to-day examining the establishment with apparent delight.

The Indian department is a specialty at Hampton. There are now sixty of these people, male and female, under training here. Fifteen came from among the prisoners at St. Augustine, Florida, and the remainder were brought from their wild homes in the north-west. The Wigwam, a brick hall of three stories, built at a cost of $18,000, serves for their dormitory. Some twenty of the colored students volunteered as missionaries of civilization to go each into a room with a chum of the red color; and each is now expressing much satisfaction with the other. In the chapel and at the table the races intermingle. The red students are getting along well in their studies. They also take readily to work under the industrial plan. The government pays $167 per capita a year toward the expense of board, tuition, clothing, and books.

The industrial is the peculiar feature of the institute. It is proving a great success in affording the opportunity to young people to help themselves, and in developing the habits and the skill of labor. These people need to be educated out of the idea that work is degrading. The farm is simply a model. It is just now receiving in the northern markets $6.25 for a dozen bunches of asparagus. Peaches, pears, cherries, peas, greens, etc., bring in turn their early prices. The twenty-three cows of blooded stock furnish a surplus of milk for the local market. Sheep and hogs and horses play their part. A portable steam-engine in the model barn threshes, grinds, cuts, and steams the fodder, then runs out to saw wood, and in the fall goes around to do threshing for the neighbors. Every particle of fertilizing is saved. The Indians have a separate shop and a patch of their own for cultivation. Printing, machine-knitting, tailoring, trimming, blacksmithing, and carpentering are carried on. A steam-engine in Virginia Hall washes, cooks, prints, and heats. Gas is made for home consumption. The smokestack is now going up for a sixty-horse engine which Mr. Corliss has given to the institute. This is to drive a planing, sawing, and matching mill. The canning of fruits, crabs, and oysters is also to be carried on by that steam. A monthly paper, *The Workman*, is published at one dollar a year. Job printing pays well. The series of "Hampton Tracts for the People" has reached No. 6. They are: The Health Laws of Moses; The Duty of Teachers; Preventable Diseases; Who Found Jamie? A Haunted House; and Woman's

Work in Reform. All are upon sanitary topics, and are as good for white savages as for red and black. Another farm of a hundred acres, near by, purchased and presented by a lady friend, is to be used for stock and agricultural purposes. Young men who offer themselves and yet have no money are set to work a year on this farm or in the sawmill, and so get something ahead on which to start at school. Meanwhile they will be gaining some knowledge by absorption. Rarely can one find a more beautiful piece of educational philanthropy than this; and then to have been so quickly and so grandly developed, that is the wonder. Surely the guilty nation does well to make haste in securing some partial restitution to these injured races. To repress the crowd at Commencement, tickets have to be issued. The assembly room endures a jam of twelve hundred. Rev. Dr. Hoge, of Richmond, accepts the invitation to follow with an address the presentation of diplomas by the president of the board, Rev. Dr. M. E. Strieby.

LETTER LXVII.

THE FISK UNIVERSITY. — THE JUBILEE HALL. — JUBILEE SINGERS.

NASHVILLE, Tenn., May 22, 1879.

PASSING through the city in 1865 on my tour of exploration, I found here General C. B. Fisk, serving as commissioner of the Freedmen's Bureau for two or three states. Just then Messrs. E. P. Smith and E. M. Cravath came along under the auspices of the American Missionary Association, to open a school for colored people in Nashville. General Fisk entered heartily into the work and used his influence to secure from the government the hospital buildings near the Chattanooga depot. The American Missionary Association bought the ground for $16,000. The Fisk School was opened January 9, 1866, and during the year the number of students ran up to ten hundred. In 1857 the Fisk University was chartered by the state. In 1871, as the old buildings were going to decay, and as they were ill-situated for a school, the idea was conceived by Mr. George L. White that his little band of trained singers should go out with him as the Jubilee Singers to earn money for a new building. I heard them, as unheralded they made their *début* before the National Congregational Council at Oberlin. That dignified body, taken by surprise, was now melted to tears and now lifted to jubilation. After the struggle of months, they at last won success in a money way. They carried the hearts of the lovers of song in America and in Europe. They gained the audience of kings, queens, and crown princes, and the patronage of the Old World's noblest men. As the result of seven years of labor they purchased the present site of twenty-five acres and built the majestic Jubilee Hall, putting into the whole one hundred and fifty thousand dollars. Jubilee Hall is on the site of old Fort Gillem, on the verge of the city and in full view of Vanderbilt University, having one of the most commanding and beautiful locations on the hill-surrounded city. Its own campus of eight acres is walled in with stone and is laid out with walks and drives and set with grass and trees. The hall is supplied throughout with steam, gas, and water. It stands upon bed-rock. Its architecture is superb and is admired quite as much as that of the Vanderbilt. It is finished in the native color of white pine, the wainscoting on the first floor being in a variety of hard woods from Africa, sawed in the mills of the Mendi Mission. By the efforts of Mrs. C. B. Fisk the rooms have been furnished uniformly in walnut sets. On the walls of the elegantly upholstered parlor are portraits of William Wilberforce, David Livingstone, and Lord Shaftesbury, presented to the Jubilee Singers, also a mammoth painting of the singers themselves and fine crayons of General Fisk and the lamented Reverends E. P. Smith and G. D. Pike, D.D., and other living workers. "To what purpose is this waste?" Does not the friend of the oppressed answer: "They have wrought a good work upon me"? It was fitting that one such monument to emancipation should be built, itself a song in crystallization. It was well that the young people just out of the house of bondage should set up in behalf of their race one testimonial of their capacity. The American Missionary Association has no other such structure. All its other buildings, present and prospective, are planned upon the most rigid idea of economy and durability.

The Baptist Roger Williams College and the Methodist Central Tennessee College, both located in this city, are devoted to the education of the colored youth. They have each good, large buildings and are doing a grand work. If all these institutions were dependent upon local patronage, they would lack of course in constituency. But as they draw from the several states around here, they have plenty of material. Schools sometimes seek a center just as business does. Then each one serves as a stimulus to the others. Fisk University no doubt has done a good deal in provoking good works. The late governor and the superintendent of public schools in Tennessee have both furnished testimonials to the high quality of work done at Fisk. In March last the legislature, having attended in a body a literary entertainment gotten up by the students at Jubilee Hall, passed a joint resolution, expressing thanks to the scholars and commendation of the university to the colored people of the state. Last summer Fisk sent out one hundred and fifty vacation teachers. Four have gone from this place as missionaries to Africa. In Texas, Mississippi, and in other southern states I have come across the influence of the Fisk students.

The eleventh anniversary has just been observed. It seemed just like any commencement at the north. The examinations, lasting through three days, led by written questions, were of a most thorough and satisfactory character. This college aims to magnify the classical course; and it is no longer a question whether these sable scholars can excel in the higher studies. The departments are the common school, the normal, the higher normal, the collegiate, and the theological. Reverend Dr. W. H. Willcox, representing Mrs. Valeria G. Stone, of Malden, Mass., upon a recent visit to Fisk, made a pledge of $60,000 to build the Livingstone Hall for chapel, library, class-room, and dormitory purposes. This is a portion of the $200,000 which he is assigning to the schools in the south. No better direction could be given to such munificence.

PERIOD IX.

IN THE SOUTH, 1880–82.

Berea. — National Cemeteries at the South. — Prohibition in North Carolina. — East Tennessee. — Anniston. — Memphis. — The Congregational Methodists. — A July Vacation. — Atlanta Cotton Exposition. — Crossing Boston Mountain. — Confederate Memorial Day in New Orleans. — Presbyterian Missions in the South. — North and South: Some Things in Common. — Colored Work of Southern Churches.

LETTER LXVIII.

BEREA COLLEGE.

BEREA, Ky., March 1, 1880.

I REALIZE the wisdom of providence in tucking this early mission into such an out-of-the-way locality, though it is really in the heart of the commonwealth. It is just on the border between the wealthy blue-grass region, where the negroes are now, as heretofore, very numerous, and the mountain district, where there are scarcely any colored people. Out of a population of forty-five thousand in Jackson County there are only fifty-one colored. So the college lays one hand upon the rich plains and the other upon the mountains; and Berea is the first institution at the south to secure the co-education of the races, though all schools of this system are open to all classes irrespective of color. The young people of the union-loving but poor mountain people find that here they can get the best of educational facilities for one third of the cost at other colleges. They have their prejudice to overcome, but they find it easier to bear such mortification than to endure the manners of the aristocratic students. So Berea runs from year to year with about equal numbers of white and black. The last year the catalogue counted one hundred and thirty whites and one hundred and forty-four blacks, with the sexes in nearly equal numbers. The Bereans, with their open Bible and its principles of equality, have access to the Sunday-school conventions, teachers' institutes, and churches of these mountains. President E. H. Fairchild made a tour of six weeks through these hill counties, lecturing and preaching, every-where meeting a cordial reception. Commencements bring out the immense multitudes of white and black, the rich coming in carriages from the blue-grass country, and the poor coming down from the mountains, afoot, on horse-back, on donkeys, and in carts. Last summer eight hundred and fifty horses came out and neighed and stamped under the shade of the college forest to which they had brought from two to three hundred people. In the great congregation, on the platform, and among the speakers the white and the black are about in equal numbers.

Recently Rev. John G. Fee, the founder, upon invitation, preached in the Presbyterian church in Richmond, the blue-grass county seat. The local paper reported the sermon in full with commendation, saying that it was the first time that Mr. Fee had ever preached in that town, although he had lived in that county for twenty-five years. It also said: "One could but recall the trying years of the past when the speaker fearlessly combated race-prejudice and slavery, when his enemies persecuted him and even threatened to take his life — one could but recall those stormy days and at the same time remember that when the war was over and Mr. Fee's party was in the ascendency, he had no man punished, he sought to revenge no personal grievance, but went on with his life-work in his quiet, unobtrusive way, remembering his enemies only to forgive them." It was in that same Richmond that a convention, held but twenty years ago, appointed a committee of "the most wealthy and respectable citizens" to wait upon the Bereans and warn them to leave the state in ten days. On horse-back, in martial array, those sixty "organized gentlemen" drew up before the homes of these unoffending families, and their orders had to be obeyed. Now some of the *élite* of Richmond come to commencement. They exchange courteous visits with our college people. At the table of the president I have dined with a gentleman who came in his carriage with his wife and daughters, and who had been of the number of those sixty, and the visit was reciprocated. The county seat courts the trade and banking of Berea. It sends out carriage-loads of visitors to show them the Yankee college.

Twenty years ago one of the daughters of Kentucky, equally related to both races, saw fit to use her liberty and run away to Chicago. At that time I had my family at the Orient Hotel. Her husband was its steward, and she the mistress of its laundry. Her master had come for her. The biped blood-hound, with U. S. on his collar, rushed into the office and demanded his prey. The proprietor, a democrat, turned the baying hound off the trail by saying that she was not there, and then rushed down into the laundry and told Mrs. Webb that she must leave instantly. We took her up-stairs into our own suite for two days and nights, hiding her in a closet behind the secretary.

LETTER LXIX.

THE NATIONAL CEMETERIES AT THE SOUTH.

ATLANTA, Ga., May 30, 1880.

As my brother, Charles A. Roy, had come on to Chicago to be mustered in, I wrote our mother inquiring what would be her wish as to his body in case he should lose his life. She replied: "Let him be buried where he falls." He survived his four years of service. Many other patriotic mothers desired that the remains of their sons should mingle with the soil on which they should die for the life of the nation. But they did not imagine that the precious dust of their sons would be gathered into such noble cemeteries as these, there to have surviving comrades as their wardens, with the Stars and Stripes ever afloat above them. It was an inspiration on the part of the man who conceived the idea of these national burial-places over the south.

Before the war I had known a deacon in Indiana who went into the service. After I came to reside in this city, his widow wrote me that he had been buried on the spot where he fell on the side of Kenesaw Mountain, and requested me to learn, if possible whether the grave with its simple headboard could yet be recognized. She had known nothing of the system of national cemeteries over the south, and so nothing of that one at Marietta within three miles of the grave she was inquiring about. I went out to that camp of sleeping patriots. The superintendent took his book and found the name, the regiment, the company of Indiana soldiers, and the tier and the number of his grave. I went out and followed along the rows of white marble memorials that stand a foot and a half above the ground, until I came to the right place, and there I read the name of my friend, my own heart overflowing with gratitude for the paternal care thus manifested by the government for its patriot dead. I wrote the facts to the widow. She answered in over-joy. If she should come down to visit the grave of her husband, arriving at Marietta, she would find herself in one of the most pleasant towns in the land — itself eleven hundred feet above the sea, and so, with its balmy and bracing air, one of the most attractive health resorts for summer and winter. Just there only two miles away is Kenesaw; and there is Lone Mountain; and there Altoona. And here only half a mile from the railway station, upon a lofty swell of land, is the cemetery, the site itself the gift of a Union eastern man, whose home was just across the way, whose fine hotel had been burned by the rebels, and whose body now rests along with those of the soldiers to whom he had proffered such hospitality. The hundred-acre lot is enclosed with a solid stone wall laid up in mortar. The drives, walks, and the adornments of trees, shrubs, flowers, and grass are such as we find in our home cemeteries. The Bermuda grass, with its tenacity of root, survives the heat of these seasons and prevents the wash of these red clay hills. In long circling tiers you see the headstones of marble, on each of which is inscribed the name, the title, and the regiment of the deceased. You come to the crest and there find the flag-staff with the colors flying, and columbiads planted in the earth, standing as the sentries of the place. You come to the lodge of the superintendent and you find it a beautiful rustic cottage, embowered in vine and bloom. You enter the office, record your name, inspect the records of interments, and find them to number in all 10,142, of which 2,963 are "unrecognized."

You make the acquaintance of the official and find him a gentleman, a wounded brave, detailed from the army for this service. You see the squad of men kept at work upon the grounds. You discover here and there among the headstones the monuments which loving friends have put in place. You read the placarded laws of Congress for the protection and management of these cemeteries. And you retire under a fresh impulse of love for the republic which thus marks its gratitude to the men who for its life gave up their own. This is a specimen. I have visited several others. At Chattanooga it is an immense area of hill and slope, encircled with a wall of stone-masonry; its well-shaven lawns are a delight. Here under their country's flag, with Lookout Mountain and Missionary Ridge standing guard about them, sleep 12,962 patriots, awaiting the reveille of the resurrection morn. Over the neutral ground of Kentucky, Fort Nelson stood guard, in its impregnable position, within the horseshoe bend of the Kentucky River, which flows through a cañon of three hundred feet of perpendicular rock, all the way round. That is now a camp of the dead, whose keeper, a hardy German, is a mutilated soldier.

I give the full statistics. There are eighty-two of these national cemeteries. Virginia has seventeen; Tennessee, seven; Kentucky, six; Lousiana, Maryland, Illinois, and North Carolina, each four — sixteen; Mississippi, Arkansas, and Missouri, each three — nine; District of Columbia, South Carolina, Georgia, Florida, Texas, Kansas, Indiana, New York, Pennsylvania, and New Jersey, each two — twenty; West Virginia, Alabama, Iowa, Nebraska, Montana, and Indian Territory, each one — six. The most numerously tenanted are: —

Vicksburg, Miss.	16,600	Stone River, Tenn.	6,145
Nashville, Tenn.	16,526	Corinth, Miss.	5,716
Arlington, Va.	16,264	Soldiers' Home, D. C.	5,602
Fredericksburg, Va.	15,257	Little Rock, Ark.	5,602
Memphis, Tenn.	13,977	Hampton, Va.	5,424
Andersonville, Ga.	13,714	Mound City, Ill.	5,226
Chattanooga, Tenn.	12,962	Antietam, Md.	4,671
Chalurette, La.	12,511	Winchester, Va.	4,459
Salisbury, N. C.	12,126	Port Hudson, La.	3,819
Jefferson Barracks, Mo.	11,490	Pittsburg Landing, Tenn.	3,590
Marietta, Ga.	10,142	Gettysburg, Penn.	3,575
Beaufort, N. C.	9,241	Newberne, N. C.	3,254
Richmond, Va.	6,542		
Poplar Grove, Va.	6,199	Total,	329,369

Of these there are "known," 173,088; "unknown," 148,281. There are, of civilians, "known," 6,900; "unknown," 1,500. And of the total there are of confederate, "known," 6,110; "unknown," 3,200. The confederates are mostly at Elmira, New York, and Finn's Point, New Jersey. Of course this summary does not include all those who were not brought home for burial. Many, buried where they fell, were not discovered for re-interment in the cemeteries. These grand cemeteries remind us also of the soldiers' homes, soldiers' colleges, the pensions, the homesteads, and the pay provided by a grateful nation. And this in turn suggests the utter lack of all these rewards on the part of the confederate soldiers. They have no such cemeteries. Many were buried in the local city of the dead. Their pay was in confederate money, which was "not worth a continental." No soldiers' homes, no pensions, no homesteads, no colleges for their children!

But who at the south shall be found on Decoration day, to scatter flowers on these scores of thousands of Union graves? Oh, that is all provided for! In this part of the country there are millions of souls that never drew a disloyal breath. They are easily known by the color given them by their Creator, and these are the people who decorate our cemetery graves. No more grateful and loving tributes are paid up north on these days than by our dusky orators down here. At Atlanta they celebrate every returning Memorial day, going out to Marietta, nineteen miles, by special train. And the patriot north is grateful to them for these delicate attentions to its soldier dead. But of their own 178,896 colored heroes, they have 80,000 graves to be decorated. And what shall be done to these sable loyalists? Make good their rights. Reverence their manhood. Help them to all Christian enlightenment. And they in turn will buttress our civil fabric.

LETTER LXX.

SNOW. — COLD. — NORTH CAROLINA ON PROHIBITION.

ATLANTA, Ga., January 17, 1881.

AT last the south and the north have been sleeping under the same blanket. Nor was the covering narrower than that they could wrap themselves in it, for it lapped over on Canada and was tucked under at Galveston on the Gulf. For thirty years never was known so much snow at the south nor so much cold. But time, the weaver, has in loom a counterpane that will yet serve these two bedfellows throughout the year, the coming of national good feeling. May the shuttle fly fast!

For the last ten days I was scouring along the way from New York to this gate city. I found the capital of the old north state a-buzz, not so much with the gossip of the legislature, as with the deeply earnest talk of the prohibition convention which had been going on for two days and which was striving to get prohibition submitted to the vote of the people. I had to verify my reckonings to see if I had not drifted out to Kansas or up to Maine. At the hotels, on the streets, every-where, prohibition was the theme. Convention men were stirring up their representatives, many of whom were in the convention meetings and participants in the same. Mammoth petitions were pouring in. One county presented a roll of twenty-six hundred voters. The ex-United States Senator Merriman filled two hours of one evening with the tersest eloquence upon the legal and financial bearings of the case, stating that the social considerations came too near him to allow him to dwell upon them. His own son had been ruined by drink. The ninety-four counties of the state were all represented. Strangely, it was said, that every one of the western counties, where the "moon-shiners" and the blockaders have their hidden stills, would vote for the law. Free whiskey was startling the people. This is well, in the old commonwealth which boasts a declaration of independence prior to 1776.[1] A look into the legislature found two dignified, business-like bodies. The colored members numbered twenty, surely no undue proportion for a people that now count up in the state a population of 530,000. Much has been said in horror of those early "nigger legislatures." It is yet a fact that in that noted legislature there were only seventeen colored members. And of the whites the mass were native southerners. The grand Mogul who was said to have bought the legislators of both houses was a democrat, and the man who received five hundred of the bonds was another. "Let not pot call kettle black."

[1] That election snowed under the constitutional amendment. But the people are at it again by the local option plan. The colored people will not be deceived again as they were on that first vote. As it was, those of them who had been under the influence of the mission schools and churches voted on the right side.

LETTER LXXI.

EAST TENNESSEE.

MARYVILLE, February 11, 1881.

BETWEEN the Smoky Mountains or the Blue Ridge on the east and the Cumberland Mountains on the west there is a broad trough extending diagonally across the state. Through it runs the Tennessee River, which, at Chattanooga, cleaves the western chain, passing between the abutments of Lookout Mountain and Walden's Ridge, then coming westward to swing back and cross the state again, from south to north. Through this valley also runs the East Tennessee Railroad, connecting the north-east with the south-west by the Kenesaw route. But it is a valley made up of hills and vales and mountain affluents. It has its beds of coal and iron and marble. In one quarry of marble, now being opened, on the bank of the river and near the rail track, there are found eight mottled varieties, assorted and arranged in nature's own cabinet. It has a rich, strong soil, fitted to the grasses, fruits, and cereals. Cattle, horses, and mules are a staple, and their market is found in the cotton regions below. In four months Atlanta sold 14,500 horses and mules, mostly from Tennessee. Of course such a country is extremely healthy. In general, it is like western Pennsylvania, with a mild climate.

Maryville, a county seat, is the present terminus of a railroad, which, coming from Knoxville, is to be carried on over the mountains to Augusta, Ga. During the war General Wheeler came with a force to dislodge some twenty Union men, who had fortified themselves in the brick court-house. Not being able to reach the garrison on account of the flying of patriot bullets, he set fire to a house near by, expecting it to communicate with the seat of county justice. But the wind shifted, saved the Unionists, and swept away several confederate homes. Then a resort to a cannonade brought the beleaguered to a surrender, which, it came out, was upon the firing of the last round of ammunition. Burnside was cooped up in Knoxville; Sherman, coming to his rescue, had got as far as Maryville when the siege was raised. Sherman's encampment was upon a farm of a hundred acres, which was a single lofty and perfect dome, adjoining the town. From this spot you view for long distances the east and the west mountain ranges, whose crests are one hundred miles apart. That farm has been changed into a cedar park, that sweet-smelling evergreen having come up spontaneously over the whole area; and its summit has exchanged the encampment for the three stately structures of the Maryville College, which, up to the end of the war, had occupied its contracted village lot, and which, during the war, had furnished a rendezvous alternately for confederate and federal forces. In 1819 the college was founded by the Rev. Dr. Isaac Anderson. At the time of the great Presbyterian excision the synod, to which the institution belonged, went with the new school; and now it abides with the general assembly of the north. In its day the college has educated more than one hundred and twenty ministers, nearly all of whom are natives of East Tennessee. These mountains produce a good deal of ministerial timber. In my class of 1853, at Union Seminary, J. G. Lamar, George Caldwell, and John McCampbell were of this stock. As George was finishing the reading of Uncle Tom's Cabin in the serial of *The National Era,* I looked over his shoulder in the reading-room and asked him if he were going back south to take the part of his namesake in that story. He answered encouragingly. However, in the great strife he went with his section, and is now pastor at Bristol, Tenn. McCampbell lost his life at Granada during the recent pestilence. Lamar has served his Alma Mater through all these years as a professor. In our class was also Peter Mason Bartlett, who for the last twelve years has been the president of this institution. A brother of his, Alexander, from Oberlin, is also a professor.

After the war General Howard appropriated $16,000 toward the new buildings, on condition that colored students should be allowed free access to the college. With not a little of effervescence the covenant has been kept. Two most excellent colored young men, whom I have been visiting with reference to a missionary life-work in Africa, were educated here and in the theological department of Howard University. I find two talented fellows of African descent now studying here. Dropping in upon President Bartlett's class in geology, I saw one of the two haul out of his pocket for inspection a lot of crystal quartz, which he had gathered up in the mountains where he had been teaching school.

In 1821 the synod of Tennessee, replying to an address of the Manumission Society, said : —

We lament the existence of slavery in our otherwise free and happy country as the greatest natural and moral evil that has ever existed in our country. We firmly believe it is such an evil as will ruin our country most inevitably, unless prevented by a gracious God. The principles of slavery are at war with all the natural rights of men and hostile to all the principles of natural and revealed religion. We can not doubt for a moment but that God will one day plead the cause of the oppressed, either by causing the power of his holy religion to be so felt that the people shall be willing to let the oppressed go free ; or he will unbind their burden by his own almighty hand, and by his righteous judgments set the captive at liberty.

I quote this from an alumni address of Professor Crawford, himself a native Tennessecan, who thus fortifies the present rule of the college. He also says that President Anderson, in his day, brought colored young men into the college, and even kept them in his own house, without any objection being made.

LETTER LXXII.

WOODSTOCK IRON COMPANY.

ANNISTON, Ala., March 17, 1881.

IT is but a few years since the site of this town was a red-hilled, gullied, cheerless old plantation. It was bought by the Woodstock Iron Company, and now it has two furnaces that turn out daily forty tons of charcoal pig-iron, a cotton factory that turns five thousand spindles, which will be increased to ten thousand, and has recently declined an order of a thousand bales (one million yards) for the China market. It has a large grist-mill, a steam-ginnery, a planing-mill, a country store that carries an immense stock of all kinds of goods. The company is now putting in water-works at an expense of thirty thousand dollars, and is building a macadamized road over the mountain into the Chocollocco Valley at a cost of one hundred and five thousand dollars. The town is finely laid out with worked streets and well-set shade-trees. The homes of the proprietors are palatial. Of the estate of twenty thousand acres five hundred are under cultivation as a model farm, with Alderney cows upon green pastures. Before the company has opened its lots for sale the population has come up to fourteen hundred.

As soon as the town is opened to the public there will be a grand rush. An immense car-wheel foundry and a car-factory are coming here. A grand winter hotel is to be built. The colored people, who are the operatives, are provided with a church and school by the American Missionary Association. General Tyler, of Connecticut, and his son, and the Noble brothers, are at the head of all this.

LETTER LXXIII.

THE CONGREGATIONAL METHODISTS.

ATLANTA, Ga., May 13, 1881.

AT the National Council in St. Louis fraternal delegates were appointed to visit some of the southern ecclesiastical bodies. Doctors Sturtevant and Goodell were to visit the Presbyterian General Assembly South, and Dr. F. A. Noble and Rev. T. L. Day to visit the General Conference of Congregational Methodists. As the last-named delegation were not able to come I was glad to comply with the request to serve as a substitute. I found the body in session at Fredonia, Ga. I was received with a royal welcome by mine host, a native Georgian whose farm was that of a thrifty Yankee, and also by the conference. Congregational Methodism took its rise in this state twenty-nine years ago, in 1852. It came up as a protest against the peculiar elements in the government of the Methodist Episcopal Church. And now they boast since their secession both branches of the old church, north and south, have put in lay delegation, have increased the duration of the local pastorate, and have given up, at least in that region, the week-day preachings of the itinerants, against which they rebelled. The Congregational Methodist churches are all in country places. Their people are generally among the poor. They have, as a rule, with exceptions, monthly Sabbath preaching, one minister serving one, two, or three or four churches. They now have state conferences in Georgia, Alabama, Texas, Mississippi, and Missouri. They number one hundred and twenty-five churches and about as many ministers, with about ten thousand members. They have the beginning of a college at Harpersville, Miss., under Rev. J. F. N. Huddleston and his son. They have a paper, *The Congregational Methodist*, at Cave Spring, Ga., near Rome, published by L. J. Jones, Esq., who was the moderator of the conference. It is an able journal, a worthy organ. At first they took the name of Independent Methodists, but they soon found that they needed fellowship, and so changed to the name which carries that idea. They have but one order in the ministry. Pastors are chosen by the churches, to remain by mutual approval. Their constitution has a strong article on temperance, and they stand by it nobly. They say that the regular Methodists ignore them as much as though they were missionaries to the freedmen. They have a history of their church by Rev. S. C. McDaniel, of Griffin, Ga. They are Methodistic in doctrine and mode of worship, and Congregational in polity. The admirable letter of Mr. Day to the conference followed his Christian, Congregational, and patriotic sentiments with a commendation of the workers of the American Missionary Association and with the suggestion: "If any of you who are our brethren in the faith should ever come to see the good results from their efforts and should be moved to speak the word of sympathy to those engaged in this lonely and difficult work, it will surely be reckoned to you by our Lord and Master as the cup of cold water in the name of a disciple." And then, as if to answer in deed as well as in word, the conference made haste to receive the visiting brother with a welcoming address, to assign to him a preaching appointment, and to seek his views in matters of Congregational polity. By their rule, at the communion, members may receive it in a sitting, kneeling, or standing posture. They give up the Episcopal and Methodist order of serving the minister first. An old colored disciple at the last came forward alone. It was touching to see the grace with which the venerable men officiating, before being served themselves, became his servants for Christ's sake, and to hear the hearty response to his ejaculations as he turned away. He was the only colored member left in those churches. I found that the brethren would be glad of outside fellowship, but they had no idea of becoming associated with any other denomination.

LETTER LXXIV.

CLIFTON SPRINGS, N. Y., July 31, 1881.
"ONCE at Clifton, always there." That is a proverb. Well, why not? Dr. Cuyler boasts of his thirty years at Saratoga Springs; and he has been a tolerably healthy man, able to do some work in preaching and writing for the newspapers. Multitudes of other people go to the same place year after year for rest and recuperation; and so do many find it to their inclination and profit to come to these springs season after season. The make-up of Dr. Foster's sanitarium develops a peculiar home feeling. The judicious medical treatment, if needed, is an attrac-

tion. The water, with its sulphates of lime and magnesia and soda, has in many cases a remedial quality. I think that within the time I get more revivification here than I could get anywhere else, and so I am now on my fourth summer at Clifton.

Nor can I refrain from saying that I find a peculiar pleasure in coming back to this place, where, during two years of enforced respite from labor, God was preparing my mind for the transition in his life-plan for me, by which I was to be taken from my own dear west and set to doing much the same work at the south, which I had already learned to love. Here I told the Lord that if he would let me up so that I could again preach the gospel of his dear Son, I would go anywhere, even to the ends of the earth. But I may as well confess that when he took me at my word and pointed out the field, it did cost a struggle, a night without sleep. Up north to have been a good friend of the slave was one thing; to go down and put one's self by the side of the depressed ex-bondman, to take chances with him, to try to lift him up, that was another. Now I bless God for the joy of the work. It is a missionary service without the labor of acquiring and using a strange language. It is in some sense the work of a foreign missionary without going from under the flag of one's own country. I feel unworthy of the gratitude of these people, of whom the Master speaks as "these my brethren." These two years I have gone every-where, from Virginia to Texas, without receiving one word or act of discourtesy, but with many tokens of approbation from my white fellow-citizens.

In the review, this seems yet the exigent work of the time. It is not the caring for one, two, or three new territories or states at a time, but for five millions of people scattered over fifteen states, who are needing, all at once, the helping hand. This going back and forth makes one realize that this is all one country, with one language, with one history, with one Christian religion, with one interblended destiny; that the comfort of the whole body must depend upon the welfare of every member; and that so our common patriotism requires the uplifting of these lowly poor. This glance back over the field brings immense encouragement as to the results of this evangelizing process; brings assurance that, if it is only prosecuted with vigor, there need be no fear as to the outcome of the great act of emancipation; and brings evidence of cheerfulness and happiness among the hundreds of workers, northern and native, male and female.

As my eye takes its usual course on the map and sweeps around the coast from the point where the old Mason and Dixon's line struck the Atlantic to the boundary of Mexico, all the way I am reminded of colleges and academies, and normal institutes and high schools, which are sources of light, fountains of blessing; of the hundreds upon hundreds of primary schools in which, during the last year, the native teachers of our own training were instructing one hundred and fifty thousand pupils; of the seventy churches of the primitive faith, which are the outgrowth of that educational scheme, and which, as to their influence for good, by their character are multiplying their number many times; of the multitudes of youth in those higher schools, who are ambitiously taking on a Christian cultivation that they may use it for the good of their people; of those Christian congregations so hungry for the Word of God, so anxious for the best things in church life; of those masses, beset with ignorance and superstition and unthrift, who need to be rallied by some worthy aspiration. And then I turn with all hope to that corps of men and women, who, under God, have wrought such great things already, whose excelling in the passive virtues has commanded respect, and made it so comfortable for those of us who come to join them now, and whose service for the republic and the kingdom makes them high benefactors in our time and land.

LETTER LXXV.

THE COTTON EXPOSITION.

ATLANTA, Ga., December 7, 1881.

THE International Cotton Exposition is a grand success, in its make-up and in its influence. Eli Whitney made cotton king. Edward Atkinson invented this idea. Atlanta sent for him and put him into the Opera House. He spoke to the people on political matters in a saucy way, but yet carried them for the great show. With money from the north and with the engineering of a Yankee director, H. I. Kimball, who has done more for rebuilding Atlanta than any other man, the Atkinsonian idea is now a fact. The extent of the buildings and of the exhibit has surprised almost every one who has come to see for himself. The opening was a grand affair, with prayer, the chorus singing of a hundred voices, led by Mr. C. M. Cady, and with the addresses of men from the north and the south. All of these were aglow with patriotism. The speech of Colonel Breckenridge, of Kentucky, was a gem in its elocution and its devout and national sentiment. The attendance is running now at about nineteen or twenty thousand a day. This is planters' week. Their association is now in session here. Before that body I heard this morning Commissioner Loring's admirable address upon the mutual relation of our national industries. On the twenty-sixth of this month is to come Freedmen's day, with Fred Douglass as orator.

Through the season upon the grounds had been cultivated a field of cotton as a specimen. Some of it was picked, ginned, spun, woven, and made into a suit of clothes, all in one day, for Governor Colquitt, and worn by him at the reception that same night. All the implements for the culture and the manufacture of this product are on exhibition. Whitney's gin, which works with many circular saws, set upon a cylinder, finds after nearly a hundred years a competitor, which pulls the lint off from the seed instead of cutting it off, and so prevents the breaking of the fiber. Here is the improved machinery for cleaning out the dust, sand, and broken pods. Formerly the seed was wasted, now it is utilized. One machine plucks off the remnant of the cotton, and another grinds the seed, separating the hulls to be used for fertilizing, from the meat which is to be pressed into oil. Cotton-seed oil is now a great business. It is offered as a substitute for lard. It is used in all forms of mixture. I have seen ships on the Atlantic coast loading with raw cotton-seed which was to be shipped to the Mediterranean, and there to be made into "pure olive oil" and shipped back to this country as an article of table luxury. But now we make our own olive oil without the trouble and expense of shipping it across the ocean and back again. Before our eyes goes on the process of ginning, cleaning, carding, spinning, and weaving. As a happy thought, by the side of these automatic machines, a half-dozen country women are carding, spinning, and weaving with their old apparatus. The production of spool cotton is the constant wonder of the crowd. After Professor Francis had taken the students of Atlanta University through the apartments, the thread proprietor sent them over two hundred and fifty boxes of his spool cotton. Nothing on the grounds was a more notable representation than this company of genteel young people who are enjoying the opportunity of higher education; even as it was a worthy exhibit at the Centennial when the American Missionary Association hung up a great map of our country, starred with its hundreds of schools in the south.

Three or four of the southern railroads have made a wonderful display of the products along their line — the grains, the fruits, the ores, the coal, the minerals, the stone, the marble, the timber. These mountains are full of riches. As the barb-wire of Washburn, Moen & Co. is made before our eyes by its own machinery, I call to mind my once going into the works of the inventor, Mr. Glidden, of DeKalb, Illinois, where he was making this wire in the old-fashioned rope-walk way, twisting the wires and putting in the barbs by hand.

The other day Governor Colquitt took over to the Atlanta University fifteen of the cotton-spinners, who left as a token of good-will $700, which in a few days was increased to $1,123. So the Cotton Exposition has been spinning and weaving a web of good feeling. Indeed, a common remark is: "It is the greatest thing in the world for the sake of harmony." I hear the southerners saying on the cars, "Why, when these Yankees come down here and find that we do not eat them up, they go back with better feeling toward the south"; not observing that any part of the change has been made in themselves. And I hear the northerners remark: "When the southerners find that we have no hoofs nor horns they think better of us."

LETTER LXXVI.

CROSSING BOSTON MOUNTAIN IN ARKANSAS.

FORT SMITH, Ark., March 4, 1882.

AT the time of the taking of Arkansas Post, I was on a sanitary boat in the fleet of steamers that could be accommodated in the White River near its mouth. Between Memphis and Little Rock I have crossed the river by a railway bridge that furnishes a draw for passing steamboats. Rising in the mountains of Arkansas, it takes a notion to frisk away up into Missouri before returning to take its diagonal shoot across its native state. Just now it is assuming to be the pathfinder for the Arkansas division of the Frisco Railroad, as that line seeks to find a way southward over the Boston Mountain, which runs east and west in a range across the southern part of Washington County, thirty or forty miles long, and ten or twelve wide. So, as the railway, six miles south of Fayetteville, struck the west fork of the White, I was glad to make the acquaintance of its upper waters and its source. A laughing mill-stream it is. For six miles further on it coquets with the steam-horse. Then by stage we follow along its course, as it swings back and forth within its own beautiful valley, gradually diminishing, and all the time increasing in elevation, until it is found to be only such a spring as would answer for a single household ; and it has led the path of the iron-horse up the side of the Boston Mountain, until we leave the engineers boring a tunnel through which to shoot across to the other side, while our coach and four climb on to the very summit, giving us, as we ascend, a splendid view into that very mouth of the earth. All the way on the other bank hundreds of men and teams are preparing the rock-based grade. In the midst of this rainy winter the hauling of ties and cement and stone, and of forage and supplies for the string of extempore villages of cabin and tent, up on one side and down on the other, has cut up the road so that it has become inconceivably execrable. But reaching the top at sunset, we are rewarded with a view of surrounding and still higher points, and breathe an air that is 1,878 feet above the level of the sea. The keeper of the Mountain House tells us that last winter he had thirty-three snow-storms, one of which measured fifteen inches of snow-fall, while the mercury once touched eighteen degrees below. But this winter, with him, is open and warm.

In the darkness, with only our two candles in the lantern to light us down the mountain-side, with the road deep in mud, rutted and full of chuck holes, with jagged rock corduroying the way, we set out for the descent. We scarcely measure the length of our team and coach before we come near ditching the whole concern. We swing to the right side or the left to balance up. One or two leap out upon the break to bear down. Soon the most of us dismount and walk, in mud and among briers, brush, and stocks, down the two miles of the toughest of the way. We get in. It is a tempestuous voyage for our pitching craft. Of course one thinks of brother Pickett's fatal mountain stage-ride. As we pass along before bed-time, the cheery lights of the cabins and tents of the army of graders only tantalize us with their symbol of rest and safety, while we are straining every nerve to keep ourselves in position and in equilibrium.

It is half-past one. We have been six hours coming twelve miles. But we are over the worst. For a way the road is a little bit smooth; when lo, over goes the coach with a crash, upon one side. Eight men are jumbled together. Up through the hillside sash we crawl, and find that all are slightly hurt but none seriously. We turn back the vehicle and make repairs and adjustments. The sachels and the mail are back in the boot again. One lamp is smashed, but the air is so quiet that its candle burns on without the glass. "But what is this here on the ground?" "It is George's," they say; and he picks it up and puts it back into his pocket again, a nearly emptied flask of whiskey, and he gets back to his place with the driver and we start on. How strange that, having passed over the worst, we should now go over where there was a plain and open way. We had driven out of the road and up a bank where the tip was inevitable; but it was not upon the frightful rocks nor down a precipice.

I call to mind that George, a deputy United States marshal at the stable, had said to Dave, the driver, that he had made one driver drunk, because it made him drive the better. Bravely Dave replied: "I would like to see you make me drunk." A skillful, trusted man he was. Like Uncle Tom, he did not have the smell of horses come upon him. He was a gentleman of the gloves and ribbons. His horses were taken from him and brought back to him in order. But at the first shanty saloon, both got down from the box and went in to drink. At the next it was the same. The flask up in that sly dark place was doing its work, so that the man who had brought us safely over the worst part of the way, when the whiskey had dulled his sense, ran up a bank in clear sailing.

It is four miles further on at Mountainburg and its post-office. All see the stupefying effect and propose that we go on to the woods, light a fire, and wait for day, for Frog Mountain is ahead of us, with its zigzagging road up the precipitous way for a mile. But once started, on we go. George has turned into the coach to sleep off his drunkenness. Another who knows the way gets up with the driver to hold the candle lamp. This writer prefers to walk up that mountain by the side of the horses in the midst of their splashing in the deep mud. They know the way, the noble brutes, and, stopping by their own sweet wills to breathe, at last they take the long inspiration of the mountain-top. A mile further on my fellow-passengers at last are all asleep. There is one sentinel on the box, and one within, with an eye on the wheel-track. "You are out of the road" is the warning. The next moment a heavy thud reveals that we are brought up against a large stump, with a clear way at hand and both lamps burning. I alight. Stupidly the driver says, "I don't believe that I know what I am about." It is now four o'clock. We have made twenty miles in eight and a half hours. We kindle a fire and wait for day, and then in we come. Of course I report the case to the proprietor, who may have occasion, with other people, to learn that many an accident, so-called, is a willful crime, and so the "crossing of Boston Mountain" has its moral.

LETTER LXXVII.

GEORGE W. CABLE. — CONFEDERATE MEMORIAL DAY.

NEW ORLEANS, La., April 10, 1882.

THIS is the home of George W. Cable, the ex-confederate soldier, the son and the grandson of a slave-holder. He is known here as a simple-hearted Christian. He gives himself to humanitarian services in the city, which endears him to the people. Meeting him the other day, as I congratulated him upon his rising literary fame, he responded only as to his sense of responsibility to use his opportunity for doing good. Last year I was present at the anniversary of the New Orleans Sunday-school Association, when the addresses were on the several parts of the lesson for the next Lord's day, which happened to be that of the Good Samaritan. The meeting was in a large hall and the choice Christian people were there. To Mr. Cable, as his part, was assigned "The Unfortunate Victim." He read a paper which in its literary finish was ready for the printer, and which in its exegesis was critical and philanthropic and plucky as it was true. That victim he now found in an amalgam of the red, the yellow, and the black man on our continent, specifying, as to the last, that he ought to be welcomed to our church pews, and not left to the second table at the Lord's Supper, nor crowded up into the gallery, nor into a corner.

I am here just at the time of the confederate memorial service. It is useless to attempt to describe the display of flowers at the monuments of the army of northern Virginia and of Stonewall Jackson. The telling thing was the overture of peace from the Grand Army of the

Republic. At one monument they had a stack of arms, made all of flowers, and resting upon a base of bloom. At the other they had a howitzer resting upon a platform of bloom and green, and itself belted with exquisite flowers, while across its mouth a bird's nest was suspended, with two birdies holding up their open bills, into which the parent, perched upon the upper edge, was dropping a morsel, and that bird was a blue-jay, to symbolize the boys in blue.

Here at this time I realize the mighty flood that is bearing down from the Mississippi Valley upon this delta, deluging houses, estates, cities, and small empires. Here the argument for federal aid in shoring up the banks of the great river seems to submerge all the theories of the inviolability of states' rights. The destruction of the sugar crop and the general damage are simply dreadful. Returning from Texas by way of Little Rock I came into the middle of the floods at White River, where to reach Memphis we were obliged to leave the rail and to go down that river one hundred and seventy-five miles to its mouth, and then two hundred miles up the Mississippi, to make the eighty-seven miles over from that break. Rarely did we come in sight of land. At one place we landed passengers on the top of a house to go ashore by boat. We saw cattle huddled together on the levees and on rafts. And we saw men in canoes cutting cane brush and barking the trees for forage to keep those cattle alive. For most of the way the river was forty miles wide.

LETTER LXXVIII.

PRESBYTERIAN MISSIONS AMONG THE FREEDMEN.

ATLANTA, Ga., May 30, 1882.

I HAVE visited some of the Presbyterian schools and churches. At Chester, S. C., I found my seminary classmate, Rev. Samuel Loomis. Ten years ago he came down there and took things in chaos, and it is strange that he has created so much out of it. He has developed his Brainard Institute, and around it in the country nine Presbyterian churches using as ministers for the same, young men who have been trained in his school, and himself serving as bishop. In Chester and the three adjoining counties there is a colored population of about forty thousand. Last year he reported two hundred and sixty-nine scholars in his institute. He has bought a fine piece of land and is about to start an industrial department, intending to furnish milk, eggs, and vegetables for the local market. He has commanded the respect of the best citizens. He has a normal institute whose members pledge themselves to abstain from all intoxicating drinks, tobacco, and profane and vulgar language. His churches bear such names as Hermon, Salem, Olivet, Tabor, Carmel, Hebron, Bethlehem. His son, Leverett M. Loomis (in addition to his duties as teacher), from sporting with a gun for health, is putting the science of ornithology under obligation to him in a work which he is preparing, "The Birds of South Carolina and the South Atlantic Coast." Rev. William Richardson, at Winnsboro', of the same state, in his Fairfield Institute, enrolls over three hundred scholars, and has the oversight of five churches. At Charleston I found the Wallingford Academy doing a good work.

I was glad to visit the principal Presbyterian institution for the colored people, Biddle University, at Charlotte, N. C. My childhood's playmate, now Rev. Dr. John H. Shedd, had been a professor there several years, between his former and his present service in the Nestorian Mission. Rev. Dr. S. Mattoon, who to twenty years of mission work in India is yet, we hope, to add many in this line of home missionary service, is the president and the professor of theology, church history and government. The catalogue reports eight theologians, twenty-one collegians, nineteen preps, and over one hundred academics.

The religious work of Biddle appears in a whole presbytery of thirty churches, raised up in the region round about. The professors go out and organize and take the supervision of the young preachers, whom they train and send along to supply the churches. Dr. Mattoon administered the ordinances of fourteen churches on fourteen successive Sundays, running out on Saturday and back in time for the routine of teaching during the week.

Western North Carolina furnishes a congenial soil for such church planting. In ante-bellum times it was a region of Presbyterianism and Unionism. After the war the colored members were disposed to come off by themselves and organize separately. Along this Piedmont belt reconstruction has gone on more rapidly than in the low country. The smaller plantations could be more readily adapted to the free-labor system. Then the farmers themselves were accustomed to work as the big planters were not. The colored people, too, of this region, accustomed to work by the side of the master and his sons, came thereby into contact with more civilization than did those of the great plantations, who were worked by overseers, and so are found, in general, a better material for the school and church process. And then theology does tell, even upon such masses of low-down people. A while ago the ladies of the Ladies' Missionary Society of the Presbyterian church in Charlotte were regretting that they could not have the presence of a live missionary in their meeting to awaken more interest among them. But at that same time there were in their city these two returned missionaries, Rev. Doctors Mattoon and Shedd, who could have poured ever so much light upon their meetings. They were not thought of, or, if thought of, they belonged to an ostracized class. If they had come from Africa they would not only have been treated with courtesy, but would have been honored by these same good ladies. Dr. Shedd has now gone back to that semi-enlightened country where his family, as with all missionaries abroad, will have the *élite* of foreign residents for their friends, and where their society will be courted. It was pitiable to hear that in one of those old-time Presbyterian pulpits the divinity of slavery was yet maintained, the pastor having bemoaned the depravity of the times that had overthrown one of God's institutions — the domestic — and was going on to serve others the same way. Let us learn the true cause of the overthrow of slavery. That subject was discussed by the opening sermon of the presbytery in Wilmington, N. C., during the last year, as reported to me by a northern minister who was present. The cause, according to this preacher, was the idolizing of the institution. To prove this he cited that the people hereabout kept their slaves at home and sent their sons into the war to be slaughtered, and the fact that they gave up all their money to save slavery. God must take away all idols! The Thanksgiving sermon last fall in another Presbyterian pulpit, the leading one of a southern city, as reported to me by a northern minister that heard it, declared it as one occasion of gratitude that it was as well with them as it was; "for," said he, "history does not give us another case where the rebels were not either hanged or banished. We did not suffer in either of those ways. We thank God for that. This is now our country. We ought to make it an enlightened country, one that we can love, one in which God shall be honored and obeyed."

LETTER LXXIX.

NORTH AND SOUTH. — SOME THINGS IN COMMON.

CLIFTON SPRINGS, N. Y., July 1, 1882.

1. ONE common possession is that of our English inheritance. We are of the Anglo-Saxon stock. We speak the English language. We have the common inheritance of the principles of constitutional government, of trial by jury, of *habeas corpus*, and of civil and religious liberty. We are joint heirs to the matchless English literature, and to a history that has made England the leading nation of Christendom.

2. We have had a common share in the domination, physical and political, of this country. Of the two companies chartered by James the First in 1606, the London, at Jamestown, was a success; the Plymouth, at the mouth of the Kennebec, was a failure, which the coming of the Puritans and the Pilgrims retrieved. In the subduing of successive territories there has been a constant interblending of stock. All my life I have known of this mixture in the interior and the western states. And now

as I am traveling every-whither in Dixie I am surprised to find how much it has of northern blood, how much of its business, how much of its enterprise.

3. We hold in common the glories of our revolutionary period. We share in the joys of the birth of a nation. We have the same traditions of patriotism. We have a mutual pride in Washington, Jefferson, and the Adamses, and in all the other fathers of the republic. Our national centennial gave occasion for the revival of this national feeling. Masses of our brethren who had become estranged were glad of the opportunity to share in the thrill inspired by the world's recognition of our country's greatness. Charleston has had her patriotic centennial celebration. The streets of Savannah were ablaze with loyal bunting at the celebration of the Jasper Memorial. Thousands of people met at King's Mountain, in North Carolina, to honor the revolutionary battle fought at that place. The Cowpens, in South Carolina, afforded another such occasion January 17, 1881, and, in the October following, all the country came to Yorktown to glorify the great consummation.

4. We share in the essentials of the reformed church life. The Pilgrims and the Puritans did their work from New England westward. Much of the blood by which the southern states were stocked was of the reformed quality. The Presbyterians were Puritans. The Scotch had a large share of this leavening. The Scotch and the Scotch-Irish element in this region has been large and largely influential. I am surprised to find how much of the Covenanter stock has been tucked away into the mountain and the hill country of the south. The Huguenots, who were the contribution of France to the Reformation, have had a large representation in the south.

Sixty years before the Pilgrims had landed, they had made two settlements on the coast of South Carolina which were annihilated by the persecuting power that followed them to the wilderness continent. They tried again and made a lodgment where Charleston now is, and there to this day the "Huguenot Church" abides in the integrity of character and worship. Out in the state, and in other places in the south, the Huguenots have given names to the leading families and towns, and tone and caste to society. The south has had but a small portion of foreign immigration, and so has felt less the influence of the continental views as to the Sabbath, so that the holy day seems to be more strictly observed here than at the north. The orthodoxy of the south is well known. It has had less activity in theological discussion, and so abides more in the old forms of doctrinal statement — so much so that the people are hungering for a more ethical and spiritual preaching. In the coming conflict with infidelity this theological soundness may be the late coming of Blücher to our Waterloo.

5. We have a common sympathy in Protestantism. The early French and Spanish occupation of Louisiana and in some cities of the other states has made them strong Catholic centers. But Romanism is not so generally a prevailing power in the south as in the north. The drift of later foreign immigration has made this difference. Rome's chance at the south is now not with foreigners, but with natives, the Africo-Americans, and she will make the most of that. But just here comes in our unity of Protestant views. Southern Christians are anxious lest the display and the mystery of the Romish system should captivate these simple children of nature. They are as anxious as the people of the north that the

same providence which delivered our land from the early domination of Catholic nationalities may save it from again coming under the supremacy of that spiritual despotism.

LETTER LXXX.

DEDICATION OF LIVINGSTONE HALL.

NASHVILLE, Tenn., October 31, 1882.

FROM the annual meeting at Cleveland there came down to this city, as a delegation to participate in this service, Rev. Doctors Strieby, Pike, O. H. White, Roy, and A. G. Haygood, secretary of the Slater Fund, Prof. C. C. Painter, President Ware, General C. B. Fisk, and directly from New Haven, Prof. Cyrus Northrop, to make the dedicatory address. Many local celebrities were present. Bishop Cain, of the African Methodist Episcopal Church, led in the opening devotions. The Mozart Society, made up of students and led by Prof. A. K. Spence, rendered the Hallelujah Chorus and other classical music, while Ella Shepherd, of the Jubilee Singers, aided in rendering some of the wonders of song. President Cravath made the historic statement, by which it appeared that sixty thousand dollars had been given by Mrs. Stone for the erection of a hall which was to be named after Mr. Livingstone. Bishop McTyeire, of the Methodist Episcopal Church South, extended welcome and congratulation to the educators and philanthropists who had come from afar, and greetings in the name of thousands who are to be benefited, to the elect lady by whose wisdom and bounty this elegant hall had been built.

The president, introducing Professor Northrop, said that

he represented an institution whose next commencement would be the one hundred and eighty-second, while the next of Fisk would be the seventeenth. Of the professor's oratory it can be said that it is like the song of a canary — it just sings itself. Such an example of chaste English, of masculine thought, of fervid eloquence, was a good object-lesson for Yale to set before the colleges for both races represented on this occasion. The professor urged that the nation must take hold of the national problem of education at the south. It was a masterly argument on that line. Yet for the higher education he said we must turn away from the state to personal beneficence. The American Missionary Association illustrates this. A society that has been able to call into existence and to develop to their present proportions such institutions as Fisk, Atlanta, Straight, Talladega, Berea, and Hampton, may view its own work with the highest satisfaction, for it has demonstrated the power of organized Christian charity to supply schools for the higher education, when all other forces had failed. Dr. Haygood rejoiced in the Livingstone Hall and reported $61,000,000 as given the last decade for education. As a boy he had been more thrilled with admiration for Livingstone than for any other man. This hall was a grander memorial than his tablet in Westminster. General Fisk in glowing strains sought to stimulate young men by the example of Livingstone, the weaver's son; and the young women, by that of the frugality and the beneficence of Mrs. Stone. It was fitting that to Secretary Strieby should fall the part of offering the finished structure to the Lord in dedicatory prayer, which in its grasp and glow seemed almost the words of an inspired prophet.

LETTER LXXXI.

WORK OF THE SOUTHERN CHURCHES AMONG THE NEGROES.

ATLANTA, Ga., November 10, 1882.

IT is one of the encouraging things as to moral reconstruction at the south that the old churches are beginning to take hold of the gospel work among the colored people. They find that they had made a mistake in letting go of them. The Episcopal Conference in Virginia this fall discussed the subject. The Southern Presbyterian General Assembly started a few years ago an institution at Tuscaloosa, Ala., for the training of colored ministers. I have visited the school. In a small way it is doing good work. Here and there we find a colored church of that connection. Atlanta has one under the care of Atlanta Presbytery, which raised the money for the church edifice, recently dedicated. It has an educated pastor from the Lincoln University. The Methodist Episcopal Church South has set off its colored members as "the colored Methodist Episcopal Church of America," giving them all the church property they had in use. Its General Conference has recently set to work to plant an institute for colored preachers at Augusta. One southern man has given twenty-five thousand dollars toward the enterprise, and the conference is pushing the endowment.

PERIOD X.

IN THE SOUTH, 1883-84.

Miss Willard in the South. — Secretary Dunning. — The New Birmingham. — Canon Farrar. — Concord Council. — Mountain Work. — Wesleyans and German Reformed in North Carolina. — The Georgia Association in Charleston, S. C.

LETTER LXXXII.

MISS WILLARD AND TEMPERANCE WORK IN THE SOUTH.

ATLANTA, Ga., January 15, 1883.

THE "Women's Crusade" was a burst of agony that could be endured in silence no longer. That movement has not died out; it has only changed its form. That impulse has been transformed into principle; that spasm of action, into a settled organism, instinct with life, tremulous with power — "The National Woman's Christian Temperance Union." It has spread over thirty-eight states and territories of the nation. It has its own Thirty-nine Articles, or departments of work. It is moving upon all legislatures to secure the legal requirement of temperance instruction in the schools. And the impersonation of this uprising is Miss Frances E. Willard, an orator, with womanly grace; an organizer of the Napoleonic pattern; a lecturing tourist, at a touch of whose genius state after state falls into line across to the Golden Gate and down to the Gulf. May the Lord make her our Miriam, our Deborah, to sing the song of triumph over the Pharaoh, the Jabin of the liquor despotism.

She has just been organizing the Georgia Union, auxiliary to the National. Her great speech was on "Personal Liberty." Rev. Dr. C. A. Evans, pastor of the First Methodist Episcopal Church South, and ex-confederate general, remarked to me his great delight with that address. When she first came to this city, two years ago, at a large Sunday night union service, Governor Colquitt followed her address with a hearty endorsement, saying that it was well known that the south, even the southern Methodists, had been very conservative upon the matter of woman's appearing upon the platform; and then in his gushing way he pronounced a benison upon her. Last fall, coming south, I fell in at Louisville upon the annual meeting of the Woman's Christian Temperance Union. It was a glorious sight. A large church filled with noble women was a-flutter with silken Stars and Stripes; and almost every state in the Union was represented by its delegation seated together, with its name emblazoned across its great patriotic shield. And so this blessed cause is helping to grow over the ugly gash cut into the tree of our national life. I counted it an honor to be invited to address that body.

A year ago I found the Lone Star state surrendering to this lone woman. Like a true conqueror, she had her campaign well laid out. At Little Rock, Ark., falling into her line of advance, I found her printed scheme for Texas. It had appointments for every day in February except two, and those were scattered all over that whilom republic so as to take in the principal cities, and so necessitating night and day travel over these green roads, rough as corduroy by the recent floods. Politicians on the stump rarely accomplish a greater feat of canvassing. So runs the list: Marshall, Jefferson, Clarkville, Paris, Sherman, Dennison, McKinney, Dallas, Fort Worth, Cleburne, Wacco, Austin, San Antonio, Houston, Galveston · and there are two appointments for each place, with three in several. Following her at Paris, Dennison, and Austin, and overtaking her at San Antonio, I have had opportunity to observe the impression left behind. At every place she is spoken of in the highest terms. The secular papers advertise her fully and report her fairly with much praise. She is entertained by the best of families. She secures union meetings. She is attended by her secretary, Miss Gordon, of Boston, who also takes a hand in the addresses, burning alcohol in her talks to children. Miss Willard's influence is not that of a stray shower; but, organizing as she goes along, it is that of new fountains. It is to be hoped that these will be such as is that of the river San Antonio, which at the city of that name, where I overtook her, bursts forth from the rock a very torrent, watering the city, irrigating the plain around, and turning mills. Nor was that campaign enough to satisfy this fair conqueror. From Galveston she leaped across the Gulf into New Orleans, and thence marched up through Mississippi, Alabama, and Georgia.

Miss Willard is true to the colored people. In our city she visited and addressed the students of Atlanta University. The foremost lady of Savannah, who entertained her, imbibing the spirit of her leader and becoming the head of the local union, visited our colored church there to inspire their temperance meeting by her presence, proffering the pastor all helpful coöperation. Precisely this was the process at Charleston. At Paris, Texas, our pastor's wife, the president of the colored Woman's Christian Temperance Union, handed me an autograph letter which Miss Willard had sent her, regretting that a washout had prevented her from going to speak to them. At Austin she addressed the colored people. At Little Rock her work must have done not a little to confirm the people of the fifth ward of that city, which alone of all its wards had voted local option and had put out of its portion of the municipality every one of the several saloons. And the great majority of the voters in that ward are colored people.[1]

LETTER LXXXIII.

THE NEW BIRMINGHAM. — ALABAMA ANNIVERSARIES. — SECRETARY DUNNING. — CANON FARRAR.

BIRMINGHAM, Ala., February 12, 1883.

RARELY is a new-world town more true to the idea of its old-world namesake than this. Here is a nice city of iron and coal and of iron-works and cotton factories. Twelve years ago it was a gullied red-clay farm; now it is a place of eleven thousand people, with its magnificent courthouse, its system of water-supply of two million gallons from a reservoir on the mountain, its sewers going in, its telephone exchange, its fire department, its gas lamps, and its telegraph business of eight thousand dollars per annum. The town lies in a valley that is four miles wide. In the mountain on the west is the coal in five-foot seams, in the eastern range is iron, and both are of inexhaustible supply. Here are five iron furnaces that employ fifteen hundred men and turn out five hundred tons of pig-

---

[1] Texas, in July, 1887, voted on an amendment to the constitution, and defeated it by a majority of seventy-five thousand. But the temperance people, nothing daunted, are renewing the contest, and will yet carry it.

iron a day. Here is a rolling-mill that works four hundred and fifty men with twenty-four puddling furnaces. Then a half-dozen iron-works for the manufacture of engines, boilers, and all sorts of machinery. Then three or four companies for mining coal and iron. The Louisville & Nashville has here general shops that employ one thousand men. Then come the planing-mills, flouring-mills, brick machines, furniture factories, two banks, and one hundred and fifty mercantile houses. One cotton-mill is already running, and another is projected with a northern capital of a quarter of a million. Here is the crossing of the two great trunk lines of railway, the Louisville & Nashville, reaching on by way of Montgomery and Mobile, and the Alabama Great Southern, which is a link in the Cincinnati Southern, which, branching at Meridian, runs on to New Orleans and by Vicksburg on to Texas. Then the Georgia Pacific from Atlanta crosses here, going on to the Mississippi.

Nor is there a neglect in the educational line. Public schools for the colored as well as for the white are run nine months in the year. Three of the Talladega students are teaching the colored youth. The several denominations are represented here by their churches, the last to be set up being the Congregational. Canon Farrar thinks that the last chapter of Paul's letter to the church at Rome does not belong to that Epistle, but rather to the one sent to the Ephesians, because, as he says, "It is strange that Saint Paul should salute twenty-six people in a church which he had never visited, and address them in terms of peculiar intimacy and affection, when he salutes only one or two in churches which he had founded." If the queen's chaplain had only been a home missionary superintendent, he could see very well how the apostle should send salutations to so many of the dear Christian friends of the several churches which he had organized, who by their enterprise had rushed into that Roman capital. I was surprised to find, upon my first visit to this wide-awake western-like town, that all the Congregational people there, whom I had already known and loved, had come in from our several churches and schools in Alabama as mechanics of a half-dozen different trades to build up their own fortunes along with that of the new city. The young Talladega pastor on his first day found a dozen of his old friends. So that either of us in a previous apostolic letter might have made out a list of the names of those to be saluted almost equal to that of the great apostle who wrote to his old friends then settled at Rome.

TALLADEGA, March 23, 1883.

The Alabama anniversaries have just been held in this place. It was a revelation to these southern Congregationalists that there was such a Sunday-School Society as that one in Boston, and that it had such a wide-awake Secretary as Rev. A. E. Dunning has proved himself to be, the first Secretary who had ever come down to attend an association in Dixie. He preached the opening sermon of the Sunday-school convention, rousing us by his apostolic fervor. He nourished the Sunday-school by his words. He was given Sunday evening to set forth the blessed work proposed by his Society. As it was Easter Sunday, at the morning service he was greatly delighted with a spontaneous real negro spiritual appropriate to the occasion. It was this: —

> Dust, dust an' ashes fly over on my grave,
> Dust, dust an' ashes fly over on my grave,
> An' de Lord shall bear my spirit home,
> An' de Lord shall bear my spirit home.

> Dey crucified my Saviour, an' nailed him to the cross,
> Dey crucified my Saviour, an' nailed him to the cross,
> An' de Lord shall bear my spirit home,
> An' de Lord shall bear my spirit home.
>
> He rose, he rose, he rose from the dead,
> He rose, he rose, he rose from the dead,
> An' de Lord shall bear my spirit home,
> An' de Lord shall bear my spirit home.

On the last night we ordained by council a young man of this college. He traced his conversion to a couple of the early lady workers here, and paid a high tribute to his Presbyterian mistress, who had taught her colored children to read, had made them learn the catechism, had kept them steadily at church and Sunday-school, and was so particular about their keeping the Sabbath that upon their getting home from church, she would change their Sunday rig for linsey-woolsey so that they would be ashamed to appear on the streets. With uplifted eye and faltering voice, he said that he believed that if there was a good woman in heaven, it was she. I have heard his brother tell the same story and then go on reeling off the catechism until I said, That is enough.

LETTER LXXXIV.

THE CONCORD NATIONAL COUNCIL. — ITS BREADTH IN TERRITORY AND IN RACES REPRESENTED.

CONCORD, N. H., October 15, 1883.

IT was a congress of an ocean-bound ecclesiastical republic. Its delegates came from the Aroostook of the north-east and from Puget Sound of the far north-west; from the Red River of the north and from the Gulf of the south. The veteran from the new north-west, whose foreign mission field had turned into one of the home-mission sort, had found his first leisure after a service of forty-five years to return to the states, and that only because the Northern Pacific had reached him in time to bring him back over the Rocky Mountains. The city of the Golden Gate from her back door had sent a silver-tongued pastor across the continent. The deep interior joined hands with the solid east. The south, from New Orleans to the federal capital, was there in right hearty allegiance. The germ of this system, which for a long time rested in the conservatory spot of New England, has now spread "throughout the mainland from sea to sea." As a tide rising above its native metes and bounds, it first crept up along all the Presbyterian creeks and coves until, flushing them, it overflowed into its broad expanse. So far as denominational interest is concerned, it did seem that these were the Lord's foolish people thus to pour so much of their Puritan blood into other ecclesiastical veins; but as relates to a grand Christian development, the turning of this life current of New England ideas and theology into the stream of the national life has been a wondrous gain. He that will lose his life shall save it. The New England zone is now broadening itself out over the south. My fellow-townsman at Atlanta, Ga., Senator Joseph E. Brown, says that Yale and Harvard are molding the whole country now. By these two institutions he means the principles which they and all other such represent. An ex-confederate officer chided me because we of the northwest did not fall in with the south. I confessed that we of that region had felt not a little of sympathy with them, because we, too, had been subjugated by those same Yankees, only that we were vanquished by their ideas and they by their bayonets. And now, Colonel, said I, you will have to take their ideas too.

Of the five races of the human family, this council represented four of them: the Caucasian, the Mongolian, the African, the American. The white race was conspicuous. The Mongolian, of the Pacific slope, with its nineteen schools, its forty teachers, its two thousand eight hundred and eighty-three scholars, and with its five or six hundred who have turned from Confucius to Christ, stood there in the person of its California substitute. For the American, stood up his missionary from Fort Berthold, on the Upper Missouri. The African race had three of her sons upon that floor, educated Christian ministers, who were welcomed to their seats, and whose voice in speech and prayer and song was joyfully heard. The people of the more favored race seemed to look upon those of the other three not as wards of charity, but as brothers in the one family whose Father is the Creator of all. And the Association, which by the Congregational churches had been put in trust with the spiritual welfare of these three depressed families that dwell within our borders, stood there to give account of its stewardship and to be cheered, in the renewal of its Christly work, with a hearty "Well done." In the enjoyment of such a fellowship how does all manifestation of the caste spirit stand out as a censure upon the Creator and a libel upon our common humanity! And how does this gathering of messengers of the churches of like faith and polity and of these four race affinities from the length and breadth of the continent for fellowship in doctrine, work, and experience, confirm the wisdom and necessity of this National Council as a bond of union and as an instrumentality for propagating the kingdom of God in our country and throughout the world.

LETTER LXXXV.

MOUNTAIN WORK.

WILLIAMSBURG, Ky., March 20, 1884.
THIS place is the center of the new series of missionary operations in the mountains of Kentucky. It is the old-time county seat of Whitley County, on the Cumberland River, in the south-east part of the state. The country is healthful and abounds in coal and the best of hard woods, and is good for fruit and farming. When I first came here I found at one mill eight million feet of seasoned walnut, and at another six million feet, waiting for the coming of the railway to carry it off. The logs are floated down from all the affluents above. The little sleepy old town has waked up from its doze of seventy years, during which time it had not built a meeting-house, and is now putting on the thrift of a western town. Two years ago Rev. A. A. Myers came in from Michigan, finding not a northern man here; but, going to work, he gathered a church, and then got under way a project for a "church house." Going ahead, and saying, "Come on, boys!" he led the people in getting the stone for the foundation and the logs for the lumber. And we now find a beautiful sanctuary, acknowledged to be the best in the mountains, thirty-two by fifty feet, with a tower, stained-glass windows, and interior finishing to match, costing in all $3,025, and not a dollar of this came from the north.

Meantime the Williamsburg Academy had come along. The time had come for the dedication of the twin institutions, and so on the last Sabbath and Monday they were duly set apart for their Christian uses. President Fairchild and Professor Dodge, of Berea, and Rev. Doctors W.

H. Ward and James Powell, of New York, and the superintendent, were here to join in the solemnities. Wishing to extend the influence of our metropolitan visitors and to make them somewhat acquainted with this mountain scheme, we had planned for them a series of meetings in three or four places where our work is taking hold. So we had them roughing it at Woodbine and Barbourville and Pleasant View and Jellico, closing with a rousing service in the colored church in Knoxville.

With great enthusiasm Mr. Myers espoused the temperance cause, and now the public sale of liquor has been driven out of the county. He has also built, or has under plan, five other edifices, which are to be used for church and high school purposes. Three are along the new line of the Louisville & Nashville road to Knoxville. It is now clearer than ever before that the solution of this mountain evangelization as to method is in the union of the church and school process. This will develop character that will stand. If it were not for the color question [1] we could soon capture and captivate the people of these mountains; and I suppose the same might have been said of the Saviour and the mountain people of his land. Yet He chose the slower and surer principle and process. Our organic testimony in these anti-caste institutions is of more importance than the securing of a much larger area of native mind for a training that leaves out the brotherhood of man in Jesus Christ.[2]

[1] One year later three or four colored young people came in, whereupon there was a stampede, by which the number of pupils was brought down from one hundred and twenty to forty. The academy went steadily along. Gradually the scholars worked back, and now for the year ending June, 1886, the catalogue enrolls two hundred and twenty scholars.

[2] On six consecutive days in December, 1887, six meeting-houses were dedicated on this field along the line of a new railroad opened, those of South Williamsburg, Pleasant View, Jellico, Rockhold, Woodbine, and Corbin. One young man of the

LETTER LXXXVI.

MORE MOUNTAIN WORK.

GRAND VIEW, Tenn., June 18, 1884.
AND it is a "grand view," indeed. I first came to it last March. Leaving the rail at Sparta, on the west side of the Cumberland Plateau, I had climbed and crossed it for a distance of fifty-six miles. Through deep mud, thrice dipping water in our buggy at the fording of swollen streams, and thrice replacing small bridges before they could be crossed, and climbing up and down the rocky mountain roads, at the end of a dark and raw day we came to turn in at the house of Squire Abbott for the night, knowing nothing of the view round about. Stepping out in the bright morning upon the upper veranda, the transcendent vision opens on me as a surprise. I am on the crest of the Waldron's Ridge, eight hundred feet above the five-mile-wide Tennessee Valley below. I take in a bird's-eye view of the best farms of the state. I see the trains of the Cincinnati Southern running up and down their track in the valley, their plumes of steam falling far

mountains was also ordained by council during that campaign. The local churches and the ministers, Superintendent Myers and Pastor Jenkins, were assisted by Reverends C. J. Ryder, A. F. Beard, D.D., G. S. Pope, S. E. Lathrop, and Joseph E. Roy. And just about that time a fine building for church and academic purposes was dedicated at Pleasant Hill in the mountains of east Tennessee. The church dedicated at Rockhold was within a stone's-throw of the old farm-house where Rev. J. C. Richardson, in 1857, had been seized and bound by the postmaster, Charles Rockhold, and his two sons, and was called The Richardson Memorial Church, the bell within its tower having been procured by the widow of that missionary among friends at Perry Center, N. Y. Such is the revenge of love. The only person remaining in the neighborhood to bear the name of Rockhold is Green Rockhold, who had been the only slave of the family, and who was the only man in the neighborhood to speak a word of approbation to the Elliots for delivering the missionary; while the three Elliot brothers and their families remain to be influential members in the new Congregational church and society.

behind before we hear the report of the signal. I see the little narrow gauge at my feet, climbing up the face of the Ridge. I take in the course of the river in its windings, traced by the fog hanging over it and shimmering in the sun, a veritable river in the air, with a pillar of smoke streaming above from the occasional passing steamer. In the distant east, over a series of smaller mountains, called the "wash-board," I see rising on the horizon the lofty ranges over in the Carolinas; and down fifty miles to Chattanooga I find the Lookout Mountain looming up in view.

At the site of that historic city by the Tennessee River, that mountain is cleft asunder from Waldron's Ridge, which runs on up in its almost perpendicular front for seventy miles, to the gap that nature made for the passage of the Emery River and the great railroad which the Queen City drops down to the Crescent City for a binding of the Union. Singularly the great plateau at its lower end for fifty miles is divided in the middle for the beautiful Sequatchee Valley, whose river-head is in Grassy Cove, a bowl of three by four miles, dropped down into the mountain surface, the Sequatchee literally finding its way out by running under the mountain for several miles to the head of the valley. All this country, covered with timber, is underlaid with coal and iron. This narrow gauge climbs up the face of these southern palisades to get over in back to such mines with the intent of crossing the plateau. At Dayton, Rockwood, and other such places on the railroad in the valley, the flaming furnaces are bringing together the fuel and the ore. Fruit is the specialty of this region. The plateau falls to the era of sandstone. Its soil is thin and poor, but, taken in its pristine state and treated fairly as to fertilization and rotation of crops, it does well in the cereals and in the grasses; so that with the extended mountain range it excels in the raising of stock, cattle, hogs, and sheep. Valley farmers drive their herds up here to be fattened through the summer under the care of herdsmen. But the principal commodity seems to be health. The common saying is: "Our country is poor, but it is healthy." Since the war northern people have been sifting themselves in here, and also sifting themselves out. At Grand View thirty northern families have made their homes, the most of them for the benefit secured from the climate. In Texas the first question asked of a newcomer is: "What did you do?" or, "What was your name before you came here?" The natural query here as to a newcomer is: "What was the matter with you?" The native citizens round about and back in the mountains get on well with the Yankees. An academy has been taken hold of here.[1]

And so at Sherwood among the mountains of this state on the Nashville & Chattanooga Railroad, fifty miles north of the latter city, another academy and church are under way. The town was named for ex-Lieutenant-Governor Sherwood, of Minnesota, who settled there himself with a colony largely by way of that state from New England. Then Scott County, lying upon the Cumberland Plateau, where the Cincinnati Southern crosses, has loomed up into a missionary prominence that has secured for it the sobriquet, "The state of Scott." The six stations of the railway within its borders have all been occupied by Sunday-school, preaching, and temperance operations, and this is only a base line of a movement into

---

[1] Rev. C. B. Riggs, a nephew of Dr. Riggs, of Constantinople, is now in charge of the academy, which has come on to have one hundred and twenty-six students, and of the church which he has organized — the whole a beautiful specimen of what may be done and ought to be done more and more in these mountains.

the regions beyond. Whereas there had formerly been in the county twenty-seven saloons to two Sunday-schools, now there are twenty-five Sunday-schools to two saloons. The Congregational Sunday-School and Publishing Society, which in more distant parts of the south has coöperated with the American Missionary Association in furnishing Sunday-school literature, has been doing the same in Scott, sending also a colporter for two or three months and detailing Secretary Dunning for a special visit. The headquarters of that work are at Robbins, whose resident proprietor, Captain A. J. C. Robbins, as a contractor, had built the three hundred thousand dollar tunnel near by bearing his name, and who, from having been one of John Morgan's thieves and an unbeliever, is now in the office of a deacon, to which I had the pleasure of ordaining him, as loyal to his country, now, as he is to his church. The following letter which Dr. Dunning received from him is as true as it is characteristic : [2]

Up to last fall I was a "heathen and an infidel," or rather, made no profession of religion. Having been for seventeen years a rough railroad contractor, and all my associations of the rougher kind, I took little thought about religion ; and it was only on one or two of my trips home, when my little daughter Ernie took me to the "new Sunday-school," that I commenced thinking about it. I professed religion in September last ; and now we have a little church organization of seventeen members, and I am a deacon in the church and superintendent of the Sunday-school. The church is Congregational in its belief. So you see we are progressing. Much interest is manifested here, and our Sunday-school is on a firm basis.

No, I do not shrink from Christ, but glory in him and know that he is my dearest, best friend. God is good to us ; and you can not realize

---

[2] The county has now three Congregational churches. It has had the ministerial services of Mr. Rufus Taft and of Rev. W. E. Barton. And now Rev. G. Stanley Pope, many years at the head of Tougaloo University, Mississippi, is located on that field as superintendent; his familiarity with southern people and his genius for work will make him a greatly effective man in those mountains.

how much we all thank you and your people for the kind interest you have taken in us.

We have just started a ten months' school. It is the first one ever started, to run that long at a time, in the history of Scott County. Still there are so many here who can not read or write, and who know not that Jesus is the Son of God and Saviour of mankind. It makes one sick at heart to see how it is. But light is breaking from the east, and I hope the time will soon come when we will be enjoying the " perfect day."

The old stage-road from Louisville to Nashville crossed the plateau above this point. On my first trip passing over that stage line I was entertained in two ancient houses which had been stage stands, both of which, as the tradition goes, General Jackson had honored as a guest. In the diversion of travel by railways the four-horse stage has gone down to be the great United States buck-board, which is apt to break down and be exchanged for the dashing mail-boys on horseback, who cross over the plateau every day both ways. Along this line on the central portion of the plateau are the villages, Pleasant Hill, Pomona, Howard Springs, Crosville, and Northville. And this line has been taken up for schools and churches. At Pleasant Hill, Rev. Benjamin Dodge has an academy and a church; and at Pomona, a church. It is wonderful how he is getting hold of the people. It is all by his making himself one of them in sympathy and interest.

LETTER LXXXVII.

THE WESLEYANS AND THE GERMAN REFORMED IN NORTH CAROLINA.

SALISBURY, N. C., September 15, 1884.
WORKING along back from New York to Atlanta I drop off and inquire for the Salisbury Prison, and learn that when the Yankees came in here they burned down the old ware-house which had served that purpose, and that the site of the old pen had been built over. So disappear the material signs of that contest, but not the wounds of hearts and homes. I find in this west end of the old north state the remnant of a Wesleyan Methodist conference, for whose people, before and since the war, nothing has been done in any special way for education. Before the war, as will be remembered by old abolitionists, Rev. Daniel Worth, a native of the state and in it at one time a justice of the peace, engaged in preaching under the American Missionary Association, was arrested and thrown into prison at Greensboro', out of which he was brought only by the raising among the friends at the north of three thousand dollars to cover his bonds. He had eight little churches. The bitterness of feeling then engendered against him and his people still abides, so that these Wesleyans are yet called "nigger equalizers." In that early day one of the preachers was seized by the throat in the pulpit and hurried off to prison. Other deeds of violence have been suffered by them. Many of their best families after the war worked out west. They desire to have a school of their own, as they do not feel free to go to the institutions of the aristocratic people who, having been secessionists, look down upon

them, as they believe. In spite of their disabilities they have come on to have a conference of seven or eight hundred members, a dozen ministers and as many plain meeting-houses, with three times that number of appointments, but nearly all of them in country places. All of their preachers have to support themselves in part on their farms or otherwise. They were Union people during the war and are all now of one political party. They go strong for temperance and are opposed to secret societies, having the courage to preach as they believe. I had the pleasure of attending their conference. I enjoyed it greatly. In order to secure an educational institution and some supplemental aid for their preachers, they raised the question of putting their conference into connection with our National Council, retaining their present title or changing it slightly. They were encouraged that such aid would be given again on condition that their schools and churches would be open to colored scholars and members. To this last condition they agreed. But in the end they decided to remain in their present standing.

On that North Carolina slope of the mountain range I came across a classis of German reformed churches. From 1750 on to the Revolution they were coming down from Pennsylvania, settling in the Indian country as it then was. Some of them were in as patriots at the battle of King's Mountain. They early set up their own churches, relying upon the mother state for their ministers. As early as 1830 they had their North Carolina classis. But, like the Welsh, adhering exclusively to service in their own language, they have always been losing their young people, and so to a considerable extent have become absorbed in the other denominations. But still they have held on their way. Their native language long since passed into disuse. Their classis now numbers thirty-one churches and two thousand two hundred and ninety-two members, and twelve ministers, who each serve two or three or four churches, and who largely support themselves by farming and other occupation. Their people are thoroughly respectable and influential, and many of them are well-to-do. They went largely for the Union; they are strong for temperance; they are decidedly evangelical, having separated themselves in 1852 from the General Synod on account of the sacramentarian drift of that body. After the war they were re-united with it, though remaining as strong as ever in their doctrinal position. Rev. G. W. Walker, D.D., who has been on his field in Guilford County for forty years, is one of the grandest of men in ability, spirit, and courage for moral reform. Not a few of the Union men did he help to keep out of the rebel conscription.

Thirty years ago this people, feeling the need of a Christian college, in order to self-preservation, undertook to found one at Newton. It was chartered as Catawba College. When I first heard of it, I thought that its name smacked of a possible love for the wine of that grape. But I find in its catalogue that in the town, the county seat of Catawba County, "the sale of intoxicating liquors is prohibited by chartered rights and by public opinion." "Every student, before entering school, is required to pledge himself not to keep or use intoxicating liquors as a beverage." It turns out that Catawba was the name of an Indian tribe which gave name to the fine river that runs through the county, and that this is the native home of that noble grape for whose ripening our northern seasons so often fall short. Before the war a subscription of $30,000 was secured toward an endowment. But this was swept down by that torrent of blood. Though the institution once graduated a college class and has been preparing young men for entering sophomore and junior classes elsewhere, it is now pretending only to do high school and normal work. In this line it has been doing a great deal of good among the young people of its own churches and of that region. If it were only better equipped, it would serve the people of the mountain slope grandly; and it would develop the needed supply of ministers. For the present needs it has an ample supply of buildings. The president is Rev. J. C. Clapp, D.D., who, growing up in the region here, was prepared for Amherst College, where he was graduated in the class behind that of his friend, the Rev. William Hayes Ward, D.D. He is a noble man, and is assisted by one professor and two ladies, who also join the professor in serving four or five of their churches in circuits of long Sabbath-day journeys. Going north to solicit endowment among the reformed people, and failing of success, he called upon his old friend the editor, through whom the matter was brought up of an alliance with the American Missionary Association and with its supporting denomination. As a result, I had the pleasure of visiting the college and of enjoying a sacramental occasion in a sort of two days' camp-meeting with the president. I was delighted with the intelligence and character and sound evangelical faith of these followers of Zwingli in the mountain region of Carolina. Dr. Strieby, coming south, also moved by affinities of blood and of history, dropped off to attend their annual meeting of classis and to enjoy a rare fellowship. Their timidity in accepting our condition that the institution should be open to any worthy colored student who should apply, broke off the negotiation.

LETTER LXXXVIII.

THE GEORGIA ASSOCIATION IN SOUTH CAROLINA.

CHARLESTON, S. C., November 17, 1884.

It has two churches in this state, and so came to hold its annual meeting with the Plymouth Church of this city. Besides the routine of business and of papers and discussions, we had a visit from Dr. James Powell. He led off on the topic of revivals. He gave us his fine lecture, "Over the Sea," and preached a glowing sermon before the communion. His theme was The Apostle Paul's Retrospect and Prospect, from the text, "I have fought the good fight." At its conclusion, with entire spontaneity, in the midst of the great congregation, a low plaintive strain was heard, but soon it was a volume of song rolling along : —

"Don't you think I'll make a soldier?
Don't you think I'll make a soldier of the cross?"

The afternoon was fading into twilight, fitting well the mellow atmosphere of the occasion ; and the striking up of that weird voice was like that of the lonely songster of the early dawn soon to be followed by the rapture of the morning concert. In the songs rendered by local choirs to illustrate his oft-repeated lecture on "Slave Music," surely Dr. Powell never found before so exquisite a rendering of the idea and ecstasy of those rhythmic gushes : —

"Yes, we think you'll make a soldier!
Secret prayer will make you a soldier of the cross."

The Rev. A. H. Missledine, pastor of the ancient Circular Congregational Church of this city, appeared and joined our body, taking part in its proceedings. He also brought with him from his church two or three fraternal delegates. It is a parental interest which the old church of nearly two hundred years takes in this Plymouth, which brought over from it more than one hundred members. Their fellowship was reciprocated by the Association, which sent Reverend Messrs. Lathrop and Roy to preach for them on the Lord's day. The body took Saturday afternoon for an excursion upon a steamer to Mount Pleasant, Sullivan's Island, and Fort Sumter. It was a sign of the times that many of the visitors who had been slaves were seen inspecting the remains of Fort Sumter.

At the closing meeting the venerated, sweet-voiced senior bishop of the African Methodist Episcopal Church, Dr. Payne, was present. The prayer he offered was a benediction. It was very touching as he alluded to the time when, having departed from his first love, he was led one morning to enter the Circular Church of that his native city to be brought back to his Saviour by a sermon from the pastor, a New England man, the Rev. Benjamin Palmer. It was this that made him love Congregationalism. Naming with gratitude the early secretaries and treasurer of the American Missionary Association, he said that he was the first person to suggest to them the need of such a church among the freedmen of Charleston. In 1834, as he was teaching school among the free negroes, he was driven out of the city and up north because of his advertising the higher branches he would teach. That was not to be allowed.

PERIOD XI.

IN THE SOUTH, 1885.

Itinerary from Austin to Corpus Christi. — Black Men and Big Pastures in Texas. — Negroes in the New Orleans Exposition. — Grant's Canal Caving in.

LETTER LXXXIX.

ITINERARY FROM AUSTIN TO CORPUS CHRISTI.

JANUARY 4, Sunday. — Assisted in organizing in the Tillotson Institute at Austin a church of twenty-one members. Lord's Supper. Prof. W. L. Gordon's two children baptized.

January 5, Monday. — At Austin depot. Waited for delayed train five hours to eight P.M.

January 6, Tuesday. — Arrived in San Antonio at one A.M. Departed for Flatonia at eight A.M., arriving at noon. Preached at night for pastor T. E. Hilson, whose second child was baptized, as the first had been by the same hand at the dedication in Luling, his alternate church.

January 7, Wednesday. — Up at four and off to Luling, arriving at daylight. Off then by livery rig, forty-five miles to Riddleville.

January 8, Thursday. — On to Helena, fifteen miles. Rode out with freedman, three miles, to our Colony Church. Lectured at night for Pastor Thompson.

January 9, Friday. — Half a day of writing. Visited at another freedman's home, taking supper. Preached at night.

January 10, Saturday. — Brother Thompson, with another colored man and myself, started for Corpus, eighty miles, reaching Goliad, thirty-five miles, at night. We were entertained at Pastor T. Benson's.

January 11, Sunday. — In the morning, Sunday-school, preaching, and communion. At night, preaching. Conferring all day, between times, and being called upon even after retiring at night.

January 12, Monday. — Up and off before daylight, without breakfast. But Mrs. Benson had provided for us a grand lunch-box that lasted us three for the two days through to Corpus. No place on the way to put up; no chance to buy eatables. Our "boss" had planned to reach the halfway spot on the Popolota for camping. The day wore away, and it was ten o'clock before we came to the halting-place. For the last three hours brother Thompson led the way, lantern in hand, splashing through the mud and water. We turned under a live-oak, took out and fed the jaded horses, and ate our snack, and committed ourselves to the heavenly Father, and at eleven o'clock turned in for the night, brother Thompson on the ground under the hack, and brother Eding and I in the hack, doubled like a couple of jackknives into four feet square of space, and all being of a color. By our side the ponies through the night crunched their corn, and, by turns, we jumped up to drive off the cows from stealing their hay.

January 13, Tuesday. — Up and off by daybreak. We camped for breakfast lunch. We camped for dinner lunch. As we consumed the fragments, how we did bless Mrs. Benson! When, at her own table, we had praised her baking and cooking, she responded: "Oh, I learned that at Talladega College." Then I had to tell Dr. Strieby's story of the native preacher who thanked him for the good wife who had been trained in one of the American Missionary Association schools, saying that he had gotten more than he had anticipated — a good cook and housekeeper. On, on we trudged through the heavy mud. Night had come, and we were yet seven miles from Corpus, and, as we had been fearing, the cold "wet norther" that had been drizzling upon us all day, at last broke upon us. Again brother Thompson was on the lead, lantern in hand, through the slush, though he had walked more than half the way through the day. The black-waxy mud was heavy for the wheels, and slippery for the poor old freedman ponies that had no shoes. Pastor J. W. Strong, who for four years has manfully held this extreme south-western outpost of Congregationalism, having learned of our approach from a dashing country rider, came along in the dark, one mile out to meet us, in Oriental style. After our salaams, he galloped back to town to make the final arrangements for our entertainment. It was now 8.30 P.M., too late for the preaching, and for once the preacher was glad that the storm had kept the people away from the appointment. But the next night they made it up, and the preacher tried to make it up, too. When Mr. Thompson brought me down six years ago we came straight through by fording, belly-deep to the horses, across the reef, three miles long, that forms the nexus between the Nueces Bay and the Corpus Christi Bay. On either side was deep water or miring sand. Once since that he has had to *tote* his passengers out on his back. The reef has been washed out in spots. Lo! this time we went up around the head of the bay, ten miles farther. Brother Thompson claims that he can endure such jaunts without wear or much weariness because he is so abstemious as not to drink tea or coffee nor to eat meat. And everybody knows him to be a true, pure, and high-minded Christian minister, who, though he has had but little schooling, has been so taught of God in the Word, that after these eleven years in the same parish at Helena he is yet confided in, there, as an able pulpit teacher. In old times his people were Presbyterians. Blood will tell, and doctrine too.

LETTER XC.

ROMISH PRE-OCCUPATION — BLACK MEN "RISING." — BIG PASTURES. — IRELAND'S GRIEVANCE GROWING UP HERE.

CORPUS CHRISTI, Texas, January 15, 1885.
THE sacred name of this city indicates the religious enthusiasm of the Spaniards who once held claim to a large part of our continent. The City of Mexico has a street named for the Holy Ghost; and so it uses nearly all of the holy titles. Such is the nomenclature of the whole Pacific coast. These names suggest the big job which our English-speaking Protestantism has had, and still has before it, to engross and assimilate the continent. For now, in the manifest destiny of Providence, with our railroads, our national treaties, our missions, and the leavening influence of our Republic all at work upon the remnant of Mexico, it is only a question of time when that whole country shall become a trophy to English-speaking Protestantism.

Texas is also taking a hand in the "negro problem." And the negro, all unmindful of the wrinkling of the white man's brow over the question, is working away at his part of the same. He is putting himself in condition to command respect. On our overland journey of one hundred and seventy-five miles from the last railroad on the north of this city, we passed the ranch of Joe Brothers, who, my driver said, is worth $20,000; and who, having managed his mistress' business in the old times, has "since freedom" in part supported his master's family. Another, mine host, with a great name, Gabriel Washington, must be worth well on to $10,000 in lands and stock. Of two large farmers in our church in Paris, both deacons, one, mine host, told me that a few years ago, meeting an old neighbor, he was thus accosted : "Well, Solomon, how are you getting along now?" "Quite well." "Not so well," said he, "as under your old master; I can see starvation in your eye." "Not so," said the ex-chattel, "I have sixty acres of as good land as there is in Texas, all paid for; I have fifteen hundred pounds of 'meat' all cured; I have six hundred bushels of corn in the crib; and when I want beef, I have only to shoot one down out of my herd." In the "Colony" Church at Helena on my way I found mine host one of several well-to-do farmers, with a nine months' school, and a pure and faithful pastor. Of course these are exceptional cases. The masses of colored people are very ignorant and low down.

"Who was that man that got out of the hack?" was a question I heard on the way with its answer, "He's the nigger preacher." If the query had been put to me, I could have answered, He's a man who is not above his title nor his work. That title does n't hurt him. When he was pastor of the Plymouth Church of Chicago, he was called a "nigger preacher." *The Savannah News* has repeatedly called him "a colored preacher." The only insult that he has ever received in seven years' travel at the south was at a Texas hotel table a year ago. But coming this time to the same hotel he heard from a colored man that the offenders had said to him, "The gentleman was insulted, and we are sorry for it." So the traveler is "optimistic" still.

From Texarkana, in the north-east corner, it is eight hundred and sixty-nine miles by rail to El Paso in the north-west corner, and five hundred and ninety-four to Laredo in the south-west, while by rail from Orange in the south-east to El Paso, it is nine hundred and fifty-three miles. Texas has now six thousand miles of rail, and of this all but one thousand miles has been built in the last ten years. Robert West's "Empire of the Southwest" must be seen to be appreciated. It is easy to write down 1,500,000 head of cattle as the annual export, worth $50,000,000. But to realize these figures you must ride by rail for some hundreds of miles among the grazing herds, and then strike off overland, as I did, for one hundred and seventy-five miles, every mile of the way through "pastures," except the first twenty-two and except the passage through the only two towns on the way. When Bryant, fifty years ago, came out to visit his brother at Princeton, Ill., he sang of our western prairies as "the unreaped fields, boundless and beautiful." You would think that these were still "boundless," only that every five or ten miles you have to alight to open a gate through a barb-wire fence that marks the domain of some cattle king. "The cattle upon a thousand hills" no longer seems a poetic license. They are all here. There is one of these pastures that has 60,000 acres and 37,000 head of cattle.

But here again is Ireland's grievance growing apace — land monopoly. The grazing land is pretty much all shut up. This not only keeps out the new settlers from this new country with its rich soil and a delightful climate, but it squeezes out the old settlers. The cattle kings, taking in their great areas, enclose the actual residents, who for years have been farming and raising stock. Shut in, annoyed in numberless ways, their cattle branded into the great herd, they must sell out and go. Yet none but the big men will buy, and so they make their own terms, and the smaller men flee from the meshes of the barbed wire, leaving their homesteads to fall into disuse and decay save as grazing ground. Not a few counties are thus decreasing in population. A lone settler told me that once they had a church of sixty members, a school and a store, but now all are gone. Having lost his negroes, he came in there after the war to make up his loss in stock. But of this he had lost a hundred head that had been worked into the big drove. Villages once flourishing are dried up in the same way. Cattle are taking the place of people, who would pay taxes, make society, build school-houses and churches. It was this crowding of the small farmers and the cutting off of the cowboy's occupation that led to the frenzy of fence cutting, whereby hundreds of thousands of cattle were turned loose. It was this that called an extra session of the Texas legislature the last year. Heavy penalties were assessed for fence cutting and the big stockmen were required to run fences around the premises of the small farmers. But this does not satisfy. It does not stop the exodus of residents from before the march of the Pharaoh of land monopoly.

For the ferriage of the Neuces River the charge was forty cents, but when the driver told the two ferry-girls that the traveler was a clergyman, they said their father never charged ministers. Then, as they had walked a quarter of a mile from their home through the black-waxy mud and through the cold drizzle, I offered them a quarter each, but they replied: "Oh, no, we don't want the money; ministers need it more than we do." It was a Christian family out upon the ranch, but the older girl had been away to a ladies' seminary, and lady-like she was.

It is a funny "den" that you "meet up" with frequently along the way. It is about the size of a musk-rat house, from two to three feet high, built around the roots of a cactus clump or a mesquite bunch, with twigs, old bark, cattle chips, etc. And whose house is that? It was built by the wood-rat, which is as large as a squirrel, and there he lives. He also takes in the brown squirrel as a tenant, and, strange to say, the rattlesnake also. A former driver opened a den to show me the occupants. Only the rat and the squirrel were at home. But my friend told me that he had once killed a rattlesnake five feet long just as he was coming out of the den. It is said that these tenants live together in peace, only that the snake eats the young of his associates. When parents take into their home that creature that "biteth like a serpent and stingeth like an adder," though they themselves may get along with him, let them look out lest their young be destroyed.

LETTER XCI.

THE EXHIBITS OF NEGROES IN THE WORLD'S EXPOSITION AT NEW ORLEANS.

NEW ORLEANS, January 20, 1885.

ONE of the first schools for freedmen in New Orleans, named for Frederick Douglass, was kept in an old negro trader's slave-mart that yet bore the ill-disguised sign,

"Virginia Negroes for Sale." And now they come into this World's Industrial Palace with their fruits of scholarship, of ingenuity, of industry, of art; as citizens, as cosmopolitans, they come. Ample and conspicuous space is accorded them. And mightily to their credit does their exhibit testify.

Some of the articles on exhibition are worthy of special mention — a black-walnut pulpit, in design and finish as beautiful and tasteful as any church could wish; a sofa, finely upholstered, and the covering embroidered with artistically executed needlework, showing four prominent events in the life of Toussaint l'Ouverture; a chandelier, very beautiful in design and finely finished; a complete set of dentist's instruments, in polish and finish remarkable; a little engine, made by a silversmith of Knoxville, who was a slave, and who has become a skilled workman of local reputation. He never worked in a shop till he had one of his own. He learned the use of tools without any instruction. These articles would certainly merit attention even if put in competition with similar specimens of the very best workmanship.

Examination papers from schools were numerous, showing proficiency in penmanship, spelling, arithmetic, algebra, geometry, free drawing, grammar, and translations from the classics; fine needlework of all kinds; millinery, dressmaking, tailoring; portrait and landscape painting in oil, water-colors, and crayon; photography; sculpture; models of steamboats, locomotives, stationary engines, and railway cars; cotton presses, plows, cultivators, and reaping-machines; wagons, buggies; tools of almost all kinds, from the hammer of the carpenter to the finely wrought forceps of the dentist; piano and organ (both pipe and reed) making; carpentry, cabinet-making; upholstery;

tinsmithing; blacksmithing; boot and shoe making; basket and broom making; pottery, plain and glazed; brick-making; agricultural products, including all the cereals and fruits raised in the country; silk-worm culture; fruit preserving; flour from a mill, and machinery from a foundry owned by a colored man; patented inventions and improvements, nearly all of them useful and practical, were quite numerous; drugs and medicines; stationery; printing and publishing.

Their gallery of paintings is greatly creditable. They presented not a few ingenious inventions. Besides evidences of scholarship, the show of the products of the industrial departments in the schools maintained for them was most gratifying to all classes of people. Before the war nearly all the mechanical work at the south was done by slaves. A man with a good trade was worth twice as much as without one. Since the war, while those old mechanics have been dying off, but few colored young men have been learning trades. White bosses would not take them, and colored bosses had not the capital with which to use them. At this rate soon there would be no colored mechanics, and then their place would be filled by those imported from the north or from abroad, and the black people would be driven to the wall, left to be mere hewers of wood and drawers of water, at thirty-three cents per day and rations. What must be done? Bring into the school process the industrial lines. Train the hand as well as the brain. Teach the girls sewing, cooking, nursing, telegraphy, etc. Teach the boys practical agriculture, blacksmithing, carpentering, tinning, printing, harness-making, etc. These rudiments of trades will start them off for final success, and will give them at once and increasingly the better positions and pay of artisans. So is it with the philanthropist as with Job: "The cause which I knew not, I searched out."

In this way industrial training is made prominent. At Tougaloo, Miss., a large farm, besides cultivating vegetables and cereals, raises fine fruits for the Chicago market, fine blooded cattle for the region, and a blacksmith shop, a tin shop, and a carpenter shop and a brickyard are run by the young men under competent teachers, while the girls are drilled in cooking and sewing; at Talladega, Atlanta, and Hampton, farms are run and trades are taught; and so also at Fisk University, the LeMoyne Institute, Memphis, the Lewis High School, Macon, Ga., and at other places: sixteen in all. At Atlanta, in the Knowles Industrial Building, built at a cost of six thousand dollars from a legacy left for the purpose by Mrs. L. J. Knowles, of Worcester, Mass., wood-working and iron-working are carried on. From the John F. Slater Fund, under the management of Rev. Dr. A. G. Haygood, aid is received for such work at seven of these institutions.

LETTER XCII.

GRANT'S CANAL AT VICKSBURG.

VICKSBURG, Miss., April 20, 1885.

IN the fall it will be twenty years since Doctors I. P. Warren and G. S. F. Savage, and Pilgrim, were here to see what the American Tract Society of Boston and the American Home Missionary Society, under the bidding of the Boston National Council, could do for the supplementing of the war. Rev. J. W. Alvord was with us a part of the time of that tour of three months, organizing branches of the Freedmen's Savings Bank. I see here now in large letters across a prominent building the legend, "FREEDMEN'S SAVINGS BANK." All was perfectly safe as he was planting these institutions, for government bonds alone were to be the security. Alas, for the day when Congress altered the charter so as to allow the funds to be loaned on real estate!

By the bend opposite the city, General Grant's flotilla, in passing down the river, had to run twice under the rebel guns. Grant's Canal failed to turn the river across that bend; but six years ago the Mississippi took a notion to go across there, any way. Disdaining the help of man it struck in three hundred yards below and in a single night did up the job. The engineer of *The Natchez* now here tells me that coming up that night on *The Katie*, a mammoth vessel, built at a cost of $200,000, and striking the mighty current of the break they were three times turned around by it before they knew what the matter was. Now, the Vicksburg landing is three miles below; and in front of the city, where was once sixty feet of water, willows and grass are growing, on which cattle are feeding, and the old bend for three miles up the river is a beautiful lake.

This Father of Waters retains all of his riparian right to go anywhere he pleases within his valley. The noted Davis bend has been cut off to become an island. A planter, seeing his sixty thousand dollar plantation falling into the river, sold it for three thousand, whereupon the current stopped cutting, and turned to restoring the land. I was up at Greenville, a fine county-seat on the east bank of the river, and found the town tumbling into the flood. Within ten years six hundred feet have been cut away, and of this one hundred and fifty feet have fallen this very winter. I found that house-moving was a regular business, *a la* Chicago. My hotel, the only one in the town, one that had cost $18,000, being of brick, will probably take its bath within a year. Yet we organized a church there to stay.

PERIOD XII.

BACK IN THE WEST, 1885-87.

Transition. — Woman's Work for Woman at the South. — Methodist Episcopal Work Among the Freedmen. — Dakota Indian Conference. — In Colorado. — New West Commission. — Slater Fund. — Centennial of Territory of the North-west and of Louisiana Purchase. — Georgia's Prison and Chain Gang for Missionaries and Teachers. — An Old Experiment in Indian Land Severalty. — The Martyrdom of Elijah P. Lovejoy.

LETTER XCIII.

TRANSITION.

CHICAGO, June 8, 1885.

REALLY, in what an eventful time has this pilgrimage been made. Slavery, rebellion, war, freedom, reconstruction civil and moral — these are catch-words of the era. Mormonism, defiant, clutched by the throat, squirming; our country's population almost doubled; the deep interior explored; the "New West" discovered, and first so-named by Pilgrim in a paper read before the Boston National Council in 1865; the peace policy set up among the Indians; the new temperance revival; the enthusiasm born for the evangelizing of our cities and of our immigrants from foreign lands; the great benevolent societies marching on under the behest of the churches and pastors; moral affiiliations going on as respects our neighbors, the Indians, the negroes, and the Chinese within our borders; among these transcendent interests have we all been traveling. At the close of the war Pilgrim spent three months in rummaging about among the "peculiar institutions" of the south, and *The Independent* heard from him every week; and so for these last seven years has he been going up and down that part of our own dear land, making notes and printing 'em, growing in his love for the people there, colored and white, seeing wonders of progress, and yet oppressed with the sense of the magnitude of the work still to be done in the progress of national and Christian assimilation. It is like the rolling of a kaleidoscope to turn over the pages of these great octavo scrap-books in which Lady Pilgrim has preserved his notes by the way. The future historian of the west and of the south may find here some material.

LETTER XCIV.

WOMAN'S WORK FOR WOMAN AT THE SOUTH.

CHICAGO, July 31, 1885.

THE thrill of foreign missions for the last dozen years has come from woman's work for woman; and the one or two hundred thousand dollars a year put by the women into each of several missionary boards has been a mighty relief of their exigent exchequers. With less parade, and yet upon a much larger scale as far as the work upon the field is concerned, and with more of personal exposure and ostracism, here has been a movement on the part of women sublime indeed. It has been, too, for a people whose original paganism had been indurated by the immoralities inherent in the system of slave-holding. It has been also by the same process — school teaching, Bible reading. house-to-house visitation, instructing mothers and daughters in the duties growing out of the mysteries of their own being. And, as a result, thousands upon thousands of youth have come forward into intelligence and virtue; multitudes of homes have been purified; scores of young men have been led into the ministry; and a generation of youth by these examples have been taught a reverence for woman which has become a hidden power of their life.

When this Association, which was the first of all organizations to give the gospel of light to the benighted children of bondage, started out, it used the hand of Christian women for its introduction, and all along to this day it has shared with them in this fellowship. As early as September, 1861, under the guns of Fortress Monroe, the work began to result in the far-famed Hampton Institute. The first teacher was Mrs. Peake, a colored woman, whom the Lord had ready at hand. The next, in July, 1862, was a daughter of our missionary, Rev. J. S. Greene, of the Sandwich Islands; and the next, in the December following, was a lady who went with her husband, Rev. E. S. Williams, to St. Helena Island. Writing at that date, he says: "Mrs. Williams will go with me and teach them to sew and sweep. They need kind lectures on cleanliness and neatness." Then as the Union lines sweep on, lady missionaries are pushed forward to Norfolk, Beaufort, and to Hilton Head. As the army, in 1863, occupies Corinth, our lady recruits are hurried on to that point, to serve in the freedmen's school and hospital. And when, in the exigency of war, Corinth must be evacuated, the corps of lady workers follows soldiers and freedmen to Memphis, pursued, fired upon and nearly captured, as the weary trip of several days is made. Once in Memphis, the school and the hospital find them at work again.

And so by the fall of 1864 the Association had on its

muster-roll the names of one hundred and sixty-nine women. And then only seventeen days after our troops have entered Richmond our teachers follow, starting a school which in two weeks has fifteen hundred pupils, the most of the instructors being women. Then as the military veterans are being mustered out it is found that the Association's Army of Occupation numbers 363, of whom 261 are ladies who had enlisted not for three months or three years, but many of them for life; and these are found stationed all along the front and in fifteen different states. In 1866 the ladies muster 264; in 1867, 410. In 1870, of the 533 workers, 450 are women. The annual report of 1869 brings out the fact that up to that time 2,628 different missionary laborers had been enlisted, of whom at least 2,000 were women. From that time on to this the list of ladies has ranged from 200 to 250, so that in these twenty-five years it is a safe estimate that not less than 3,000 women have been in this service. What a multitude of gospelers! It should also be considered that the time when these numbers ran the highest was the Ku-klux period, when the brave women could stand in places where the men could not live. In Mississippi at midnight one of these heroines is waited on by a Ku-klux company in masks and gowns. After a hasty robing she is obliged to open the door. The ruffian crew are themselves abashed, as their leader breaks out: "Why, you are a lady!" and then gives her twenty-four hours in which to leave, notifying her that they will be around by that time to see that she is gone. "Low-down fellows were they," the citizens said. "No," answered she; "such men don't wear fine top-boots and have soft hands." The lone woman surrenders, saying that she scorns to tell them that, though she is an Illinois girl, she was the granddaughter of Rev. Dr. Allen, of Huntsville, Alabama. Another woman's school at Austin, Texas, is broken into by the roughs. Then the post-commander sends a guard to stand by day at her door and to escort her home at night, and back in the morning. At another place in Alabama the Ku-klux Klan draw up in line before the lady teacher's castle of a school-house home, and fire a volley of beans and shot through her windows on each side of the chair where she is sitting. But now she is entering the eighteenth year of service on that same spot. Another, having her school in an old North Carolina rebel gun-factory, when a man offered to be one of twenty to put her on the cars and send her away, gave as her response: "I was sent here by the American Missionary Association, and when that says go, I will, and not before." She is now entering on her twenty-third year of service and is as brave as ever. Time would fail us to relate of these women only such deeds of valor as have come to our ears. The best of all is that they cherish no revenge. Theirs has been the victory of the passive virtue, but a triumph as real as that of military valor. They went down south to do good to the poor and the lowly, to build something of their own noble spirit and character into the life of the outcast. Nobly have they been fulfilling their mission.

"What honor and what dignity hath been done to Mordecai for this?" said the king, as he came, in the restlessness of the night, to the record of the man who had saved his life. "There is nothing done for him," was the truthful reply. In the turning of the books of the last day, the Supreme Monarch will say of these unheralded Christian patriots: "Let royal apparel be brought, and let it be done to them as to those whom the King delighteth to honour."

The First Woman's Missionary Society dates back of the modern era of missions, and, indeed, back of the Acts of the Apostles. It was set up in the early part of the ministry of Jesus in Galilee, and here is the record of it in Luke's Gospel (8: 1-3): "And it came to pass afterward that he went throughout every city and village preaching and showing the glad tidings of the kingdom of God, and the twelve were with him. And certain women, Mary, called Magdalene, and Joanna, the wife of Chusa, Herod's steward, and Susanna, and many others, ministered unto them [Revised Version] of their substance." How were these missionaries to be subsisted? Here were our Lord and the Twelve, traveling on foot from town to town, and, as is likely, holding their evangelistic meetings every day. Our Lord did not feed his company by miracle; he did not command stones to be made bread. These Christian women had thoughtfully set themselves to aid in this matter. It seems that they had formed a circle as an auxiliary to the Saviour's missionary society, and the object of their branch was to minister of service and of substance. They were evidently of the well-to-do class, as they had "substance" to draw from. And there were not a few of them, but Mary and Joanna and Susanna and many others. Importance was attached to Mary, in her being named first, and in stating the city from which she came, Magdala. She was, perhaps, the president of the circle. (When shall we ever be done with the perfectly unauthorized aspersion that she of Magdala was not a chaste woman?) Then, as there were saints in Cæsar's household, to whom the apostle Paul sent salutations, so thus early was there at least one in Herod's home, Joanna, the wife of his steward. The emphatic thing in the history is that these women were associated for service, and that they ministered of their substance. Quite likely these and "the many," not only drew from their own purses, but called upon other sisters to enter into this fellowship of giving. And so that was a great service rendered to the gospel, as it began to be preached; and the Saviour accepted it as such in an unhesitating way, proving thereby his confidence in the purity and the faithfulness of these Galilæan friends.

And it seems to have been a continuous service, one that lasted through the Saviour's ministry; for it was upon the occasion of his last passover at Jerusalem that they followed Jesus and his company up from Galilee to minister unto them. And the evangelist Mark says that these women, who, at the crucifixion, were looking on afar off, were the same "who also, when he was in Galilee, followed him and ministered unto him." And he gives their names: "Mary Magdalene, and Mary, the mother of James the less and of Joses, and Salome, and many other women which came up with him unto Jerusalem." So, when the dear body was laid in the tomb of Joseph, the women also which came with him from Galilee followed after, and beheld the sepulcher and how his body was laid, and then returned again with their prepared spices and ointments to anoint him, only to become themselves the first witnesses to testify of his resurrection. And so when the Pentecost had come, that world's missionary prayer-meeting, these same women, and Mary, the mother of Jesus, were there. It was but natural that this enduring woman's organization should merge itself in the grand pentecostal evangelism.

Are not our woman's bureaus and boards of the present time the veritable successors of that original auxiliary, which had the benediction of the Saviour's approval and participation? Are not the women of these now ministering of service and of substance to the Lord Jesus just as much as did those of Galilee? By their prayers, their sisterly attentions, their letters of sympathy, their material offerings in behalf of the brethren and sisters of our Lord in foreign parts, or among the lowly poor of the four races who dwell in our own land, are they not following the common Master and his disciples, and ministering unto them as really as though they had been walking with them over the hills of Galilee? And surely nothing can more gratify and inspire these women in their special missionary work than to feel assured that the Saviour does thus approve and accept their loving ministry of service and of substance.

LETTER XCV.

METHODIST WORK AMONG THE FREEDMEN.

CHICAGO, August 31, 1885.

My first meeting with Bishop Gilbert Haven was in 1878, when from a sail to Africa he came into dry dock at Clifton Springs, where I had been undergoing repairs for more than a year. I was just then considering a transfer to the south. I opened the matter to him. With that catholic spirit of his he kindled at the idea. He urged my going. He cleared away some difficulties. He magnified the fact that my denomination was called upon to do much in the way of helping the south take care of its dusky citizens. If I had been a Methodist preparing to go down and work under him, he could not have been more cordial in his proffer of personal fellowship and helpfulness. When I came to meet him in Atlanta, where we were both located, his delicate attention was more than I had a right to expect. He took me into the inner circle of his social fellowship. Much did he aid me. At the Clark University I greatly enjoyed his scholarly and vigorous baccalaureate and also a theological lecture which was a marvel in its comprehensiveness, its profundity, and yet its simplicity. That institution itself, I believe, was a child of his own brain and heart. Seeing things big, he located upon several hundred acres of land outside of the city. But the late shooting of a new railroad by the campus into the city and the working of two great thoroughfares out in that direction, with street-cars, have now quite brought it into the town. The Clark is steadily advancing in its quality and in its extent. A son-in-law of the bishop is now at the head of the theological department. Besides the literary, theological, classical departments, it has the industrial. From the city the smokestacks of its shops make it look like a factory. The young men are taught work in iron, wood, and tin. Some of their own buildings have been put up by the students. The young women are taught cooking, sewing and, I think, nursing.

In the Clark there is Professor Crogman, a graduate of our Atlanta University, of whom we are quite fond. He is a rare instructor, an orator with not a little genius. Eight years ago at our annual meeting in this city, when we gave an evening to speakers of the four races, red, yellow, black, and white, he represented the negro; as he did also in Madison, Wis., at the National Teachers' Association. At both places he carried the award of genuine eloquence and of noble sentiment. In his address for us, referring to the mixture of blood down there, he said that sometimes you could hardly tell where Ham left off and Shem began. At our thanksgiving service in Atlanta, following the election of President Cleveland, after I had been gathering some occasion for thanksgiving from the fact that the leading southern people had been putting themselves on record as the very best friends of the black people, the professor came forward and said: "Yes, but we will try them. Two little birds sat singing on the fence. One sang, 'I love you'; and the other sang, 'Show it.' So let them declare their love. We will see if they show it."

Bishop Warren, too, I have heard upon that same commencement platform, delivering one of his elegant addresses, without any apparent lowering of its tone to meet his congregation. Indeed, these people are good hearers, as slavery had cultivated their attentiveness and their memory. They were accustomed not only to the pulpit but also to the rostrum, where they took in the spirit of our American institutions and so became better qualified to exercise the elective franchise — at once their education and their defence — than the masses of the people landed upon our shores from the monarchies of the old world.

Every-where over the south I found that the colored people knew of Bishop Haven and held him in great reverence for his heroic devotion to their welfare. Eminently had he the courage of his convictions. The "Illustrated History of Methodism" says that he was "one of the most admired and best hated men in America." His final departure was a triumph.

I have repeatedly visited the Claflin University at Orangeburg, S. C. It is a beautiful affair. It has the normal, classical, and theological departments, and has an adjunct of a farm of a hundred or more acres, where the boys are trained in fine agriculture and horticulture. The state pays $4,000 a year out of its United States agricultural fund toward the running expenses, on the ground of its normal work. Others of these institutions I have visited. They are all worthy of the largest confidence, of still larger endowments.

LETTER XCVI.

THE DAKOTA INDIAN CONFERENCE.

ASCENSION, D. T., September 29, 1885.

It has been to me a delight, coming from the Dakota General Association, where the Indian missionaries, pastors, delegates, and teachers appeared as members, to turn in at the annual meeting of the General Conference of the Dakotas. It is here upon the Sisseton Reservation, which is along the middle of the east line of the territory, a wedge of land fifty or sixty miles long and averaging a dozen miles in width. It is a beautiful region, with hills, and gulches of trees, and springs, and a good soil. This remnant of the Sissetons, a band of the Sioux, numbers sixteen hundred. They have taken up farms, have cabins and frame-houses, and teams and cattle. They are doing quite well in their experiment. The agent of the government, Colonel Thompson, is a worthy Christian man, a Presbyterian elder. But the people are now practically independent, having no annuity and no rations, receiving only each fall a small supply of clothing.

We meet ten miles away from the agency, at the Ascension Church, Rev. John B. Renville, pastor. This name was not taken from the Catholic calendar, but from the fact that here the Sioux coming westward ascended the Coteau, the plateau of rough, rolling country.

This convocation represents a part of the fruitage of the planting of the American Board half a century ago under Stevens, Riggs, and Williamson. These churches are upon the Sisseton, the Yankton, the Santee, the Teeton, and Devil's Lake, Ree, and Mandan Reservations, with one in Montana and one in Canada, thirteen in all, with over one thousand members. They are now under the care of the Presbyterian Boards and of the American Missionary Association.

The first two days were given to a theological institute for the native pastors and candidates and teachers, led by Reverend Messrs. J. P. Williamson, A. L. Riggs, T. L. Riggs, and C. L. Hall. There are thirty-five of the institute men, and eight or ten of the lady teachers have come along to help to make up the occasion and to enjoy it. The topics are of the practical sort, such as Sermon-making, Exegesis of the Word, Personal Character, Financial Management of the Churches, Schools, and Societies. Great good is gained by the young men from these instructions and discussions. As to the entire program, I find that it is our Alabama convocation over again: theological institute, conference of the churches, anniversaries of the Dakota Native Missionary Society, of the Woman's Missionary Society, and of the Young Men's Christian Association.

In the conference, first we have the salutations of the messengers of the churches and their pastors, and of the visiting friends. Colonel Thompson, in behalf of the people of his agency, welcomes those from all the others, and testifies that it is only the Christian religion that could have civilized them so. He said that he had had only one case of petit larceny, and that was tried by one of the justices elected by the people. Pilgrim gave the greetings of the Presbyterian and Congregational people, who, for half a century, had been helping the Dakotas. He was also put on upon the topics, The Power of Character in the Religious Teacher and Preacher, and Work among the Colored People, A. L. Riggs and Williamson interpreting. Some of the subjects discussed were: Duties of the Young Men's Christian Association; How much Land can a Man retain Permanently? What should Parents be willing to deny themselves for the Education of their Children? How to secure the Spiritual Growth of a Church; Methods for raising Money for Church and Missionary Purposes. As to land, the sentiment ran: Only so much as a man can cultivate.

Their missionary society is now ten years old. In that time they have raised $5,449. In the last six years they have raised an average of $819. For their thousand members this swells up, the last three years, well on to a dollar for each. Looking over the treasurer's book for these ten years I find that each church is represented almost every year in the money column. They have a regular organization, with a constitution and three directors, who appoint missionaries and appropriate the funds. They are supporting two native missionaries at Devil's Lake, and one at the Cheyenne Agency. What a lesson here for the hundreds and hundreds of our churches at home, which are not reported in the missionary column! And what a rebuke to those churches which say, We are so poor we must use up every thing at home! These are poor people just redeemed from heathenism. They have to support the gospel at home, but they want to give it to those who have it not. Of that $1,161 given the last year, $541 came from the Woman's Auxiliary, $100 from the Young Men's Christian Association, and

$520 from the churches. So, even among the Christian Indians, the women are even with the churches and many may go ahead of them, as their white sisters are doing.

Mr. Williams, a representative of the Young Men's Christian Association system, was here to receive this one into fellowship. Sermons were interspersed along the program. The Sabbath, the fourth day of the conference, is the great day of the feast, with the Lord's Supper, and abundant preaching.

It is a beautiful thing that the sons of Doctors Williamson and Riggs are following in the footsteps of their fathers. Besides these, Robert Riggs, married to one of the lady teachers, has settled near Fort Sully, and so is at hand for sympathy and help. The daughter Martha, Mrs. Morris, has been associated for fifteen years with her husband in the Good Will Boarding School at the Sisseton Agency. Isabella is at the North China Mission. The burden of all these missionaries is for recruits. Who will volunteer?

Will it pay to enlist and give money in this process of Indian Christianization? Yes. This experiment proves it. The settlement of the people in severalty of land and in citizenship can no longer be called an experiment. Look on this convocation of dignified worshipers, clad in citizen's dress and clothed and in their right mind; take account of these societies and of the churches out of which they have grown; see the beaming of character under Christian training, and say not again that there is no use to try to save these native Americans. The exigency of the people favors the undertaking. Their game is gone. They must take the white man's way. The flood of emigration has thrown them into islands of reservation, so that they can be the more easily assimilated into the Christian nation. They are only a quarter of a million, anyhow. Why make a long job of it?

But what can be shown for the half-century of this Dakota Mission? I have been studying that question closely. See this convocation. Observe the devotion to it marked by the fact that two of these delegates have come six hundred miles; another three hundred; that a dozen families have driven their own teams over two hundred miles, taking over a week of time to reach this Jerusalem; and that sixty or seventy *teepees* (tents) are pitched here, each by the side of a good wagon, with its own horses, oxen, and colts, feeding; hard by, a camp-meeting with four hundred counted guests. Surely it belongs to the Church Militant! Then add to this our own Santee Industrial and Normal Boarding School and half a dozen of a lower grade; add the first-class boarding school of this agency. Then consider that the Indian work of the Episcopalians among the Sioux has fattened upon the literature, which the way-wise and converted people furnished to their hand by this mission. Count in the Flandreau and Brown Earth settlements of a hundred Sioux Christian families, citizenized. Count in the capital of a prepared people at Devil's Lake, laid hold of by the Catholics. Reckon in that colony in Montana, and that larger one in Canada. Take also into the inventory the Riggs Dakota Bible, his grammar and dictionary, the hymn-books, the school-books, the translation of Bunyan's Pilgrim and other such works, to the number of forty-two, as soon to be shown by a Smithsonian Bibliography under the index name of "Riggs." Put down the Dakota newspaper, the *Iapi Oaye*, and also the English-Dakota Dictionary, which John P. Williamson is now preparing, and who shall say that this has not been a paying mission?

Corollary: Mr. Williamson says that fifty children have been born to the Dakota missionaries, that he knows them all, that not one of them has turned out badly, and that nearly all have become Christians and are making useful people. Even under unpropitious conditions God's covenant holds good.

LETTER XCVII.

COLORADO AND "NEW WEST" WORK.

SOUTH PUEBLO, Colorado, October 29, 1885.

THIRTEEN years ago, on a tour through Colorado, I came to Pueblo, and found it a town of adobe houses, on the Arkansas, at the then southern terminus of the Denver & Rio Grande Railway. The pastor of the Presbyterian church told me that he had a membership of Congregational people. So I looked over the river, upon the fine plateau, and prophesied a South Pueblo and a place for a Congregational church. Turner, of Missouri, could see a Congregational church in one old woman. Pilgrim could see one in a virgin prairie. And now, in South Pueblo, he finds not only one, but two Congregational churches, the first of which royally entertained the General Association. He also finds here a city of 15,000 people, nearly half of whom are on the south side, with water-works, with street-cars, electric lights, the largest smelter in the world, and another smaller, with a third going in; also, a steel-rail rolling-mill, a great foundry, and other factories. The Denver & Rio Grande has branched its narrow gauge out over the crest of the continent, to the total of over two thousand miles. The smelters here, by their central location, are able to secure such a variety of ores as to furnish their own flux, without the extra expense of procuring the necessary fluxing material.

Pueblo means simply a village. So when the Spaniards discovered here in the heart of the continent a tribe of Indians who were not nomadic, but who lived in villages, they called them Pueblos. Of these, in New Mexico, there are now over 10,000, who live in nineteen villages. It is for these that the University of New Mexico is providing a special department, which the American Missionary Association is helping to sustain.

Colorado College, with Professor Strieby serving as acting president, is getting out of the woods. The college administration is running satisfactorily. It has an able corps of instructors and a fine body of students. It has a superb campus and a grand building. It is properly located. It is an essential to this Rocky Mountain region. It has an unusually sympathetic and helpful constituency in the local community. It deserves patronage and endowment. It has at hand, as foster-mother, the second Congregational church of the state.

The mutual relation of Christian colleges and home missions has become an axiom in the problem of the evangelization of our new territories and states that are settled by the people of the older portions of our country. My experience in our southern work has profoundly impressed me with the wisdom of the New West Commission in its movement for primary and academic education in the midst of our Mormon and Spanish-American regions. We have found at the south that the school process is absolutely essential to any sound church development. The old people who came out of their bondage in Egypt soon passed away. Their children took forty years of training under Moses for their exalted mission.

Our hope as to this latter race of ex-bondsmen is in the intellectual and moral nurture of their children. We find that they readily take on our ideas. They soon grow up. They make the best and about the only material for our church fellowship. In this way the American Missionary Association, since the war, has developed one hundred and twenty churches, which, in the main, are a delight to our Christian workers.

The same process is needed in those territories where Mormonism and Romanism predominate. The other nascent states will themselves take up the regular public school process. But in these the American idea of education must be fostered *ab extra*. Yet in this new undertaking there is the mighty advantage of having Christian schools, with the Bible in them and its system of morality and religion. Our teachers for the south are beforehand tested as to their Christian character and missionary spirit. In this way we draw out a grade of consecrated talent which the mere business of teaching could never reach. Christly souls, hungering to do their share under the great commission of the Master, find here the opportunity to become the most effective missionaries. They have had the honor of leading multitudes of souls to the Saviour; they have brought out most of the young men who are now the cultured pastors of the churches; they have led the way in organizing the most of those same churches. By no means could they have gained such results, and — as to themselves — such privilege, such honor. Precisely this is the process by which these Christian teachers are to lead out the children of Utah and New Mexico into intelligence and into character, into church membership and into worthy citizenship.

And so naturally comes along the relation of this new

scheme to the grand scheme of the American Home Missionary Society — the same as that of the old order of Christian colleges, only that it starts in farther back. The superintendents and preachers of the Society will counsel and help the school-workers of the Commission. The school-houses will become preaching stations. The lady teacher, with her Sunday-school, will become the nucleus of the Church itself, which, under the culture of the Spirit, will be a growth out of the Christian school. And so the leaven, the mustard-seed of the Gospel, will come to mighty proportions.

That old Society, which our churches have used in spanning the continent, and which we of the west delight to honor as the "mother of us all," may well welcome this new coadjutor, leaving to it the school business, while coöperating in the same, and then going on in its own heaven-blessed mission and building up the churches of Jesus Christ. The planting of superintendents in the Rocky Mountain regions shows her purpose to embrace the opportunity to meet the exigency. In adjusting the relations there has been need of wisdom, but now the deck has been cleared for action, the lines re-formed for a renewal of the warfare. And we of the southern work, saluting the banners of the right wing as they dip into the valleys and rise to the mountain-tops of the New West, will, on the left, take courage to drive on our "March to the Sea."

The work of the Commission for the academic year 1885–86 is given below: —

Schools of all grades		35
Number of teachers		63
,,	,, pupils	2,560
,,	,, Mormons	764

Number of apostates 541
,,   ,, Mexicans 142
,,   ,, Sabbath-schools 29
,,   ,, attendance estimated in Sabbath-schools . 2,200

The chartered academies are those at Salt Lake, Albuquerque, Las Vegas, and Trinidad, and others at Lehi, Park City, and Ogden. These figures attest the grip which this young society has laid upon this last of the twin relics. That it has at once leaped into an acknowledged position, with $50,000 a year, attests the exigent need of this agency. Its teachers go back and forth, a dozen at a time, on their way to or from the campaign. Carlyle had no place in his book of heroes for the name of a woman. But if he should pass by Joan of Arc, he might have found true heroines among the missionary women who go to do battle with pollution and savagery. All hail to these women who are holding the fastnesses of the mountains for their country and for Christ! Their leader, Secretary Charles R. Bliss, is their Great Heart.

LETTER XCVIII.

THE JOHN F. SLATER FUND.

CHICAGO, July 2, 1886.

MR. SLATER, of Norwich, Conn., having had in mind for some years a plan for devoting a large sum of money to the education of the freedmen, in March, 1882, put the same into shape by an ably drawn letter addressed to the men whom he had selected to be trustees of the fund. These men were ex-President R. B. Hayes, Chief Justice M. R. Waite, William E. Dodge, Rev. Phillips Brooks, Daniel C. Gilman, John A. Stewart, Alfred H. Colquitt,

Morris K. Jessup, James P. Boyce, and William A. Slater. By his stipulation it was to be a "Christian education" by which he would seek to bestow blessings upon the emancipated people. The trustees held their first meeting in New York, May 18, 1882. A charter from the state of New York was accepted. R. B. Hayes was elected president, M. R. Waite, vice-president, M. K. Jessup, treasurer, and D. C. Gilman, secretary. Mr. Slater, being present, paid over to the trustees one million dollars. Something more than half of this was in railway bonds drawing five and six per cent. interest, and the remainder in cash, which was also invested in bonds. By the charter in New York these funds are to be exempt from tax, except such as are in real estate. At the first a small sum was set apart, to be increased until it should reach $100,000, as a guarantee fund, and this, by the report of 1886, has reached $86,068, an increase beyond the clean million. Clearly this fund has no debtors such as the states of Tennessee and Florida, whose bonds turned over to the Peabody Fund to the amount of hundreds of thousands of dollars have been repudiated, even while appropriations from the fund to the sum of many thousands of dollars a year had been received by them, until the trustees decided, after labor had with these defaulting commonwealths, that they should be stricken from the list of beneficiaries.

The board, with the approval of Mr. Slater, at its next meeting in October, 1882, appointed as General Agent of the fund, Rev. Atticus G. Haygood, D.D., LL.D., president of Emory College in Georgia. This, as it seemed at the time and has since been proved, was an appointment eminently fit to be made. Dr. Haygood by some has been termed the Luther of the south. Such comprehension had he of the work of the missionary teachers and preachers at the south that long before he entered upon the same he had pronounced "immortal honor" upon them, and had said: "Suppose that these northern teachers had not come, that nobody had taught the negroes, set free and made citizens! The south would have been uninhabitable by this time." His own views have doubtless had a process of development, and wisely he has kept himself in an attitude to educate and lead along the public sentiment of his section. He has thus been in a position to lay his hands both upon the north and the south, and so to make peace. It is this that has made him so eminently useful in the office which he holds under the Slater Corporation. He is leading the southern people into an appreciation of our work and workers among them as no northern man could have done; and at the same time he has carried along the confidence of the missionaries and their supporters.

Mr. Slater, although connected with a Congregational society, provided that his gratuity should be administered without respect to denominations. Only this would he insist upon, a "Christian education." And so upon the board there was put only one member of the ecclesiastical system to which he was attached, and he the president of a non-denominational university, Dr. D. C. Gilman, of the Johns Hopkins. And so, in the appropriations, schools in all branches of the church that had been doing eminent work among the colored people are made recipients, as will appear in the report appended. The trustees started out with the theory of aiding such institutions as should give special prominence to the subject of industrial training, and such scholars as should be trained in some manual occupation simultaneously with their mental and moral instruction. The system with this feature in it is working well. It puts the aided institutions upon their best endeavor in the line both of scholastic and industrial training. Dr. Haygood's last report counts eight thousand colored youth indirectly aided and over three hundred teachers in the schools connected with the Slater Fund. It has also stimulated the raising at the south and at the north for such work to an amount in the last eighteen months, as he estimated it, of $60,000.

For the year ending October, 1883, the fund appropriated $16,250; for 1884, $17,106; and for 1885, $36,764, a total of $100,120. For the current year the sum of $40,000 is appropriated. While this is a magnificent charity in itself, it scarcely brings any relief to the exchequers of the several missionary societies, for it gives that more may be given. Thus of the twenty-nine institutions aided last year the seven that are under the American Missionary Association received $8,700, which necessitated about as much additional outlay. And then that amount, generous in itself, is but a small proportion of the $208,211, of expenditures at the south by the Association for the same year. So will it be with all of the other societies; and so the friends of each, while encouraged by this auxiliary fund, will yet not find themselves relieved at all in the matter of personal contributions to this cause. Below is given the schedule of appropriations for the school year of 1884–85, with an indication of the denomination or society to which each school belongs: —

Atlanta University, Atlanta, Ga., A. M. A.	$2,000.00
Austin High School, Knoxville, Tenn., Ind.	500.00
Benedict Institute, Columbia, S. C., Bap.	1,000.00
Brainerd Institute, Chester, S. C., Pres.	500.00
Central Tennessee College, Nashville, Tenn., M. E.	1,500.00
Claflin University, Orangeburg, S. C., M. E.	2,000.00
Clark University, Atlanta, Ga., M. E.	2,000.00
Fisk University, Nashville, Tenn., A. M. A.	2,000.00
Hampton Institute, Hampton, Va., Ind.	2,000.00
Hartshorn Memorial Institute, Richmond, Va., Bap.	1,000.00
Howard University, Washington, D. C., Ind.	1,000.00
Kentucky Normal University, Louisville, Ky., State.	1,000.00
Leland University, New Orleans, La., Bap.	14,000.00
LeMoyne Institute, Memphis, Tenn., A. M. A.	1,200.00
Leonard Medical School, Raleigh, N. C., Bap.	1,000.00
Lewis Normal Institute, Macon, Ga., A. M. A.	500.00
Lincoln Normal University, Marion, Ala., State.	1,000.00
Meharry Medical College, Nashville, Tenn., M. E.	1,000.00
Mount Albion State Normal School, Franklinton, N. C., State	400.00
Mount Hermon Female Seminary, Clinton, Miss., Ind.	1,000.00
Roger Williams University, Nashville, Tenn., Bap.	1,400.00
Scotia Female Seminary, Concord, N. C., Pres.	1,000.00
Shaw University, Raleigh, N. C., Bap.	2,000.00
Spelman Female Seminary, Atlanta, Ga., Bap.	2,314.10
State Normal School, Huntsville, Ala., State.	1,000.00
State Normal School, Tuskegee, Ala., State.	1,000.00
Talladega College, Talladega, Ala., A. M. A.	2,000.00
Tillotson Institute, Austin, Texas, A. M. A.	600.00
Tougaloo University, Tougaloo, Miss., A. M. A.	1,000.00
To special students	450.00
Total,	$36,764.10

LETTER XCIX.

THE NORTH-WESTERN CENTENNIAL. — THE LOUISIANA PURCHASE.

CHICAGO, July 15, 1886.

APRIL 7, 1888, will come our great north-western centennial. The ordinance for organizing the territory north of the Ohio was passed July 13, 1787. The next year the first settlement was made at Marietta, Ohio, and there the centenary celebration is to be held. By that organic act, freedom scored a great victory, for slavery was to be excluded from all the region which now makes up our five interior states; and by it the sixteenth section of every township in all this wide domain was consecrated to public schools, and subsequently the same principle was applied to all the territory acquired, reaching to the Pacific coast. Thomas Jefferson has ordinarily had the credit of having introduced that proviso for freedom. Three or four years before, he had proposed that no slavery should be allowed in the territory after 1800. For this he deserves honor. But when the ordinance was finally passed, he was not in Congress, nor was he in this country, being abroad upon public duty. The provision for freedom and education was introduced by Nathan Dane, of Massachusetts, and Rev. Dr. Manasseh Cutler, of the same state, who afterward organized the colony and came with it to Marietta, had much to do in Washington with the procuring of that beneficent act of Congress. As the centennial comes on we shall fight over again the "Toledo war," and the battle between Illinois and Wisconsin, over boundary lines. The ordinance had provided for the future setting up of three states in the region covered by Ohio, Indiana, and Illinois, and if any of the territory north of these three should be also organized separately, it was stipulated that the boundary should be a line running east and west by the lower extremity of Lake Michigan. The people of Ohio supposed that this line would strike north of Toledo, a rising sea-port which they desired, and over which their jurisdiction had been extended. But Michigan coming on claimed the line originally named which should give Toledo to the peninsula. The militia were ordered out on both sides. The federal government intervened and, as a compromise, Michigan accepted the upper peninsula lying on the lower side of Lake Superior. As it turns out, Michigan had a war that did not cost a life, and she gained a vast region of the richest iron and copper ore. I well remember the excitement over that Toledo war in Ohio when I was but a child. But Wisconsin fared worse. Illinois took a slice off from the south because she wanted a sea-port and Michigan had despoiled her of the mountains of metal.

The first and second of the articles of compact are of the nature of a bill of rights. The third is as follows: " Religion, morality, and knowledge being necessary to good government and the happiness of mankind, schools and the means of education shall forever be encouraged. The utmost good faith shall always be observed towards the Indians; their lands and property shall never be taken from them without their consent; and in their property, rights, and liberty they shall never be invaded or disturbed unless in just and lawful wars authorized by Congress; but laws founded in justice and humanity shall, from time to time, be made for preventing wrongs being done to them, and for preserving peace and friendship with them." Article VI declares: "There shall be neither slavery nor involuntary servitude in the said territory, otherwise than in the punishment of crimes, whereof the party shall have been duly convicted."

In 1903 will come the centennial of the Louisiana Purchase. President Albert Salisbury, of the Whitewater Normal, Wisconsin, has made a fine contribution to the geography of our country in a settling of the western boundary of that purchase. This was in an article of his in *The Pacific School Journal*, July, 1884. Did that purchase include Oregon and Washington and Idaho? General Walker's map in the census report of 1870 so made it. Some school histories have followed him, and notably a centennial map that aimed to show that boundary in colors. But the president proves that France never claimed any thing beyond the Rocky Mountains. The royal charter of Louis the Fourteenth to Anthony Crozat, 1712, limited Louisiana to the valley of the Mississippi. Then in 1800 Napoleon retroceded it to Spain. It was to be "with the same extent that it now has in the hands of Spain and that it had when France possessed it." Marbois, Napoleon's minister of the treasury, who as such was the negotiator in the sale, in his History of Louisiana, 1829, says: "The shores of the western ocean were certainly not included in the cession"; and again: "The first article of the treaty meant to convey nothing beyond the sources of the Missouri." As other authorities he quotes President Jefferson, John Quincy Adams as Secretary of State, and others. Mr. Adams made our title to Oregon rest on: 1. The discovery of the Columbia by Captain Grey, 1792; 2. The exploration of Lewis and Clark, 1805; 3. The settlement at Astoria, 1811. So there is no foundation in international law nor in history for a French claim to any country beyond the crest of the Rockies. Bryant's Popular History of the United States reports the matter according to the idea of this article, giving it credit. So also do Anderson and Swinton in their histories.

LETTER C.

GEORGIA'S PRISON FOR HER MISSIONARIES TO THE CHEROKEES, AND CHAIN-GANG FOR HER TEACHERS OF THE NEGROES.

CHICAGO, September 1, 1887.

IN 1829 Georgia passed a law to extend her jurisdiction over the nation and the territory of the Cherokees, and so to dispossess them of their ancestral domain. Their right of possession had extended back to a period beyond the genesis of American history. This right had been recognized by the colony and the state of Georgia in six different treaties made with them, and by the United States government in fifteen treaties made with the same people. By all such treaties Georgia had had purchased for her, of Indian tribes, by the United States, 19,927,200 acres; while the Cherokees as a nation had retained for their home territory only 5,000,000 acres, which was about three hundred acres a head for the sixteen thousand who were finally removed. The execution of the law was nothing but Ahab's extending his proprietorship over Naboth's vineyard. It was an over-riding of all the rights of possession, of treaties, of legal enactments, and of the nationality of the Indians. Then the dividing up of this Cherokee country into one-hundred-and-forty-acre lots to be drawn at lottery by citizens of the state, stimulated their cupidity, even to violence, in seizing upon the houses and improvements of the Indians and of the mission stations. The law also, in order the more certainly to secure the land, provided that the missionaries of the American Board, and any other white men who should remain upon those lands, should be subject to an imprisonment for four years at hard labor.

Those missionaries, as early as 1815, had entered that field when the American Board was only three and a half years old. Rev. Cyrus Kingsbury, on his way to it from Andover, passing through Washington, laid the matter before President Madison, who ordered the Secretary of War to say that the agent for Indian affairs would erect a house for the school and one for the teachers, to be followed by others. The agent was also instructed to furnish "two plows, six hoes, and as many axes for the purpose of introducing the art of cultivation among the pupils; and when female pupils should be received, a loom, a half-dozen spinning-wheels, and as many pairs of cards." In 1819 President Monroe and General Gaines visited the mission. The President expressed himself so well pleased with all he saw, that on the spot he ordered a much better building for the girls' school, at the expense of the government. By this mission the Cherokees, in 1830, had been so advanced in civilization that one half of those in Georgia had learned to read. They had schools, courts, a legislature, eight churches, and stringent laws against the sale of strong drinks. At that time, as President Bartlett says, three fourths of all the church members in the missions of the American Board were among these and other Indians. These missionaries, knowing their rights in the Cherokee nation as secured by treaties with Georgia and the United States, and by the patronage of the government, decided to remain among their people and take the consequences.

Their arrest was by no warrant of civil process, but by the Georgia Military Guard, who went around from station to station gathering up their victims. Rev. S. A. Worcester was taken from his home while his wife was confined to her bed in sickness. Dr. Butler, the physician and catechist, had a chain fastened around his neck by a padlock, with the other end around the neck of a horse, by the side of which he walked. As night came on and the horse was kept walking at a rapid step, the doctor, being unable to see the wilderness road, and liable at any moment to fall and so be dragged by the neck until the horse should stop, was at last taken up behind the saddle, his chain being still fastened to the horse's neck, and short enough to keep his neck close to the shoulder of the guard. In this situation the horse fell and both riders came under him. The doctor was much hurt and the soldier more. Turning in at midnight, during a drenching rain, the prisoner was chained to his bedstead by his ankle. The next day he had a walk of thirty-five miles, with the chain on his neck, relieved by an occasional ride. The Rev. Mr. Trott, a Methodist missionary, and Mr. Proctor were chained to a wagon in which they were not allowed to ride, and at night chained to the wall of a house by the neck and to one another at the ankle. In this way the missionaries were brought fifty to seventy-five miles to jail at Camp Gilmer; and here is the account of their imprisonment for eleven days before their examination, given by the Report of the American Board for 1831 : —

"After lying eleven days in a miserably filthy log prison, in the middle of July, without window, bed, table, chair, or any article of furniture except a small piece of board;

with no floor to stand, sit, or sleep upon, except rough and crooked poles; being allowed to receive no letters nor send any, nor have any bundle pass out or in without being searched, nor allowed any interview with a friend except in hearing of the guard, and being forced to hear the abominably blasphemous and obscene language of the Georgia soldiers, a writ of *habeas corpus* was obtained, which, after some delay, took them out of the hands of the military and brought them before the inferior court of Gwinnette County, where they were released on giving bonds to appear at the superior court in that county in September." There had been no need of the cruelty of those chains, for these men did not wish to escape. Colonel Nelson, the officer in charge, as he turned them into jail, tauntingly said: "Fear not, little flock, for it is your Father's good pleasure to give you the kingdom." And this was echoed two or three times by others. As the jailer thrust them in, he said: "There is where all the enemies of Georgia have to land — there and in hell." Their request of Colonel Nelson that they might have religious service was derisively refused.

The trial took place in September, and the three missionaries and eight other white men were by the jury found guilty, and by Judge Clayton sentenced to four years' hard labor in the penitentiary, with a recommendation to executive clemency on condition that they would not return to live in the Cherokee country. Brought to the prison at Milledgeville, all accepted the proffered release except Worcester and Butler, who were assigned, one to the shoe-shop and the other to the cabinet-shop.

Meantime an appeal to the Supreme Court of the United States brought a reversal of the verdict and an order for the release of the prisoners, William Wirt being their attorney, and Chief Justice Marshall rendering the opinion. This decision also annulled the Georgia law as unconstitutional. Georgia refused to obey the order, and so took her place by the side of South Carolina in nullification. The prisoners appealed to President Jackson for relief, and Old Hickory answered through Lewis Cass, his Secretary of War, that the action of Georgia had rendered "inoperative" the federal authority, and he is reported to have said: "Let Marshall execute his own decree." Old Hickory, who could swear by the Eternal that South Carolina should not nullify in a matter of tariff, when slavery lifted its behest for slave soil, had to succumb. Then the prisoners, through their attorney, gave notice of an appeal to the Supreme Court for the enforcement of its decision. This notice they afterwards withdrew, not from any recognition of the rightful stand of Georgia, but from the patriotic consideration of relieving that state and the country from the consequences of coming into collision with the federal government, and of postponing the day of the fateful crash that came at Fort Sumter. While these men were in prison their wives made the long, rough journey to Milledgeville to visit them. On their way, when some Presbyterian friends tried to persuade them to advise their husbands to submit to the Georgia law they answered: "If we thought we would say one word to weaken the purpose of our husbands we would not go another step." And when the children met their fathers in prisoner's garb they shrank back from their proffered embrace, but rallied when smiled upon. While I am writing this letter I am permitted to meet a woman who was one of those little children, a daughter of Mr. Worcester, then four years old, who, growing up in the mission, was married to the

Rev. Mr. Robertson, and has been for many years laboring with the Creek nation in the Indian Territory. She showed me the New Testament translated into the language of that people by herself alone. She has a daughter who for a time was a teacher in the Atlanta University and is now again laboring among the Creeks. The mother bears a vivid recollection of those times of trial. When, after sixteen months in prison, its doors were opened to them, these men wrote Governor Lumpkin: "We beg leave respectfully to state to your Excellency that we have not been led to the adoption of this measure by any change of views in regard to the principles on which we have acted, or by any doubt of the justice of our cause or of our perfect right to a legal discharge in accordance with the decision of the Supreme Court in our favor already given." Mr. Worcester was in the line of eight generations of ministers. He and Dr. Butler had the Puritan grit. When set at liberty they went right back to their labor among their dear Cherokees in spite of the cruel law. And their wives were of the same stuff. They went back home from their visit to the prison having kept their determination that no Georgian should see their tears, lest they should construe them as regretting their husbands' course, which they never did. These missionaries and the insulted national authority waited for the infliction of retribution that came at the battle of Missionary Ridge, which was named from the very mission where such usurpation and nullification had defied the American Board and the American nation.

In Dr. Humphrey's missionary library I find a volume of the speeches made in Congress in 1830 against the bill for the removal of these Indians. They were made by Senators Theodore Frelinghuysen, Sprague, of Maine, and Robbins, of Rhode Island, and by Representatives Storrs, of New York, Ellsworth, of Connecticut, Johns, of Delaware, Bates and Edward Everett, of Massachusetts, and David Crockett, of Tennessee. The discussion lasted five days. These were masterly orations, covering the whole ground of Indian treaties and legislation back in the mother country and in the United States. These all took the side of the Cherokees against Georgia. David Crockett represented the largest district of any man in Congress except Duncan, of Illinois, having twenty-two thousand constituents. In his speech he uttered some sentiments denunciatory of the bill which might well be considered by the present legislature of Georgia. Turning away from the south to go with the north he said: "I have constituents to settle with, I am aware, and I should like to please them as well as other gentlemen. But I have also a settlement to make at the bar of my God, and what my conscience dictates to be just and right I will do, be the consequences what they may."

At Clifton Springs I was accustomed to meet General B. A. Hill, a retired veteran of the regular army. He told me the story of the driving out of these Cherokees in 1837. General Winfield Scott was sent with an army of two thousand men to do the job, Hill being then a young lieutenant. At first the people were notified to come into corral, preparatory to deportation. None came in. Then the army was divided into squads to go about and make prisoners of the families. Hill was in charge of one of those squads. He told me that he found the Indians living in a more civilized way than the crackers round about them. He described their thrift, their churches, their schools, and their temperance habits. He said that when he came to their homes he had to apologize for his hateful business by stating that he was acting under orders. He said that as the families were brought out of their homes sometimes a man would go back and put the key under the door, saying, "Surely the government will yet relent and allow us to return to our homes." As the battered soldier of many wars, after these many years, told this tale, his eyes were suffused.

As a sign of the degree of their civilization I quote from that speech of Edward Everett a summary of property besides their lands and homes: — 36 grist-mills, 13 saw-mills, 762 looms, 2,486 spinning-wheels, 172 wagons, 2,923 plows, 7,683 horses, 22,531 cattle, 42,732 swine, 2,566 sheep, 66 blacksmith shops, 9 stores, 2 tan-yards, several public roads, ferries, and turnpikes; they also had 8 churches, and 18 schools with 314 scholars, under the American Board.

It was ten months from the time of the first corraling to the arrival on the Arkansas River, and five months through the winter of rain and mud and cold and snow were consumed in the transportation over a distance of seven hundred miles; while four thousand of the people, one fourth of their entire population, were buried by the way. This was not by the severity of the army treatment, but by the incidental strain of the journey. How could a people thus depleted, maddened, and discouraged by the treatment they had had, ever again take root in a strange and uncongenial land? This is an answer to the question sometimes asked, What have you to show of established institutions for all the years of your missionary work? Yet those leading tribes of the Indian Territory are a civilized people. They have courts, a constitutional government, churches, and seminaries.

And so it is no new thing for Georgia to be pushing the Glenn Bill, which proposes a thousand-dollar fine and chain-gang service for a year upon the Atlanta professors if they persist in teaching their own little children, natives of the state, in their own university classes. But how will it look for Georgia to go on and pass and execute the law? Let us see. In that Board of Trustees of the Atlanta University are Col. E. A. Buck, General Lewis, and Rev. S. E. Lathrop. Colonel Buck left the principalship of an academy in Maine to enter the service. Since the war he has remained in the south to help build up its fortunes. He is one of the heaviest men in an Alabama iron-furnace village. He represented that state in Congress for a time. He is now in the office, held for some time at Atlanta, of clerk of the United States district court. He lives in one of the finest houses of the aristocratic Peach Tree Street. He is one of the most respected and public-spirited citizens. General Lewis carries an empty sleeve in his Atlanta store. He was the first general superintendent of the schools of Georgia, whose administration is still pointed to as the model. Mr. Lathrop was a cavalryman in the Union service, but for nine years has served as missionary pastor in connection with the Lewis Normal Institute in Macon, Georgia, so named for the general above referred to. Now, how will it look for chivalrous Georgia to treat these soldiers as is proposed by that law?

How will it look for Mr. Grady to come north to orate upon the New South, and Governor Colquitt to plead here the temperance cause, and be obliged to report that they had left behind such men, for such an offence, in the chain-gangs of Georgia?

Rev. and General Erastus Blakeslee is called to leave a

pastorate at New Haven, Conn., to take the place of E. A. Ware, the deceased president of the Atlanta University. How will it look to the Grand Army of the Republic to have him and these other comrades thrust into the penitentiary to be hired out in the coal-mines of Georgia for the crime of allowing the children of the teachers in that institution to be taught in the classes presided over by their parents?

As the students of that school have gone forth to teach in the country, some of them have been sought out by white teachers who have said: "Now we have not had any chance for normal training, and you have had the best; we want you to instruct us how to teach." Suppose, then, these white teachers, aspiring to make themselves proficient in their profession, shall say: "We will not stop with this second-hand instruction; we will go to the headquarters and put ourselves under those accomplished professors in the Atlanta University." And, really, how will it look for Governor Gordon, as the executive of the laws, to say to such: "If you do go there I will send those teachers and trustees to the convict camp and the chain-gang"?

Among the finest specimens of magnamimity in southern character has been the readiness of the Board of Examiners to rectify former opinions and to report the attainments of the colored students in that institution. At first they gave up the notion that the colored pupils could not advance into the higher branches of study, and that the mulattoes would be smarter than the blacks. In their report of 1882, expressing desire that Prof. T. N. Chase, of the chair of Greek, should be retained, they say: "We would deem it unfortunate that so important an element of education as Latin and Greek should fall into any disrepute in the Atlanta University." Again they say: "We have seen him [the colored student] quite as much at home in Latin, Greek, mathematics, ethics, mental and physical science, as in the more rudimentary studies." And again: "We do not believe that we have ever seen better teaching than we have seen in the Atlanta University." Now, how will it look to put that Professor Chase and his associates into prison and along by the side of Georgia's galley-slaves, just because he was allowing his own children and some of theirs to enjoy these rare advantages? Then, Rev. C. W. Francis, professor and pastor of the University Church, and Rev. Dr. Bumstead, acting president, both sons of Yale, will Georgia enjoy the sight of those men in the chain-gang?

Rev. Dr. Isaac Anderson, who, in 1819, founded Maryville College in East Tennessee, brought colored young men into that college, and even kept them in his own house, without objection made, as says Professor Crawford, of the same institution, himself a native Tennessean.

How it would have looked if that college president had been thrust into prison for that act! And how would it look if the present incumbent, Rev. Dr. P. M. Bartlett, should be treated in the same way, because for the last score of years a few colored young men were always to be found in that college, which has educated a large number of ministers and other professional men for all of that south-east?

People of Georgia, in presence of the Christian sentiment of the world, how will it look? It would seem to be too bad to celebrate this semi-centennial of the deportation of those outraged Cherokees by repeating a tragedy of like enormity.

LETTER CI.

AN OLD INDIAN EXPERIMENT.

CHICAGO, October 1, 1887.

QUITE in contrast with that treatment of the Cherokees was the dealing of Massachusetts with Stockbridge Indians three half-centuries ago, whereby citizenship and land-in-severalty were conferred upon those aboriginal inhabitants. Land-in-severalty for the Indians, as now provided for by a law of Congress, is not altogether a new thing. Mr. E. W. B. Canning, in *The Magazine of American History* for August, upon "Indian Land-grants in Western Massachusetts," shows that such an experiment was tried in Stockbridge nearly one hundred and fifty years ago. The mission had been doing its work. The meeting-house had its missionary and its school-master. The General Court, in 1749, ordained that upon a public notice to be posted upon that meeting-house the Indians should there assemble and make the necessary arrangements. By this plan it was found that sixty of these dusky roamers of the lower Housatonic were entitled to ownership in severalty. Among these 1,670 acres of land were divided. For others a quantity of undivided land was reserved. The six English families who had been invited to come and settle among them six years before as pattern farmers and housekeepers remained in possession of their endowments, one of whose dwellings, built in 1747, is still standing.

The same law enacted that these Indians "shall be subjected to, and receive the benefit of, the laws of this government to all intents and purposes in like manner as other his majesty's subjects of this province are subjected and do receive." Of course the influences of their church, their school, their model farmers and housekeepers, and the social habits and examples of their white co-occupants had operated to set them forward in civil status quite in advance of any of our aboriginal tribes of the present time except the Cherokees, Choctaws, Creeks, and the Sissetons and the Santees of the Sioux. They were represented among the town and church officials, bore military titles, and were enrolled among the alumni of Harvard and Dartmouth.

The experiment worked as well as could naturally have been expected. The Indians were civilized, citizenized, and for the most part Christianized. After the manner of the New England town organization, as their record book shows, they held regular annual, and many special, meetings for more than thirty years. And yet this state of things continued less than forty years. And why? The writer finds the solution of the question in the intrusion of white purchasers and settlers, by whom the little Indian commonwealth was absorbed. He presents a number of specimens of sixty votes recorded for the sale and transfer of the undivided lands. These run thus: Fifty acres to a white hotel-keeper, "in consideration of his having his ox killed; one hundred acres to another for his paying £37 to liberate Unkarring from prison; fifty acres to another to encourage him to set up his blacksmith's trade in Stockbridge." Other appropriations of land were made to make improvements in the town, to pay its debts, and to reward the services of surveyors, physicians, etc. In short, it was the stronger crowding out the weaker; the inchoate civilization yielding to the matured. And so, when the friendly Oneidas, in New York, offered them a share in their own reservation, they accepted the same and made a removal. Then they were removed to Indiana, then to Green Bay, then to Lake Winnebago, and then, forty years ago, to their present locality in Shawano County, Wisconsin. There they had some fine timber land. White speculators coveted it. But the tribe as a body would not vote to alienate their land. Then the timber sharks craftily persuaded them that land-in-severalty was the true idea. This once accomplished, the timber land was bought from individuals at nominal prices, and the birthright was thus squandered, its inheritors being then turned out to shift for themselves, which resulted in their becoming absorbed by the wilder natives of the neighborhood.

Mr. Canning says in conclusion : " To my own mind one thing is certain — that to render any experiment of land-owning in severalty effective of solid and permanent good to the Indian, *absolute prohibition of white residence among them*, save for educational purposes, should be enacted and enforced."

The Dawes Law, now to be put into execution, provides that the allotted lands shall be inalienable for twenty-five years. This, surely, in the light of the experiment here detailed, is as short a time as is wise or safe to be fixed. But this law, from which so much of good is anticipated, provides for selling the surplus lands to white settlers, which will be in the face of the theory just quoted, that all such contact must be interdicted. But, as Mr. Beecher in his Cleveland letter said of the freedmen, they would have to take the consequences of liberty, so these to be newly made citizens must take the consequences of citizenship. They will improve under the process of exercising their rights as citizens ; they will learn from the example and by the stimulus of their pale-faced neighbors.

But every body can see that in order to any success in this scheme of citizenizing the Indian he must be Christianized. He can not be legislated into character. Land-ownership is not an equivalent of enlightenment. Merely secular schools will not build up, however, nor sweeten the life of families, nor make the essential unit of the beneficent commonwealth. And in order to this civilizing, the Indians must have Christian ideas, and these come from the Bible, which the native wants in his own language. It is usurpation to take away from them their vernacular Bible, as is implied by the policy of casting out of all Indian schools instruction in the native dialect.

LETTER CII.

THE MARTYRDOM OF ELIJAH P. LOVEJOY.

CHICAGO, November 1, 1887.

It will be half a century on the seventh of this month when Elijah Parish Lovejoy, in the free state of Illinois, at Alton, became the proto-martyr to the freedom of the press and the freedom of the slave in our country. I have in hand his memoir, written by his brothers Joseph and Owen, also an account of the "Alton Trials," written by a lawyer at that time, and a "Narrative of the Riots at Alton," by Rev. Edward Beecher, D.D., then president of Illinois College. In one of these is a picture of the stone warehouse at Alton, and of the mob as they were assaulting it. The only portrait of Mr. Lovejoy extant, a silhouette, is in the possession of his sister, the wife of the Rev. Henry L. Hammond, of this city. As the half-century memorial is at hand, and as a generation has come on since that eventful day, it may be worth while to reproduce the leading facts in the tragedy.

Mr. Lovejoy's grandfather, Francis, had removed from New Hampshire to Maine in 1790, and his father, Daniel, was a Congregational minister in that state. He was graduated with the highest honors at Waterville College, in 1826, presenting at that time a poem on the "Inspiration of the Muse." This and other poems written before and after that date show that he had himself not a little of the gift of the Muse. On his departing for St. Louis, in 1827, his farewell had these heroic strains: —

> Thy sons are noble, in whose veins there runs
> A richer tide than Europe's kings can boast,
> The blood of free men; blood which oft has flowed
> In Freedom's holiest cause; and ready yet to flow,
> If need should be, ere it would curdle down
> To the slow, sluggish stream of slavery.

Arriving in that city, he fell to teaching school, and then to the editing and publishing of a political paper, advocating Henry Clay for President. His prospects for political elevation became flattering indeed. But in January, 1832, under the ministry of Rev. W. S. Potts, he took upon himself the yoke of Christ. He then struck for Princeton Seminary to study for the ministry. Licensed by a Philadelphia Presbytery he supplied for a time at Newport, Rhode Island, and in the Spring Street Church, New York. But his heart was upon the west, and the thought of the west was upon him. Christian friends in St. Louis, feeling greatly the need of a religious weekly paper, urged him to return and become the editor of it, pledging him a salary of $500, and a capital of $1,200. And so, in November, 1833, the first number of *The St. Louis Observer* was issued. The tone was that of a Christian journal, and not of an abolition propagandist. Indeed, Mr. Lovejoy was not at that time in favor of immediate abolition, and was rather inclined to the colonization scheme. But dwelling in the midst of slavery, his quick sense of the right soon ripened his views to favor immediate abolition.

Along in 1834 a convention was proposed for amending the constitution of Missouri so as to abolish slavery in a gradual way. To this, even, *The St. Louis Republican* committed itself, and its position was used by the *Observer* to push on the anti-slavery sentiment. Meantime Mr. Lovejoy was urging the duty of Christian masters towards their slaves. He could not help denouncing the act of a state's attorney who had whipped a female slave nearly to death, and of another man who did whip the life out of a slave, and who, being tried, was not condemned, as negro testimony was not allowed in court. A case of cruelty had also stirred his righteous indignation. Two men, suspected of abducting slaves from Missouri, had been brought back and scourged nearly to death by "most respectable citizens," one of the suspects proving to have been totally innocent. Then a case of lynching had aroused his denunciation, the victim, a colored man, having been burned to death. And to his mind, worse than all was the complicity of Presbyterian elders with such things. The proprietors of the paper became frightened. They undertook to lock Mr. Lovejoy's lips. This could not be done. When the abolitionists were charged with favoring amalgamation, he could not help retorting that he saw evidence enough of such practice in the bleached faces of thousands of people upon the streets. Among those who begged him to desist was Dr. Potts. The mob tore down his office. And then, as Alton offered him an asylum, he decided to remove his paper to that city.

But no sooner was his press landed upon the wharf at Alton than it was seized, broken in pieces, and thrown into the Mississippi. Another press was secured in July, 1836, and this was run until August of the next year, when it also was destroyed by the mob. A third press was secured and this also was soon made to follow into the river. The anti-slavery people being aroused, a convention was held at Alton to organize an anti-slavery society. The mobbites, taking advantage of the opportunity offered for free discussion, came in and perverted the meeting, after which the abolitionists by themselves organized their society. In the fall of 1837 a fourth press had been ordered from Cincinnati. It was to come by steamer and to be landed and stored in the ware-house of Godfrey, Gilman & Co., that Mr. Gilman being the father of Secretary Gilman of the Bible Society, and of President Gilman of the Johns Hopkins University. The friends had sought the protection of the mayor for the landing of the press. He recognized their right to protect their property, and agreed to authorize them as an armed posse. About forty or fifty of them assembled at the ware-house for this purpose. At ten o'clock at night several retired, leaving thirty on guard. At three in the morning the boat arrived and delivered the press. No resistance was offered at that time except the firing of a few stones. The danger was thought to be over, and so President Beecher, who had remained over from the anti-slavery convention till that morning, supposing that there was no further need of his services, returned by stage to Jacksonville. On the next night only twelve remained at the ware-house, among them Mr. Lovejoy, who alternated with his brother Owen in standing guard. Pretty soon the mob appeared, armed with stones, guns, and pistols. After they had fired two or three shots into the building the defenders fired back, and one of the mob, Bishop, was mortally wounded. Whereupon the rioters, reinforced from the rum-shops, put up ladders against the stone walls to set fire to the roof. Five of the defenders volunteered to come down to drive away the assailants and did for the time disperse them. Returning into the store they reloaded and came out for a second assault. By this time some of the rabble, having concealed themselves behind a pile of lumber, fired a volley into the assailing party, when Mr. Lovejoy received six balls, three in his breast, one on the left and one on the right side, and one in the abdomen. Turning quickly back into the store, he ran up-stairs and came into the counting-room and fell, exclaiming, "O God! I am shot, I am shot!" and expired in a few moments. Another one of the defenders, Mr. Weller, was wounded, but not fatally. When it was announced to the mob that Lovejoy was dead they sent up a yell of exultation, and swore that his comrades also should find a grave where they were. The mayor coming around, so far from serving as an officer of protection, became a messenger to bear the terms of the mob to the beleaguered men. When the next morning the bloody remains of the martyr were being removed to his dwelling, their attendants were saluted with jeers and scoffs. It was here that Owen Lovejoy, over the body of the martyred brother, took his vow of ceaseless opposition to that great criminal, the slave-holding system. On Thursday, the ninth of November, 1837, just thirty-five years from the day of his birth, the proto-martyr was borne to his grave. His devoted wife, whom he had married at St. Charles, Mo., and who with her husband had been mobbed in that town, was not at home at the time of his death, having left the city in delicate health to avoid the continual alarm. When informed that he had been killed she fell down senseless, "trembling," says one present, "as though an arrow had pierced her heart." Mr. Lovejoy had been moderator of the presbytery of St. Louis, and at the time of the murder was moderator of the presbytery of Alton.

The memoir of Mr. Lovejoy contains reports of meetings held in many cities of the north to denounce the crime, and also gives the spirit of the secular and religious press as a whirlwind of indignation. *The New York Observer*, true to itself, gave faint praise to the martyr of liberty. But *The New York Evangelist*, under the grand Joshua Leavitt, and *The Boston Recorder* took the very highest ground. Clearly, as John Brown said of himself, Mr. Lovejoy was "worth more to die than to live." The enemies of freedom by their insane act had set forward the cause of anti-slavery many years.

It was a travesty of justice by which the grand jury indicted for a riot the men who stood for the defence of their property and lives as well as for the freedom of the press. Mr. Gilman, one of the owners of the ware-house, and who was himself in the thick of the fray, was the only one of the indicted men who was tried. When the verdict of "not guilty" was rendered a *nolle prosequi* was entered as to the others. And so when the mobbites were tried under an indictment from the same grand jury, they too were cleared. But the jury of the American people long since tried and executed the supreme criminal, that system which made merchandise of the image of God.

This semi-centennial memorial of the martyrdom of

Lovejoy seems a fitting conclusion of this series of letters which have been strung upon the string of the anti-slavery issue. It took us a hundred years to make good the Declaration of Independence that all men are created equal. It was a weary and bloody accomplishment. By Mr. William F. Poole's volume on "Anti-Slavery Opinions before 1800," it appears that there were in the United States, before that date, sixteen abolition societies, of which ten were in slave-holding states. Mr. Poole gives Dr. George Buchanan's oration, delivered in Baltimore, July 4, 1791, and dedicated to Thomas Jefferson, Secretary of State, upon "The Moral and Political Evil of Slavery," at a public meeting of the "Maryland Society for promoting the abolition of slavery, and the relief of free negroes and others unlawfully held in bondage." I have already referred (Letter LXX) to the Manumission Society in Tennessee, in 1821, and (Letter III) to the Manumission Society of North Carolina, in 1830.

But, all of that finally accomplished, we have new covenants to make good, the citizenship of the negro, his suffrage, and his Christian enlightenment. To these God will hold us, if it takes another hundred or a thousand years. The sooner the spirit and the practice of the accursed system of caste are put away we shall have enduring concord, the peace of righteousness. As to the method of meeting this new crisis in the anti-slavery cause, we can not do better than to give heed to the almost inspired and prophetic injunction of one who was a signer of the Declaration and a member of Congress, Dr. Benjamin Rush, president of the Abolition Society of Chestertown, Maryland, in an address sent out within the last century to the abolition societies of the United States. He says: "When we have broken his chains and restored the African to the enjoyment of his rights, the great work of justice and benevolence is not accomplished. The newborn citizen must receive that instruction and those powerful impressions of moral and religious truths which will render him capable and desirous of filling the varied duties he owes to himself and to his country. By educating some in the higher branches, and all in the higher parts of learning and in the precepts of religion and morality, we shall not only do away with the reproach and calumny so unjustly lavished upon us, but confound the enemies of truth by evincing that the unhappy sons of Africa, in spite of the degrading influence of slavery, are in no wise inferior to the more fortunate inhabitants of Europe and America."

The martyrdom of Lovejoy has its bearing upon our next great moral issue, that of temperance. This cause already numbers its three or four martyrs, George C. Haddock, the preacher, Dr. Northrop, the political organizer, the constable of Des Moines, Iowa, and Gambrell, the editor at Jackson, Miss. As once slavery claimed the right to rule the nation, so now the saloon system is seeking the same preëminence by throttling the politics of the nation. The seven hundred millions paid annually for the dram-bill of our country, as reported by United States officials, together with the hundreds of millions invested in this business, make a total in amount beyond that of the old slave-power. And this evil is right among us every-where, and not, as was the other, off down south where we could whack away at it in safety. The conspiracy of the saloon interest of the "saloon statesmen" is as patent as was that which sought in secession to break down the nation. The challenge is accepted. The battle is set in array. Remember Lovejoy! Remember Haddock, and Northrop, and Gambrell! And may God give victory to the right!

FINIS.

INDEX.

A. H. M. S., 24, 55, 57, 75, 132, 152, 249, 270.
A. M. A., 23, 55, 75, 88, 102, 116, 132, 150, 152, 157, 174, 195, 201, 231, 233, 256, 263, 269.
Abbott, Mr., 228.
Acadians, 165.
A. C. U., 75, 132.
Adair, 66.
Adams, John Quincy, 278.
Alabama Anniversary Week, 171.
Alabama Legislature, 96.
Allen, Brigadier-General, 117.
Allen, Wm. T., 12.
Allen, Rev. Dr., 256.
Alexander, Dr. W. S., 164.
Alloucz, Father, 123.
Alvord, Rev. J. W., 89, 94, 99, 102, 249.
American Board, 145, 263, 280, 281, 284, 286.
American Tract Society, 84, 249.
Andrews, Rev. D., 33.
Andrews, Prof. E. B., 32.
Andrews, Dr. Edmund, 41, 42.
Andrews, Rev. Dr. G. W., 160, 172.
Anderson, Dr. Isaac, 191, 289.
Andersonville Prison, 66.
Andrus, Rev. E., 93.
Anniston, Ala., 193.
Arkansas Post, 38, 202.
Armstrong, Gen. S. C., 174.
Arnold, Hon. Isaac N., 117.
Ashley, Rev. S. S., 165.
Atlanta, Ga., 86, 156.
Atlanta Cotton Exposition, 199.
Atlanta University, 288, 289.
Aunt Lizzie Aiken, 38.
Austin, Mr., of Texas, 149.
Avery, Rev. John T., 30.

Bacon, Dr. Leonard, 77, 113, 126.
Bacon, Lord, 47.
Badger, Dr. Milton, 57, 81, 152.
Baker, Rev. J. D., 33.
Banks, General, 38, 92.
Baldwin, Dr. Theron, 110, 111, 137, 152.
Baptist Work among Freedmen, 275.
Barbed Wire, 244, 245.
Barber, 16.
Barnes, Rev. H. E., 33.
Barton, Rev. W. E., 231.

Barrows, Dr. William, 134.
Bartlett, Pres. P. M. 192, 280, 289.
Bascom, Dr. Flavel, 56, 172.
Bates, of Mass., 285.
Beard, Dr. A. F., 228.
Beecher, Dr. Edward, 54, 121, 126, 292, 293, 296.
Beecher, Rev. Fred W., 113.
Beecher, Henry Ward, 46, 77, 78, 80.
Bellows, Rev. Dr., 39.
Beloit College, 32.
Beman, Dr., 144.
Berea College, 181.
Biddle University, N. C., 209.
Birmingham, Ala., 220.
Bishop, General, 297.
Bismarck, D. T., 146.
Blagden, Dr., 113.
Blakeslee, Gen. Erastus, 287.
Blatchford, E. W., 29, 36, 64, 115.
Bleeding Kansas, 11.
Bliss, Rev. Charles R., 271.
Bliss, Rev. T. E., 55.
Blue Laws of S. C., 107.
Bodwell, Rev. L., 55, 61.
Booth, William, 84.
Boston Council, 72, 78, 113, 116, 249.
Boston Mountain, Ark., 202.
Boston Recorder, 298.
Boston Tract Society, 81, 93.
Boyce, James P., 272.
Bragg, General, 81, 84.
Brainerd, Rev. David, 136.
Bradford, Conn., 135.
Brayman, General, 118.
Breckenridge, Colonel, 199.
Brice, Rev. Mr., 113.
Brockway, Captain, 58.
Brooks, Rev. Phillips, 271.
Brooks, Preston S., 101.
Bross, Col. John A., 57, 58, 118.
Bross, Gov. William, 47, 58, 145.
Brothers, Joe, 243.
Brown, John, 21, 72, 298.
Brown, Gov. Joseph E., 224.
Bryan, T. B., 52, 130.
Bryant, W. C., 244.
Bruce, Judge John, 172.
Buck, Col. A. E., 287.
Buchanan, Dr. George, 299.
Buckingham, Gov. W. A., 73.

Bumstead, Prof. Horace, 289.
Budington, Dr. W. I., 132.
Burnell, Miss Mary, 38.
Bushnell, Rev. M., 33.
Butler, Gen. B. F., 23, 69, 92, 174.
Butler, Peter, 122.
Butler, Dr., 281, 284.
Butterfield, Pres. H. Q., 132, 134.

Cable, George W., 206.
Cady, C. M., 199.
Cain, Bishop, 214.
Caldwell, Rev. George, 191.
Camp Douglas, 63, 66.
Candee, Rev. George, 20.
Canal at Vicksburg, 249.
Canning, Mr. E. W. B., 290.
Cardoza, Rev. F. L., 102.
Carpenter's Painting, 71.
Carpenter, Deacon Philo, 143, 145.
Carlyle, Thomas, 271.
Centennial, 151.
Central Tennessee College, 179.
Cass, Lewis, 283.
Chapin, Pres. A. L., 31.
Chapman, Rev. Daniel, 33.
Chandler, Senator, 49.
Charity for Chicago, 130.
Chase, Bishop, 54.
Chase, Prof. T. N., 288, 289.
Chattanooga, 161.
Charleston, S. C., 100, 212, 237.
Chetlain, General, 98, 118.
Cherokees, 280, 284, 285.
Cherokee Missionaries, 280.
Chicago, 125.
Chicago Fire, 129, 132.
Chicago Relief and Aid Society, 133.
Chicago Theological Seminary, 72.
Christian Commission, 68.
Claflin University, 261.
Clapp, Dr. A. H., 152, 153.
Clapp, Dr. J. C., 236
Clark, Dr. Joseph, 44.
Clark University, 260.
Clary, Rev. Dexter, 152.
Clay, Rev. Daniel, 167.
Clay, Henry, 94, 167, 294.
Clayton, Judge, 282.
Clendenin, Col. D. R., 52.
Clifton Springs, 196, 285.
Coan, Dr. Titus, 136.
Coe, Dr. D. B., 152, 153.
College Society, 132.
Colored Gentleman, 83.
Colored Men's Heroism, 98.
Columbus, Ky., 35.
Colt, Mrs., 38.

Colver, Dr. Nathaniel, 25.
Colquitt, Gov. A. H., 200, 201, 218, 271, 287.
Colorado, 138, 267.
Connecticut in Legislation, 134.
Congregational Methodists, 194.
Congregational Union, 75, 132.
Confederate Memorial Day, 206.
Concord Council, 223.
Cook, General, 32.
Cook, Hon. B. C., 116.
Congregational Sunday-School and Publishing Society, 222, 231.
Corliss, Mr., 176.
Cordley, Rev. Richard, 19, 55, 61, 66.
Corpus Christi, 168, 242.
Cox, General, 32, 137.
Crawford, Professor, 193.
Cravath, Pres. E. M., 177, 214
Creek Nation, 284.
Creoles, 92.
Crissey, Mr., 63.
Crockett, David, 148, 285.
Crozat, Anthony, 278.
Crogman, Professor, 200.
Cruft, General Charles, 32
Crum, Rev. Mr., 150.
Currier, Judge Warren, 72.
Cushing, Dr. C., 134.
Custer, General, 146.
Cutler, General, 117.
Cutler, Dr. Manasseh, 276.
Cuyler, Dr. T. L., 196.

Davenport, Rev. James, 135.
Davis, Jefferson, 62, 72, 102.
Davis, Rev. J. S., 21.
Dawes Law, 292.
Day, Rev. S., 33.
Day, Rev. T. L., 194.
Dakota Indian Conference, 262.
Dempster, Dr. John, 25.
Dan, 246.
Decoration Day South, 187.
De Tocqueville, 134.
Dexter, Dr. H. M., 73, 127.
Dickinson, Anna, 51.
Dickinson, Rev. Jonathan, 135.
Dill, Rev. J. H., 33.
Dix, Miss Dorothy, 173.
Dodge, Rev. B., 232.
Dodge, Professor, 226.
Dodge, William E., 271.
Doolittle, Senator, 31.
Douglass, Fred, 92, 200.
Dow, 10.
Driver Drunk, 204.
Duluth, 140.

Duncan, of Illinois, 285.
Dunn, Rev. R. C., 113.
Dunning, Dr. A. E., 220, 231.

Eastman, Hon. Zebina, 31.
East Tennessee, 190.
Eddy, Dr. T. M., 25, 118.
Edgefield, S. C., 101.
Elizabeth, N. J., 135.
Elliott Brothers, 21.
Ellis, Mr., 144.
Ellsworth, of Connecticut, 285.
Emancipation Day at Atlanta, 159.
Emigrant Aid Society, 13, 15.
Emery, Rev. S. H., 33.
England, 76.
Evangeline, 165.
Evans, Dr. C. A., 218.
Evanston Biblical Institute, 32.
Everett, Edward, 285, 286.
Everts, Dr. W. W., 25.

Fairchild, General, 117.
Fairchild, Pres. E. H., 182, 226.
Fairfield, Rev. M. W., 113.
Fallows, Brigadier-General, 117.
Farragut, 38.
Farrar, Canon, 220.
Farwell, J. V., 112.
Fee, Rev. John G., 21, 182.
F. F. V.'s, 107.
Finney, Pres. C. G., 32, 131.
First Woman's Missionary Society, 257.
Fisk, Gen. C. B., 59, 83, 84, 106, 177, 214.
Fisk University, 177.
Foote, Commodore, 36.
Foote, Hiram, 117.
Foote, Horatio K., 117.
Foster, Dr. Henry, 196.
Fort Abraham Lincoln, 146.
Fort Brady, 33.
Fort Crawford, 33.
Fort Dearborn, 33, 144.
Fort Gillem, 178.
Fort Howard, 33.
Fort Pillow, 56, 58.
Fort Smith, Ark., 202.
Fort Sully, 142.
Fort Sumter, 238, 283.
Fort Wright, 36.
Fortress Monroe, 23, 173, 254.
France, 76.
Francis, Prof. C. W., 200, 280.
Freedman's Savings Bank, 89.
French, Rev. M., 101.
Frelinghuysen, Theodore, 285.
Fry, Gen. S. S., 32.

Gaines, General, 280.
Gambrell, Editor, 300.
Garden, Alexander, 111.
Garrison, W. L., 92.
Gemmel, Rev. George B., 53.
Georgia Chain Gang, 279.
Georgia Prison, 279.
German Reform in North Carolina, 233, 234.
Gifford, John, 116.
Gilman, Pres. D. C., 271, 273, 296.
Gilman, of Alton, 298.
Gilman, Secretary, 296.
Gilmer, Camp, 281.
Glass, Peter, 68.
Glenn Bill, 287.
Glidden, Mr., 201.
Godfrey, Gilman & Co., 296.
Goliad, Texas, 170.
Goodell, Dr., 194.
Goodrich, Hon. Grant, 25.
Gookins, Hon. S. B., 25.
Gordon, Prof. W. L., 239.
Gordon, Governor, 288.
Grand View, Tenn., 228.
Grady, Editor, 287.
Grant, Rev. Joel, 33.
Grant, Gen. U. S., 38, 39, 69, 87, 118, 249.
Gray, Joseph, 49.
Greeley, Horace, 124, 140.
Green, Rev. J. S., 254.
Greensborough Jail, 19.
Griffith, Sergeant J. E., 110.
Grinnell, Hon. J. B., 125.
Gubernatorial Golgotha, 18.
Guernsy, Rev. Jesse, 152.
Guild, Rev., 66.
Gilded Deadfall, 151.
Guilford, Conn., 135, 136.
Gwinnette Co., Georgia, 282.

Hall, Dr. Charles, 152.
Hall, Rev. C. L., 263.
Haddock, Rev. George C., 300.
Hamilton, General, 117.
Hammond, Col. C. G., 56, 73.
Hammond, Rev. Henry L., 293.
Hampton Institute, 173, 254.
Hannibal, Mo., 59, 65.
Hanks, Mr., 72.
Harlow, Rev., 66.
Harper's Ferry, 21.
Harris, Gov. I. G., 84.
Harvey, Governor, 117.
Haven, Pres. E. O., 128.
Haven, Bishop Gilbert, 157, 259, 261.
Hawley, Rev. Z. K., 37, 38.

Hayes, Ex-Pres. R. B., 271.
Haygood, Dr. A. G., 214, 249, 272.
Helper's Impending Crisis, 20.
Henry, Patrick, 107.
Henshaw, Mrs. Sarah Edwards, 118.
Hickok, Professor, 106.
Hill, Gen. B. A., 285.
Hitchen, Rev. G., 91.
Hitchcock, President, 114.
Hobart, Brigadier-General, 117.
Hoge, Dr., 177.
Hoge, Mrs., 38, 70.
Hopkins, Dr. Mark, 175.
Hosford, Major, 66.
Howard, Dr., 93.
Howard, Gen. O. O., 88, 92, 94, 159, 192.
Howard, Rev. R. B., 89.
Hoyt, 16.
Hubbard, Gordon S., 145.
Huguenots in South, 212.
Humphrey, President, 136.
Humphrey, Dr. S. J., 125, 284.
Huntsville, Ala., 87.
Hurlbut, General, 118.
Hyatt, 16.
Hyde, Dr. J. T., 128.

Iapi Oaye, 143.
Illinois College, 32.
Indians at Hampton, 175.
Industrial, 176.
Interval of Silence, 151.
Indian Language in Indian Schools, 293.
Ireland's Grievance, 244.
Itineracy of Pilgrim, 239.

Jackson, Gen. Andrew, 232, 283.
Jackson, Miss., 90.
Jacobs, B. F., 164.
Jefferson, Thomas, 113, 276, 278, 299.
Jenney, Rev. E., 33.
Jessup, M. K., 272.
Jewett, Dr. Charles, 46.
Jewett, M. T., 84.
Johns Hopkins University, 273, 296.
Johns, of Delaware, 285.
Johnson, Pres. Andrew, 69, 74, 100, 112, 116.
Jones, John, 21.
Jones, L. J., 195.
Jones, Ottawa, 16.
Jubilee Singers, 131.

Kansas City, 55.
Keeler, Rev. Mr., 113.
Kendrick, William, 20.
Kent, Rev. Erastus, 152.

Kimball, H. I., 199.
Kingsbury, Rev. Cyrus, 280.
Kings Mountain, N. C., 212.
Kinney, Miss Rose M., 37.
Kirby, Superintendent, 152.
Kirk, Dr., 80.
Kitchel, Dr. H. D., 44.
Knowles, Mrs. L. J., 249.
Knox College, 32.
Knoxville, Tenn., 86.
Kokomo, 48.

Lane, General, 11, 14.
Langworthy, Dr. I. P., 134.
Larned, E. C., Esq., 43.
Lathrop, Rev. S. E., 228, 238, 287.
Lawrence, Kansas, 60.
Le Compton, 17.
Lee, Gen. Robert E., 67.
Lamar, Dr. J. G., 191.
Le Moyne, Dr., 162.
Lewis, General, 287.
Libby Prison, 66.
Lincoln, Pres. A., 25, 31, 55, 57, 62, 63, 68, 72, 82, 104, 122, 159.
Little Tad, 70, 71.
Litts, Rev. P., 91.
Livermore, Mrs., 70.
Livingston Hall, 214.
Lockwood, Rev. L. C., 23.
Logan, General, 118.
Loomis, Rev. Samuel, 208.
Loomis, Prof. L. M., 208.
Lone Star State, 147.
Louisiana Sunday-school Convention, 163.
Louisiana Purchase, 278.
Love, Dr. W. D., 117.
Lovejoy, Elijah P., 53, 293, 296, 297, 298, 300.
Lovejoy, Rev. Daniel, 294.
Lovejoy, Francis, 294.
Lovejoy, Joseph, 293.
Lovejoy, Owen, 49, 51, 53, 293, 296, 297.
Lum, Rev. S. Y., 11, 13.
Lumpkin, Governor, 284.
Lyman, W. R., 164.
Lynch, James, 101.

Madison, Pres. James, 280.
Mammoth Cave, 81.
Manumission Society of North Carolina, 20.
Manumission Society of Tennessee, 192.
Mardi Gras, 163.
Marietta College, 32.
Marsh, T. J., 13.
Marsh, Rev. Mr., 19.

Marshall, Chief Justice, 283.
Maryville College, Tennessee, 289.
Mason, Lowell, 105.
Massie, Dr. James W., 76.
Mattison, Rev. D., 33.
Mattoon, President, 209.
McClernand, General, 41, 118.
McCoy, Rev. D. C., 126.
McCampbell, Rev. Mr., 191.
McDaniel, Rev. S. C., 195.
McClean, Dr. R. G., 40.
McPherson Barracks, 158.
McTyeire, Bishop, 214.
McVicker, Pres. Peter, 66.
Medill, Joseph, 30.
Memphis, Tennessee, 162.
Menefee, Alfred, 84.
Merriman, United States Senator, 189.
Merrill, Superintendent, 152.
Methodist Work among Freedmen, 216, 259.
Mills, Rev. Samuel J., 136.
Minneapolis, 141.
Misseldine, Rev. A. H., 237.
Missionary Ridge, 85, 284.
Missionaries Ostracized, 210.
Mississippi Legislature, 90.
Mississippi River in Flood, 207.
Missionary Tour in Connecticut, 131.
Monod, Rev. Theo., 76.
Monroe, E. B., 174.
Monroe, Pres. James, 280.
Moody, D. L., 113, 164.
Moore, Sec. W. H., 134.
Morgan, Dr. John, 21.
Morgan Raid, 23, 48.
Morrill, Rev. S. S., 33.
Morris, Mrs. Martha, 265.
Morris, Rev. E., 33.
Mountain Work, 226.
Mount Gilead, Ohio, 12.
Mulligan, Colonel, 57, 118.
Myers, Rev. A. A., 226, 228.

Napier, Captain, 123.
Napoleon, 278.
National Cemeteries, 184.
Natchez, Miss., 91.
Negroes in the New Orleans Exposition, 246.
Negroes' Newspapers, 102.
Nelson, Colonel, 282.
Newark, N. J., 135.
New Amsterdam, 135.
New Britain, Conn., 175.
New England, 34.
New England Zone, 44.
New England Church, Chicago, 131.

New Iberia, La., 165.
New Orleans, 163.
Newman, Dr., 93.
New York Evangelist, 298.
New York Observer, 298.
New West Commission, 270.
Nettleton, Rev. Asahel, 136.
Neuces River, 245.
Noble Brothers, 194.
Noble, Dr. F. A., 194.
North and South. — Things in Common, 211.
Northern Michigan, 149.
Northern Pacific, 146.
Northrup, Prof. Cyrus, 214.
Northrup, Dr., 300.
Norwich, Conn., 79.
Nova Scotia, 76.
Nullification, 283.

Oak Park, 130.
Oberlin, 32.
Oberlin Council, 131, 178.
Oglesby, General, 64, 118.
Ohio River, 137, 138.
Old Indian Experiment, 290.
Old Hickory, 283.
Olmsted, Fred. Law, 39.
Oneidas, 291.
Orient Hotel, 183.
Otis, Hon. L. B., 25, 29.

Paine, General, 99.
Paine, Brigadier-General, 117.
Painter, Prof. C. C., 214.
Palmer, Dr. Benjamin, 238.
Palmer, Dr. B. M., 93, 164.
Palmer, General, 32, 118.
Paris, Texas, 149.
Parker, R. D., 19.
Pattenburg, 41.
Patton, Dr. Wm. W., 24, 25, 30, 36, 45, 50, 68.
Payne, Bishop, 238.
Peabody Fund, 272.
Peake, Mrs. Mary E., 24.
Pease, Captain, 99.
Perkins, Rev. George W., 145.
Peters, Dr. Absalom, 136, 152.
Pennsylvania Company, 154.
Petrie, Dr., 172.
Phillips, 16.
Pierce, Rev. W. G., 33.
Pike, Rev. G. D., 179, 214.
Pilgrim's Rest, 114.
Pittsburg Landing, 35.
Pleasant Hill, Tenn., 228.
Plymouth Rock, 250th Year, 126.

Poole, A. M., 155.
Poole, W. F., 299.
Porter, E. Payson, 164.
Porter, Dr. Jeremiah, 33, 37, 38, 112, 136, 145.
Pope, Rev. G. S., 228, 231.
Pope, General, 32, 36.
Potts, W. S., 294, 295.
Powell, Dr. James, 227, 237.
Pratt, Rev. C. H., 65.
Post, Rev. T. M., 44, 55, 56, 72, 127.
Presbyterian Negro Missions, 208.
Princeton College, 135.
Price, Gen Sterling, 59, 66.
Proctor, Mr., 281.
Prohibition in North Carolina, 188.
Pyrn, Dr., 93.

Quantrell's Raid, 60.
Quint, Dr. A. H., 77.

Raleigh, Dr. Alexander, 76.
Randolph, 17.
Rankin, Rev. A. L., 33, 88.
Ransom, General, 118.
Read, Superintendent, 150.
Renville, Rev. John B., 262.
Revolutionary Soldier, 64.
Reynolds, Gen. J. J., 32.
Rice, Rev., 66.
Richardson, J. C., 20, 228.
Richardson, Rev. William, 208.
Richmond, Va., 67, 79, 103, 107, 113.
Riggs, Rev. A. L., 141, 263.
Riggs, Rev. C. B., 230.
Riggs, Dr. S. R., 141.
Riggs, Rev. T. L., 142, 263.
Rob Roy, 65.
Roberts, 16.
Robbins, Captain A. J. C., 231.
Robbins, Ernie, 231.
Robbins, of Rhode Island, 285.
Robbins, Tennessee, 231.
Robertson, Rev. Mr., 284.
Robinson, Governor, 13.
Robinson, Rev., 66.
Rockhold, Mr., 20.
Rogers, Rev. J. A., 21.
Roger Williams College, 179.
Romeyn, Captain, 175.
Ross, Dr. F. A., 87.
Roy, Aaron D., 11, 61.
Roy, Charles A., 184.
Roy, Rev. Jos. E., 31, 43, 132, 228, 238.
Ruger, General, 117.
Rush, Dr. Benjamin, 200.
Ryder, Rev. C. J., 228.

Salisbury, Pres. Albert, 278.
Saloman, General, 117.
San Antonio, Texas, 168, 219.
Sandwich Islands, 174.
Sanitary Fair, 49, 71.
Sanitary Commission, North-west, 36, 44.
Sanitary Commission, United States, 34, 39, 45, 49.
Santee Agency, 142.
Savage, Dr. G. S. F., 45, 81, 128, 249.
Savannah, 102, 212.
Saxton, General, 101.
Scofield, Rev. W. C., 33.
Scott Co., Tennessee, 231.
Scott, Dred, 12.
Scott, Gen. Winfield, 144, 285.
Scudder, Dr. H. N., 125.
Schurtz, Gen. Carl, 117.
Shedd, Dr. John H., 209.
Sheffield, Rev. D. Z., 126.
Shelby Iron Works, Alabama, 161.
Sherman, Gen. W. T., 38, 94, 102, 163, 191.
Sherman, Texas, 149.
Shepherd, Ella, 214.
Sherwood, Ex-Governor, 230.
Sherwood, Tennessee, 230.
Shomber, Mr., 16.
Shurtleff College, 32.
Skinner, Hon. Mark, 25, 36.
Slater Fund Appropriations, 274.
Slater, John F., 249, 271.
Slater, William A., 272.
Slavery Idolized, 210.
Small, Robert, 102.
Smith, Rev. E. F., 147, 177.
Smith, Gov. of New Hampshire, 175.
Snow South, 188.
Soldiers of Congregational Churches in the West, 107.
Solomon, 243.
Southern Churches and the Negroes, 216.
Spence, Prof. A. K., 214.
Sprague, of Maine, 285.
Stage Drivers, 140.
Stanton, Secretary, 30.
Starkweather, Brigadier-General, 117.
Steele, Prof. A. J., 162, 163.
Stevens, Rev. J. D., 141, 263.
Stewart, John A., 271.
St. Joseph, Mo., 59, 122.
St. Louis Republican, 295.
St. Charles, Mo., 297.
Stone, Mrs. Valeria G., 180.
Stockbridge Indians, 290.
Storrs, Dr. R. S., 80.

Storrs, S. D., 19, 66.
Storrs School, Atlanta, 158.
Storrs, of New York, 285.
Strieby, Dr. M. E., 55, 56, 132, 134, 177, 214, 236.
Strieby, Prof. William, 268.
Strong, Rev. James W., of Corpus Christi, 241.
Sturtevant, Pres. J. M., 55, 56, 121, 194.
Sturtevant, J. M., Jr., 59, 74, 113.
Sugar-making, 165, 166.
Sumner, Charles, 92, 101.
Supreme Court, United States, 155.
Surgery in the Army, 42.
Swayne, Gen. Wager, 100.

Taft, Rev. Rufus, 231.
Tade, Rev. E. O., 88.
Taney, Chief Justice, 12.
Talladega College, 160.
Tappan, Arthur, 80.
Tappan, Lewis, 80.
Tarbox, Dr. Increase, 112, 113, 134.
Taylor, Dr. N. W., 136.
Terre Bonne, La., 167.
Terre Haute, Ind., 48.
Terry, General, 105.
Texarkana, Texas, 244.
Texas School Fund, 148.
The Planter, 102, 103.
Theological Seminary, Chicago, 72, 128, 145.
Thomas, Colonel, 98.
Thomas, Gen. George H., 106, 107.
Thompson, Colonel, 262, 263.
Thompson, Dr. Joseph P., 73, 128.
Thompson, Rev. M., 239.
Thornwell, Dr., 93.
Thurston, Rev. David, 80.
Tompkins, B. W., 126.
Toombs, Senator Robert, 101.
Tougaloo, Miss., 249.
Transfer South, 151.
Transfer back West, 252.
Turner, Rev. E. B., 65, 267.
Trott, Mr., 281.
Tuscaloosa, Ala., 216.
Tyler, General, 194.
Tyler, Missionary, 134.
Tyler, Pres. John, 24.

Uncle Tim, 64.
Unkarring, 291.

Vallandigham, C. L., 62.
Vanderbilt University, 178.
Van Horne, 86.
Van Lew Family, 107.

Vaughan, Dr. Robert, 76.
Vestal, Rev. Alfred, 20.
Vicksburg, 38, 41, 88, 93.
Virginia Legislature, 107.
"Virginia Negroes For Sale," 92, 247.
Virginia Flag, 52.

Waite, Chief Justice M. R., 271.
Waldo, Rev. L. F., 121.
Wales, 76.
Walker, Charles, Esq., 25.
Wallace, Governor, 118.
Wallace, Gen. Lew, 32.
Wallace, Sir William, 35, 39.
Ward, Dr. W. H., 227, 236.
Ward, Pres. Joseph, 143.
Ware, Pres. E. A., 288.
Warren, Bishop, 261.
Warren, Rev. Leroy, 150.
Warren, Dr. J. P., 81, 88, 249.
Warriner, Dr. H. A., 39.
Washburn, General, 117.
Washington, Gabriel, 243.
Washington, George, 28, 65.
Waterbury, Conn., 136.
Waterville College, 294.
Woman's Christian Temperance Union, 218.
Walker, Dr. G. W., 235.
Wells, Ralph, 164.
Wentworth, Hon. John, 43.
Wesleyans in North Carolina, 233.
Western War Books, 117.
Whateley, Judge, 95.
West Virginia, 136.
Wheaton College, 32, 145.
Wheeler, General, 190.
Whipple, Sec. George, 80.
White, George L., 178.
White, Dr. O. H., 214.
White River, 39.
Whitefield, George, 111.
Whiting, Rev. J. L., 126.
Whittier, J. G., 96.
Wild, General, 101.
Willcox, Dr. W. H., 180.
Williams, Dr. E. F., 131.
Williams, Rev. E. S., 254.
Williamsburg, Ky., 226, 227.
Williamson, Rev. John P., 141, 263.
Williamson, Dr. T. S., 141, 263.
Willard, Miss Frances E., 217.
Wilson, Hon. John M., 25.
Wise, Governor, 137.
Wirt, William, 282.
Woman's Work for Woman, 253.
Woodbine, 227.
Woodbridge, N. J., 135.

Woodstock Iron Co., 193.
Wool, General, 23.
Worcester, Rev. S. A., 281, 284.
Worth, Rev. Daniel, 19, 20, 233.
Wight, Richard R., 159.
Wright, Rev. S. G., 33, 91.
Wright, Rev. W. B., 68.

Yates, Gov. Richard, 34, 118.
Y. M. C. A. of Chicago, 113.
Y. M. C. A. Dakota Indian, 263.
Yerrington, Colonel, 98.
Yorktown, Va., 212.

www.ingramcontent.com/pod-product-compliance
Lightning Source LLC
Chambersburg PA
CBHW031906220426
43663CB00006B/792